2000

W9-CLZ-412

3 0301 00207318 3

The Holy See and the United Nations 1945–1995

Edward J. Gratsch

VANTAGE PRESS
New York

Nihil obstat:

    Rev. Robert L. Hagedorn
    April 24, 1996

Imprimatur:

    Most Rev. Carl K. Moeddel
    V.G., Auxiliary Bishop
    Archdiocese of Cincinnati
    April 25, 1996

FIRST EDITION

Copyright © 1997 by Edward J. Gratsch

Published by Vantage Press, Inc.
516 West 34th Street, New York, New York 10001

Manufactured in the United States of America
ISBN: 0-533-12206-6

Library of Congress Catalog Card No.: 96-90881

0 9 8 7 6 5 4 3 2 1

To
the Holy See and the United Nations
on the occasion of the latter's
fiftieth anniversary (1995)

Contents

Introduction

The word *See* in the title of this book is derived from the Latin word *sedes,* which means "seat," and it generally refers to the seat or residence of a Bishop who presides over a portion of the Lord's flock. Thus we speak of the See of Rome, the See of Constantinople, the See of Canterbury, and so on. In our case, the word *See* has a more personal meaning, and it refers to the Pope, the Bishop of Rome, and his representatives in the Vatican and elsewhere who assist him in carrying out the mission of the universal Church.[1] The See of the Bishop of Rome is called Holy because of its preeminence in the Catholic Church and because of the responsibility of the Pope and his representatives to mediate the holiness of Christ to the universal Church.

The United Nations is, of course, the international organization that was founded at San Francisco in 1945 and has its headquarters in New York City. The United Nations was founded to promote the peace and security of all nations, to secure the recognition of human rights, and to further social progress and higher standards of living. Major arms of the United Nations include the General Assembly, Security Council, Economic and Social Council, Trusteeship Council, Secretariat, and International Court of Justice, as well as many specialized agencies. Today the far greater number of nations with an overwhelming share of the world's population are members of the United Nations.[2]

This book is concerned with the relationship between the Holy See and the United Nations, especially from the side of the former. For the most part, that relationship has been one of mutual respect, cordiality, and cooperation. Unquestionably, the purposes and approaches of the Church and the United Nations are different. Nevertheless, the Church and the United Nations find wide areas of cooperation on the basis of their common concern for the human family. Both international entities wish to promote the establishment and preservation of true peace, the recognition of human rights, and the development of the total person.

The Holy See looks upon the United Nations as an organization that, having admitted the greater number of nations to membership, reflects the unity and solidarity of the human race. The United Nations represents "the obligatory path of modern civilization and world peace," as Pope Paul VI put it in his address to the General Assembly in 1965. In turn, the United Nations recognizes the Holy See as a powerful ally. By reason of its moral authority and worldwide influence the Holy See can significantly assist the United Nations in achieving its lofty objectives.

The contacts between the United Nations and the Holy See have been frequent and close. The Holy See maintains representatives at the headquarters of the United Nations in New York and at the headquarters of its various specialized agencies in Geneva, Rome, Paris, Vienna, and elsewhere.

The Holy See regularly takes part in meetings and conferences sponsored by the United Nations. Two Popes, Paul VI in 1965 and John Paul II in 1979 and 1995, have addressed the General Assembly in New York. In turn, the officials of the United Nations meet in audiences with the Pope in Rome and address written communications to him and his representatives.

As I write these words of introduction, several events come to mind. I think, first of all, of the visit of Pope Paul VI to the United Nations on October 4, 1965. I watched the course of his visit with several colleagues by means of television. I can still see the Pope as he traveled in an open automobile down Fifth Avenue in New York to the headquarters of the United Nations along the East River. Then I was profoundly moved as the Pope addressed the General Assembly. He was, as it were, speaking to the whole world about his hopes and dreams for the future—for the peace and security of all nations, for decent living conditions for all men and women, and for a general spirit of brotherhood and solidarity. He pledged the efforts of the worldwide communion of the Catholic Church to help achieve these noble goals. When all was said and done, I thought that October 4, 1965, was one of the most notable days in the recent history of the Catholic Church.

I think also of my own visits to the headquarters of the United Nations in recent years. Any visit to New York is memorable: the boat ride around the island of Manhattan, the spectacular views from the observation decks of the tall buildings, the beautiful houses of worship, the immensely rich museums and galleries, the variety of people, the bustle of Wall Street, the Statue of Liberty, the Staten Island ferry, and a thousand other marvels. However, the experiences that affected me most were my visits to the headquarters of the United Nations. To see the flags of the member-nations waving in the breeze along the promenade, to visit the hall of the General Assembly, where most of the nations of the earth sit as equals and brothers, to listen to the knowledgeable guides as they explain the efforts of the United Nations to preserve peace and promote the welfare of the entire human race, to breathe the atmosphere of a complex where peace and not competition are the main objectives, to view the relics of war and persecution that the United Nations seeks to eliminate—these things and many others affected me deeply.

Memorable, too, was my meeting in New York with the Permanent Observer of the Holy See at the United Nations, the Most Reverend Renato R. Martino, on September 9, 1991. His observations about the relationship between the Holy See and the United Nations were quite illuminating.

In the pages that follow I refer to many documents. I have selected these documents because I believe they are representative of others. Generally, for the sake of brevity, I have summarized and paraphrased the material in these documents, because the amount is considerable. In this case, selection, summary, and paraphrase may have been faulty, and I must accept responsibility, but I am convinced in my own mind that the general picture conveyed in this book is accurate.

For a complete text of documents issued by the Holy See one can consult the *Acta Apostolicae Sedis (AAS)* and *L'Osservatore Romano,* (English edition) both published in Vatican City, and *Paths to Peace,*[3] published by the Permanent Observer Mission of the Holy See to the United Nations, New York. For information about the United Nations one can consult the annual *Yearbook of the United Nations; Everyone's United Nations*, a basic reference book; *Basic Facts about the United Nations,* a shorter reference work; the *UN Chronicle,* which contains reports on the wide-ranging activities of the entire UN system; and a host of other publications dealing with specific topics.

These latter publications are available from the United Nations Department of Public Information, New York, NY 10017.

If this book, in some small way, renders the collaboration of the Holy See and the United Nations over the past fifty years more understandable, if it promotes the noble objectives that they have in common, then I, the author, will be amply rewarded.

1

The Holy See

As I remarked in the introduction to this book, the purposes and approaches of the Catholic Church and the United Nations are different; nevertheless, the Church and the United Nations find wide areas of cooperation on the basis of their common concern for the human family. In this chapter and the next, devoted to the Holy See and the United Nations respectively, I wish to explain this remark at greater length.

The Holy See—that is to say, the Pope and his representatives—is the principal organ of government and leadership in the Catholic Church. According to Catholic doctrine, the Catholic Church was founded by Jesus Christ in order to proclaim his teaching to the men and women of every nation and succeeding generation (Mt 28:19–20). What was the teaching of Jesus?

The Teaching of Jesus

At this point, it is not necessary to describe the teaching of Jesus in detail, but we may say that it centered on the kingdom of God, an idea with deep roots in the Old Testament and Jewish apocalyptic literature. The kingdom of God exists wherever men and women submit to the will of God (Mt 6:10; Lk 11:2). However, the kingdom of God is both a present and a future reality. The appearance of Jesus among his contemporaries meant that the kingdom was already present among them (Mk 1:15). But the kingdom of God continues to outgrow its humble origin, just as a tiny seed becomes a large tree (Mk 4:30–32). One day in the future, the kingdom will attain its final growth and perfection. The final phase of the kingdom will be inaugurated with the Second Coming of Christ at the end of human history (Mt 25:31–46). In other words, Jesus looked forward to a fulfillment of the kingdom outside of and beyond the circumstances of the present life.

What are the duties of individuals with respect to the kingdom of God? Entrance into the kingdom is essentially a gift (Mk 10:15), but at the same time it entails personal responsibility. Men and women enter the kingdom of God by submitting to his will. The will of God, according to Jesus, is expressed by the two great commandments of the Christian religion—to love God with one's whole heart and soul and mind and to love one's neighbor as another self (Mt 22:37–40). The two great commandments are further specified by the famous Ten Commandments of Moses (Lk 18:18–20), the needs of one's neighbor (Mt 25:31–46), and other commandments of Jesus such as prayer (Mt 6:9–13), the reception of baptism (Mt 28:19), and the celebration of the Lord's Supper (Lk 22:19). If men and women accept the sovereignty of God by obeying these commandments, if they repent of their sinful ways (Mk 1:15), they can enter the kingdom of God. Entrance into the kingdom of God is synonymous with entrance into eternal life. Those who enter the kingdom will be blessed with the life and joy of the kingdom (Mk 10:17–19; Mt 25:23) inchoatively in this life and completely in the life to come.

2

The Church

Quite frequently we use the word *church* to designate the building in which Christians gather to worship, but the word *church* refers primarily to the people who meet in that building—that is to say, to Christians, the followers of Jesus Christ. Jesus himself is the founder of the Church. When Jesus walked on this earth, he followed the general practice of the rabbis of his time: he gathered disciples or followers around himself in order to instruct them in greater detail. Jesus selected twelve of them to be his constant companions. These he sent to preach the good news of the gospel (Mk 3:14). By gathering disciples, by choosing the Twelve, by entrusting them with the mission of preaching to others about the kingdom, Jesus established, in effect, a religious society. In so doing, he took an initial step in the establishment of the Catholic Church, which is a group of persons who are committed to Jesus and the proclamation of his teaching.

Jesus took a second step in the establishment of his Church when he chose the apostle Peter to be the foundation and leader of the Church. At Caesarea Philippi in Palestine, Jesus said to Peter, "You are Peter [a name which means "Rock"], and upon this rock I will build my Church, and the gates of the netherworld shall not prevail against it" (Mt 16:18). In the same place, Jesus promised Peter the keys of the kingdom of heaven and the authority to bind and loose (Mt 16:19). Then, after his resurrection, Jesus explicitly made Peter the shepherd of his flock. After Peter had declared his love for Jesus, Jesus said to Peter, "Feed my lambs; tend my sheep" (Jn 21:15–16). In this way, Jesus provided his Church with visible leadership, once he had withdrawn from this earth. We see very clearly Peter's leadership of the primitive Church in the Acts of the Apostles 1–12, but the precise nature and implications of Peter's position could be known only with the passing of time.

Jesus took a third step in the establishment of his Church when, in accordance with his universal vision, he sent his representatives to the men and women of every nation and generation. They were to proclaim his message to all. Jesus said to his followers, "All power in heaven and on earth has been given to me. Go, therefore, and make disciples of all nations, baptizing them in the name of the Father, and of the Son, and of the Holy Spirit, teaching them to observe all that I have commanded you. And behold, I am with you always, until the end of the age" (Mt 28:18–20).

By a series of steps, therefore, Jesus founded the Church as a religious society. A review of these steps enables us to achieve some understanding of the nature of the Church. The Church is a community of persons committed to Jesus Christ by living and spreading his message. The message of Jesus is centered on the kingdom of God, to which we gain entrance by loving God above all else and loving our neighbor as another self. Fulfilling these conditions for entrance into the kingdom has profound implications for the present life and the life to come. The Church founded by Jesus possesses the visible leadership of Peter, the apostles, and their successors. Of course, Jesus himself remains the invisible leader of the Church "until the end of the age."

The Holy See

It is the conviction of Catholics that, according to the will of Christ, the office and function of the apostle Peter remain in the Church today. The function of the Petrine office is to furnish visible leadership to the Church, to give it unity and direction, and to do for the contemporary Church what Peter did for the primitive Church (Ac 1–2). The need for such an office is enduring. Indeed, the reference of Christ to Peter as the rock or foundation of Christ's Church (Mt 16:18) implies the permanence of Peter's position and role. Today, therefore, according to the belief of Catholics, the Church is led by the successors of Peter, the Popes, the Bishops of Rome, where Peter died and handed down the mantle of leadership. Consequently, those followers of Christ, Catholics, who recognize the authority and leadership of the Popes constitute the Church of Christ. It is this conception of the Church and of its function that guides the Holy See in its contact with others, including the United Nations.

The recognition of the Bishop of Rome as the visible head of the Catholic Church was a gradual process. Certain instances from the earliest centuries seem to suggest the primacy of the Roman Church and its Bishop. For example, circa A.D. 96 Clement I of Rome intervened in a dispute unsettling the distant community of Corinth, Greece. Some years later, in his Letter to the Romans, Ignatius, the celebrated martyr-bishop of Antioch who died circa A.D. 112 or 116, spoke of the Roman Church as "preeminent in love." Some scholars interpret this phrase to mean that the Roman Church presides over the universal Catholic Church, the congregation of love. Subsequently, Ireneaus of Lyons, who died circa A.D. 202, wrote that it was a matter of necessity "that every Church should agree with the Roman Church on account of its preeminent authority."[1] On the other hand, when the Bishop of Rome tried to set the date of Easter for the churches in Asia Minor in the second century, they paid no heed to him. Other instances of this nature could be adduced.

From a very early moment, however, there was a growing movement to recognize the claim of the Bishop of Rome, the Pope, to be the visible head of the Church. In the fourth and fifth centuries, Popes like Damasus (366–84), Siricius (384–99), Innocent (402–17), and Leo (440–61) vigorously asserted the prerogatives of the papacy in quite explicit fashion. They appealed to Matthew 16:18–19 as evidence that the Church was built on Peter, the Rock, who lived on in his successors, the Popes. As the successors of Peter, the Popes claimed a primacy of authority and jurisdiction over the Church. Acceptance of this claim by others lagged somewhat behind the claim itself, and acceptance did not always mean compliance with Roman directives; but by the fifth century and even earlier the present position of the Bishop of Rome in the Catholic Church was firmly established. Undoubtedly there was a development in this matter; but, in the judgement of Catholics, the development was justified by the words of Christ and the position of Peter in the New Testament.

The position of the Bishop of Rome, the Pope, in the Catholic Church is spelled out in the *Code of Canon Law* (1983), the official collection of laws governing the greater part of the Church. The *Code of Canon Law* reflects the teaching of the First Vatican Council (1869–70) and of the Second Vatican Council (1962–65) about the Pope. According to the code, the position of the Pope was originally conferred by Christ on the apostle Peter and was to be handed down to his successors. The Pope is the Vicar of Christ and pastor of the universal Church. He has supreme authority in the Church. No one may appeal a decision or decree of the Pope to anyone else except

God. The other Bishops of the Church help the Pope in various ways, for example, by meeting in synods to discuss Church affairs. The Cardinals of the Church and the Roman Curia also help the Pope. Ordinarily, the Pope conducts the daily affairs of the universal Church with the help of the Roman Curia. The Roman Curia includes the various congregations, tribunals, and agencies that function at his behest. The terms *Apostolic See* and *Holy See* apply not only to the Pope, but also to the institutions of the Roman Curia.[2]

When the *Code of Canon Law* speaks of the authority of the Pope or Holy See, it is evident that this authority ordinarily cannot be enforced by civil penalties, whatever the case may have been in the past. The authority of the Holy See is moral and spiritual. It is considered to have been derived from Christ, who gave his Church the "keys of the kingdom of heaven" and the power "to bind and loose" (Mt 16:19). To reject or disregard the authority of the Holy See, the supreme authority in the Church, is to reject or disregard the authority of Christ. The Holy See can obtain compliance with its teaching and directives only by speaking to the consciences of individuals who hear the voice of Christ in the voice of the Church.

Of course there are many non-Christians who do not acknowledge the authority of Christ and there are many Christians who do not accept the authority of the Church. Even so, the Holy See tries to speak to the consciences of these individuals too. Speaking of conscience, the Second Vatican Council (1962–65) declared:

In the depths of his conscience, man detects a law which he does not impose on himself, a law which holds him to obedience. Always summoning him to love good and avoid evil, the voice of conscience, when necessary, speaks to

7

his heart more specifically, saying: "Do this" or "Shun that." For man in his heart has a law written by God. To obey it is the very dignity of man, and he will be judged according to it. Conscience is the most secret core and sanctuary of man. There he is alone with God, whose voice echoes in the depths of his being. In a wonderful manner conscience reveals that law which is fulfilled by the love of God and neighbor.[3]

The Holy See strives to set forth the demands of conscience in this manner and reflect the moral conscience of humanity in the face of forces that divide individuals and nations.

The moral and spiritual authority of the Pope is not without effect in international relations, although it is sometimes measured in military terms. There is an authentic anecdote about Napoléon and his envoy to the Pope. When Napoléon as First Consul of France sent Francois Caçault to Rome, he was asked by the envoy what principle should determine his attitude toward the Pope. Napoléon told him, "Deal with the Pope as if he had 200,000 men at his command."[4]

Vatican City

One must distinguish the Holy See from Vatican City. The *Holy See,* as I noted above, refers to the Pope and the Roman Curia. Vatican City is the tiny state (108.7 acres) set in the middle of Rome over which the Pope is the temporal sovereign. Vatican City provides the Holy See with the political independence necessary for its spiritual mission.

At one time, the papacy ruled a much larger territory called the Papal States. For several centuries, the Papal

States included Rome and a greater part of central Italy. The revenues of this territory accrued to the Holy See for its support and activity. Sometimes the Pope had to rely on other countries, such as France, to defend his territory. Sometimes the Pope was driven out of his domain by civil disturbances in Rome, but the Pope retained dominion over the Papal States into the nineteenth century.

The year of revolutions, 1848, witnessed the triumph of a liberal revolution in almost every capital of Europe. That year Pope Pius IX was driven from Rome and the Papal States by Mazzini and Garibaldi, who set up a republic. The following year, however, with the help of a French army, the Pope regained his temporal sovereignty, but it was not to endure. In 1860, Victor Emmanuel II of Piedmont captured the Papal States, and in 1870 he took Rome itself. The Italian government introduced the Law of Guarantees to regulate relations between the state and the Church. The Pope refused to recognize the law because recognition would have been tantamount to renunciation of papal sovereignty over the Papal States. The Pope became, in effect, the "Prisoner of the Vatican." In 1929, Pope Pius XI settled the "Roman Question" with Benito Mussolini: Vatican City became a sovereign state, and the Church received a monetary settlement for the territorial losses it had sustained.

Catholic theologians sometimes ask if the Pope could transfer his see, let us say, from Rome to New York, the seat of the United Nations, so that the Bishop of New York would be the visible head of the Catholic Church. Some Catholic theologians reply affirmatively to the question. Just as the apostle Peter traveled from Jerusalem to Antioch and finally to Rome, so the Pope, the successor of Peter, could transfer his see to another city.

Other Catholic theologians reply negatively to the question. They believe that the apostle Peter, having been sent immediately by Christ, established the definitive location of the Holy See at Rome and it lies beyond the competence of Peter's successor to transfer it. Needless to say, the Pope could temporarily reside elsewhere and still retain his position as Bishop of Rome. As a matter of fact, the Pope did reside in Avignon in southern France during the fourteenth century because of civil unrest in Rome at that time.

One may ask whether the papacy is represented at the United Nations and its specialized agencies as the Holy See, the spiritual leader of the Catholic Church, or as the State of Vatican City, a temporal sovereignty. After an initial period of confusion, this question was answered in 1957 by an exchange of letters between the Holy See and the Secretary-General of the United Nations. It was agreed that the papacy should be represented at the United Nations as the Holy See.[5] In this regard, the Secretary-General, Dag Hammarskjöld, once remarked, "When I request an audience from the Vatican, I do not go to see the King of Vatican City, but the head of the Catholic Church." Representation at the United Nations as the Holy See emphasizes the spiritual and religious character of the papacy. Nevertheless, the Holy See retains its right to act as the governing authority of the State of Vatican City, therefore as a temporal sovereignty. Indeed, it could act in both capacities at once. The capacity in which it functions will be determined by the matter at hand.

One may also ask whether the Holy See is eligible for membership in the United Nations. It is not a full-fledged member of the United Nations, although it has been represented at the United Nations since 1964 by a

Permanent Observer. Could the Holy See become a member of the international organization? According to article 4 of the charter of the United Nations, "membership in the United Nations is open to all other peace-loving states which accept the obligations contained in the present Charter and, in the judgement of the Organization, are able and willing to carry out these obligations." The same article goes on to say that "the admission of any such state to membership in the United Nations will be effected by a decision of the General Assembly upon the recommendation of the Security Council."

Some maintain that the Holy See and the State of Vatican City are not eligible for membership in the United Nations because they are too small in comparison with other sovereign states. For the same reason, the principality of Liechtenstein was not admitted to the League of Nations.

Others, of course, hold that the Holy See is eligible for membership in the United Nations. The Holy See maintains diplomatic relations with many other states. It is already a full-fledged member of various specialized agencies of the United Nations. Moreover, it would be useful to the United Nations if the Holy See were a member because it is the spiritual leader of so many Catholics in so many member-states.

Up to this point, however, the Holy See has not sought membership in the United Nations. One can only speculate about the reasons. Perhaps membership would involve the Holy See too directly in the political and economic conflicts that sometimes erupt among the members and are not immediately related to its spiritual mission.

Papal Legates

The practice of sending legates or ambassadors abroad has been known as long as peoples and nations have come into contact with each other. Frequently legates were employed to form alliances or conclude peace. Prior to the fifteenth century, however, legates were generally sent out on an ad hoc basis. They completed their mission and returned home. With the rise of independent states, particularly in the last four centuries and even earlier, permanent diplomatic missions were sent from one country to another. The legate or ambassador was stationed at the court of a foreign ruler with a view to representing the interests of his own sovereign. At the end of the fifteenth century and the beginning of the sixteenth, the Italian republics, such as Venice and Florence, and some European nations, such as France, Spain, and England, set up permanent embassies in Rome. Later the Pope established his own embassies in Vienna, Madrid, and Lisbon, on the Italian peninsula and elsewhere. Today the Holy See continues to exchange legates or ambassadors with other nations on an even broader scale.

The function of a papal legate is detailed in the *Code of Canon Law*. The Pope claims the inherent right to send legates to particular churches and governments throughout the world. The legate is the representative of the Pope. Similarly, the delegates and observers of a papal mission represent the Holy See at international organizations and conferences. The principal duty of a papal legate is to foster unity between the Holy See and the particular church to whom he is sent. This he does by working with the local bishops for the good of all. The duty of a papal legate who is also accredited to the state is to promote good relations between the Holy See and the government.

A third type of legate, mentioned above, represents the Holy See at international organizations and conferences. If this representative has the right to vote, he is called a delegate; if he does not have the right to vote, he is called an observer.[6]

The decision of the Holy See to send either a delegate or an observer to an organization or conference depends upon the nature and circumstances of the assemblage. The Holy See currently sends a "delegate" to the International Atomic Energy Agency (IAEA) in Vienna and to other agencies. The Holy See maintains permanent "observers" at the United Nations in New York, at the Food and Agricultural Organization (FAO) in Rome, at the United Nations Educational, Scientific and Cultural Organization (UNESCO) in Paris, at the Organization of American States (OAS) in Washington, and at other organizations elsewhere.[7]

Pope Paul VI dispatched the first Permanent Observer of the Holy See to the United Nations in New York in 1964. The Permanent Observer does not take part in the deliberations unless he is invited, nor does he have a right to vote; nevertheless, his presence at the headquarters of the international organization reflects the esteem of the Holy See for the principles and purposes of the United Nations. The presence of the Observer testifies to the interest, sympathy, and sometimes concern with which the Holy See follows the deliberations and activities of the organization. Finally, his presence indicates the willingness of the Holy See to collaborate with the United Nations when such collaboration is possible and useful. In turn, the United Nations welcomes the representatives of the Holy See because of the latter's moral influence throughout the world.

2

The United Nations

Nineteenth-Century Antecedents

One can identify several antecedents in the nineteenth century that prepared the way for the League of Nations and the United Nations in the twentieth. One such was the so-called Concert of Europe. The Concert of Europe was a group of major European powers—Britain, Russia, Austria, and Prussia—that signed the treaty of Chaumont, France, in 1814. By this treaty, they agreed to act "in perfect concert" to prosecute the war against France. After Napoléon's defeat at Waterloo, the same powers renewed the provisions of the treaty of Chaumont at Paris in 1815 and agreed to hold periodic congresses where they might act together to settle the political problems of Europe. In 1818, France was admitted to the Concert on the basis of full equality.

The powers did confer many times in the course of the century—for example, in 1820 to deal with revolutions then going on in Naples and Spain; in 1832 to recognize Greek independence and choose a new King; in 1876 and 1878 to try to settle the Eastern Question, which had to do with the disintegration of the Turkish Empire; in 1884 to impose rules on the partition of Africa; and even as late as 1906 to sort out difficulties in Morocco. However, the Concert gradually disintegrated with the growing rift between the nations of Europe prior to World War I.

The political conferences of European powers became a system of diplomacy for running the continent in the nineteenth century. Two assumptions lay at the basis of this system—that serious political problems affected the entire continent and that the major powers were responsible for the preservation of peace and political stability. The system of conferences enhanced the atmosphere and skills for multilateral negotiation and produced a prototype of a major organ of modern international organization—the executive council of great powers.

A second antecedent of the League of Nations and the United Nations at the end of the nineteenth and the beginning of the twentieth centuries was the convocation of two Hague Conferences of 1899 and 1907, which also prompted the idea of international collaboration on issues of common interest. Both conferences were called upon the initiative of Czar Nicholas II of Russia and met at The Hague, the Netherlands. The conferences were notable for the number of nations represented—twenty-six, including the United States and Mexico, at the first; and forty-four at the second. Neither conference achieved its main objective, which was the reduction of armaments, but certain noteworthy results, including provisions for mitigating the horrors of war, did follow. In a sense, the conferences brought together the world's first general assembly in which small states sat on equal terms with the great powers. A Permanent Court of Arbitration emerged from the first Hague Conference. The conference formulated certain rules of international law, an initial and tentative step in that direction. Finally, the Hague Conferences suggested the need for permanent international institutions to preserve world peace. A third Hague Conference, scheduled for 1916, was canceled because of World War I.

A third antecedent of the League of Nations and the United Nations in the nineteenth century was the creation of many governmental and nongovernmental agencies for the organization of international life. International commissions were set up to control and improve conditions of navigation on the Rhine (1815) and the Danube (1856). The World's Alliance of Young Men's Christian Associations was created in 1855; and the first International Working Men's Association, commonly known as "the International," in 1864. The organization known today as the International Red Cross was formed in 1863. The International Telegraphic Union was established in 1865; and the Universal Postal Union, in 1874.

The growth and expansion of contacts among nations led to the formation of commissions and unions to regulate the trade of specific commodities such as sugar, and to halt the spread of diseases such as cholera. The Paris Convention of 1883 dealt with international protection of industrial property. International scientific congresses gave birth to a wide range of public and private organizations concerned with humanitarian, cultural, political, and commercial interests. Perhaps there were as many as three hundred international organizations in 1907. Subsequently, some of these—often in a merged or evolved form—became members of the UN "family" of organizations.

The League of Nations

The League of Nations was the immediate forerunner of the United Nations. It was the creation of the Paris Peace Conference that met in 1919 to conclude officially the hostilities of World War I. The President of the United States, Woodrow Wilson, was the chief figure behind the foundation of the league, but the United States never joined it. The basic document of the league was the covenant, an integral part of the Treaty of Versailles, and it came into force on January 10, 1920, with forty-two signatories.

The covenant of the league consisted of a preface and twenty-six articles. The preface stated the purpose of the league, which was to promote international cooperation and achieve international peace and security. Article 1 stated the conditions for membership in the league—in effect, adherence to the provisions of the covenant. Articles 2 through 7 described the principal organs of the league—an assembly composed of all the members of the world body and a council composed of the principal powers (originally the United Kingdom, France, Italy, and Japan but later adding Germany and the USSR) that were permanent members and four nonpermanent members that were elected by the assembly. Both the assembly and the council might deal "with any matter within the sphere of action of the League or affecting the peace of the world." There was also a secretariat. Geneva was chosen as the seat of the league. Article 8 recognized the need to reduce armaments, and article 9 set up a permanent commission to advise on the implementation of the preceding articles.

Article 10 expressed the intention of the members to respect and preserve against aggression the territorial integrity and independence of members. Articles 11 through 17 provided for the arbitration and conciliation of disputes, for sanctions against aggressors, and for a Permanent Court of International Justice, which was competent to hear and judge any dispute of an international character that the parties submitted to it. Articles 18 through 26 had to do with treaties, colonial mandates, international cooperation for humanitarian purposes, and amendments to the covenant.

It is evident that several streams of development in the nineteenth century came together in the covenant of the league. The league reflected the international membership of the Hague Conferences, the council of the league reestablished in a more formal way the Concert of Europe, and the Permanent Court of International Justice continued the work of the Permanent Court of Arbitration arising out of the first Hague Conference.

The league also manifested a growing realization of certain important facts—that the nations of the world could not tolerate the increasing devastation of war, that they could not leave the preservation of peace to chance, that greater international interdependence made international collaboration a necessity, and that cooperation in war should facilitate cooperation in achieving peace.

The League of Nations was not without a measure of success. In 1920–21 it mediated a dispute between Sweden and Finland over the Aland Islands; in 1925 it forestalled a war between Greece and Turkey over a boundary; and it helped rescue the disastrous financial condition of Austria. The league administered the free city of Danzig (Gdansk) from 1920 to 1939 and the Saar from 1919 to 1935. Moreover, the league encouraged and implemented many humanitarian measures having to do with the plight of refugees, the suppression of traffic in women, children, and drugs, the promotion of public health, and international cooperation in sundry areas such as labor relations and disaster relief. Also, a Permanent Court of International Justice was involved in a number of important cases.

On the debit side, however, the league made little progress in achieving disarmament, despite serious efforts on its part. Ultimately the inability of the league to prevent or cope with the lawless actions of the great powers led to its collapse. In 1923 the French occupied the Ruhr, in 1931 the Japanese invaded Manchuria, in 1935 Italy invaded Ethiopia, in 1938 Hitler seized Austria, and in 1939 Russia invaded Finland. Often the great powers simply ignored the league and went their own way. In 1946, after the United Nations had been founded in the previous year, the League of Nations dissolved itself and its property was transferred to the new international organization for which it had provided a model.

The United Nations

The United Nations is, of course, the international organization established immediately after World War II. It replaced the League of Nations. The name "United Nations" was coined by Pres. Franklin D. Roosevelt and was first used in the "Declaration by the United Nations" issued January 1, 1942, during World War II, to designate the twenty-six nations at war with the Axis Powers. These nations pledged to continue fighting together and not make peace separately.

The Charter of the United Nations was drawn up by the delegates of fifty countries meeting at San Francisco between April 25 and June 26, 1945. As the basis of their deliberations, the delegates worked with specific proposals for the new organization drafted by China, the Soviet Union, the United Kingdom, and the United States at Dumbarton Oaks between August and October 1944. (Dumbarton Oaks is an estate located in the District of Columbia.) The charter was signed at San Francisco by the delegates of fifty countries. Not represented at San Francisco, Poland signed the charter later, so that there were originally fifty-one member-states.

The United Nations officially came into existence on October 24, 1945, when the charter had been ratified by China, France, the Soviet Union, the United Kingdom, and the United States (the five permanent members of the Security Council) and by the majority of the other forty-six nations that had signed it. "United Nations Day" is observed each year on October 24. The headquarters of the United Nations is situated on a tract of land along the East River in New York City. The money to purchase the land, $8.5 million, was a gift of Mr. John D. Rockefeller, Jr.

The Charter of the United Nations consists of a preamble and nineteen chapters divided into 111 articles. Article 1 of the charter speaks of the purposes of the United Nations: to maintain international peace, to develop friendly relations among nations, to achieve international cooperation in solving international problems of an economic, social, cultural, or humanitarian character, to promote and encourage respect for human rights and for fundamental freedoms for all without distinction as to race, sex, language, or religion, and to be a center for harmonizing the actions of nations in attaining these common ends.

Article 2 of the charter speaks of the principles guiding the actions of the United Nations, stating that the

United Nations is based on the principle of the sovereign equality of all its members; all members are to fulfill in good faith their charter obligations; they are to settle their disputes by peaceful means, without endangering peace, security, and justice; they are to give the United Nations every assistance in any action it takes in accordance with the charter and shall not assist states against which the United Nations is taking preventive or enforcement action; and nothing in the charter authorizes the United Nations to intervene in matters that are essentially the domestic concern of any state.

Articles 3–6 list the conditions for membership in the United Nations. Membership is open to all peace-loving nations that accept the obligations of the charter and, in the judgment of the organization, are able to carry out these obligations. New members are admitted by the General Assembly on the recommendation of the Security Council.

Articles 7–8 speak of the principal organs of the United Nations, which are a General Assembly, a Security Council, an Economic and Social Council, a Trusteeship Council, an International Court of Justice, and a Secretariat. Necessary subsidiary organs may also be established. Both men and women are eligible to participate in all facets of the principal and subsidiary organs.

Articles 9–22 delineate the function of the General Assembly. It is the main deliberative organ of the United Nations, and it may discuss any matter within the scope of the charter. The General Assembly is composed of representatives of all member-states, each of which has one vote. Decisions on important questions, such as recommendations on peace and security, admission of new members, and budgetary matters, require a two-thirds majority of the members present and voting. Decisions on other questions are reached by a simple majority.

Articles 23–54 have to do with the Security Council. The council has fifteen members: five permanent members—China, France, Russia, the United Kingdom, and the United States—and ten nonpermanent members elected by the General Assembly for two-year terms. The Security Council has the primary responsibility to maintain peace and security. The members of the United Nations agree to accept and carry out the decisions of the Security Council. Each member of the Security Council has one vote. Decisions of the Security Council require an affirmative vote of nine members, including the concurring votes of the permanent members. The Security Council may adopt any measures—conciliatory, economic, diplomatic, or military—deemed necessary to preserve international peace and security.

Articles 55–72 have to do with international economic and social cooperation and the Economic and Social Council. The latter was established by the charter as the principal organ for coordinating the economic and social work of the United Nations and specialized agencies connected with it. The council has fifty-four members who serve for three years, eighteen being elected each year for a three-year term. Voting in the Economic and Social Council is by simple majority, and each member has one vote. According to article 71, the Economic and Social Council is also authorized to consult with nongovernmental organizations that are connected with matters within the competence of the council. Hundreds of nongovernmental organizations have consultative status with the council.

Articles 73–91 have to do with non-self-governing territories, the International Trusteeship System, and the International Trusteeship Council. The council supervises the administration of trust territories placed under the trusteeship system. The aim of the system and the council is to promote the well-being and eventual independence of territories that, for some reason or other, are not self-governing. Happily, the system and the council have largely achieved their goals.

Articles 92–96 have to do with the International Court of Justice, which is the principal judicial organ of the United Nations. The Statute of the Court is an integral part of the Charter of the United Nations. Each member of the United Nations agrees to comply with the decision of the Court in any case to which it is a party. The Security Council is authorized to effect compliance with the decisions of the Court. The Court is composed of fifteen judges elected by the General Assembly and the Security Council. No two of them may be nationals of the same state. The judges must be persons of high moral character who are qualified to hold the highest judicial offices in their own country. The seat of the Court is at The Hague, Netherlands.

Articles 97–101 have to do with the Secretariat, which consists of a Secretary-General and such staff as the organization may require. The Secretary-General is appointed by the General Assembly upon the recommendation of the Security Council. As the chief administrative officer of the United Nations, he acts in that capacity at all meetings of the General Assembly, of the Security Council, of the Economic and Social Council, and of the Trusteeship Council. Moreover, he performs any other function entrusted to him by these organs. He is also charged with bringing to the attention of the Security Council any matter that, in his opinion, may threaten international peace and security. The Secretary-General is assisted by a large staff that is recruited on a wide geographic basis and is required to work exclusively in the interest of the United Nations.

The remainder of the articles, 102–11, have to do with miscellaneous provisions, transitional security arrangements, amendments, and ratification and signature of the charter.

Since 1945, the United Nations has undergone a significant evolution. The fifty-one original members were largely Allies of World War II. Since then, the Afro-Asian group of nations has been admitted, the number of member-nations has more than tripled, and the Allied nations have lost their clear majority. As a result, there has been a marked change in voting patterns. Moreover, the role of the Secretary-General has expanded. According to the charter, he is the chief administrative officer of the United Nations, but he has also assumed an important role as peacemaker, in accordance with his authority to carry out other functions entrusted to him by the chief organs of the United Nations.

Another factor in the evolving situation has been the fluctuating support and utilization of the world body by the major powers. In some cases, such as disarmament, the major powers have not always paid much attention to the proposals and recommendations of the United Nations, while in other cases, such as the Iraqui invasion of Kuwait (August 1990), the major powers complied fully and decisively with the provisions of the charter. Simultaneously, the United Nations has expanded its activities on behalf of economic aid and technological advancement of less developed countries. As far as the future is concerned, with the end of the Cold War and the increasing number of problems that involve more than one country—problems such as drugs, terrorism, environmental damage, and AIDS—one may hope that the United Nations will experience greater unity in the pursuit of its goals.

Specialized Agencies of the United Nations

Much of the work of the United Nations aimed at improving the economic and social conditions of the peoples around the world is carried out by specialized agencies. Article 57 of the charter provides that "various specialized agencies established by intergovernmental agreement and having wide international responsibilities, as defined in their basic instruments, in economic, social, cultural, educational, health and related fields, shall be brought into relationship with the United Nations."

Among the bodies that function as specialized agencies of the United Nations but are not specifically provided for in the charter are the International Atomic Energy Agency (IAEA), the International Labor Organization (ILO), the Food and Agricultural Organization (FAO), United Nations Educational, Scientific and Cultural Organization (UNESCO), the World Health Organization (WHO), the World Bank, the International Monetary Fund (IMF), the International Civil Aviation Organization (ICAO), the Universal Postal Union (UPO), the International Telecommunication Union (ITU), the World Meteorological Organization (WMO), the International Maritime Organization (IMO), the World Intellectual Property Organization (WIPO), the International Fund for Agricultural Development (IFAD), the World Trade Organization (WTO), and the United Nations Industrial Development Organization (UNIDO).

The relationship between the United Nations and the specialized agencies is defined by individual agreements:

The specialized agencies are separate, autonomous organizations which have their own membership, legislative and executive bodies, secretariats and budgets. They work with the United Nations and each other through the coordinating machinery of the Economic and Social Council, to which they report annually under Article 64 of the Charter.[1]

Agreements between the United Nations and the specialized agencies generally follow a standard pattern. As a rule, they provide for reciprocal representations at meetings; reciprocal inclusion of agenda items when requested; exchange of information and documents; uniformity of personnel arrangements and coordination of statistical services, as well as budgetary and financial arrangements. Each specialized agency has agreed to consider any recommendation made to it by the United Nations and to report to the organization any action taken as a result of such recommendation.[2]

Perhaps we may compare the United Nations and its specialized agencies to the solar system. Just as the planets revolve around the sun without being dominated or absorbed by it, so the specialized agencies revolve around the United Nations without being dominated or absorbed by it. The specialized agencies look to the United Nations for coordination and guidance but enjoy essential freedom of action in their respective fields.

The provisions of the charter for the specialized agencies make it additionally clear that the United Nations is an organization dedicated not only to the maintenance of international peace and security, but also to the well-being of mankind in all the important areas of life that require international attention. The purposes of the United Nations, stated in article 1 of the charter, include "international cooperation in solving international problems of an economic, social, cultural or humanitarian character." To many delegates at San Francisco what the world needed was not only a collective security agency, but also a world body capable of addressing the extreme misery of so many people throughout the world. The representative of Mexico expressed the fervent hope of many when he said at one of the closing sessions at San Francisco:

> The Charter is not only an instrument of security against the horrors of war. It is also, for the people who have been fighting to uphold the principles of human dignity, an instrument of well-being and happiness against the horrors of a peace without hope, in which men would be subjected to humiliating privations and injustices. "Blood, sweat and tears" comprised the glorious but provisional rule of war. It must not become the rule of peace.[3]

The world, then, is the parish of the United Nations. There is hardly one serious human need, except the need for God, that lies outside the concern of the United Nations. The United Nations cannot concern itself with the need for God, important as it is, because the members of the world body hold widely conflicting views about the existence and nature of the Divinity. Still, the silence of the charter about God is by no means complete, since the United Nations is vitally concerned with the welfare of the human family, all of whose members, believers maintain, are made in the image and likeness of God.

3

The Catholic Church and the International Organization (I)

This chapter and the following one deal in summary fashion with the attitude and relationship of the Catholic Church to international organizations over the centuries. At the beginning of the Christian Era, the Church had to contend with an international organization, the Roman Empire, that initially was both a boon and a threat to it. The Roman Empire was a boon because it maintained civil peace and unity, which greatly facilitated the spread and development of the Church. Yet the empire was also a threat because it periodically persecuted the Church with greater or less intensity.

Subsequently, after the conversion of the Emperor Constantine, the Church entered upon a fateful alliance with the empire and, after its demise in the West, a second international organization, the Holy Roman Empire, which was the nominal successor of the Roman Empire in Western Europe. Pope and Emperor, who was now Christian, ruled the same people in the spiritual and temporal realms respectively. Often enough the two rulers succeeded in collaborating, but often each encroached upon the other's domain, to the detriment of church and state.

With the disintegration of the Holy Roman Empire and the rise of nationalism, the theologians of the Church and the Popes began to speak of the community of nations, emphasizing their interdependence and common interests. The Church applauded the rise of many international organizations, especially in the nineteenth century. Such organizations help nations and individuals live together for their mutual advantage as members of the one human family and community.

The Bible

The Bible enshrines the faith of the Church and inculcates ideas that have shaped the response of the Catholic Church to international organizations. We find these ideas in both the Old and New Testaments.

The Old Testament

Two ideas that influence the response of the Church to world bodies are the essential dignity of all men and women and the unity of the human race. According to the Book of Genesis, man was created in the image and likeness of God. Man is the image of the divine fatherhood because he is to multiply and fill the earth, and he is the image of the divine lordship because he is to subject the rest of God's creation to his dominion.[1] The human being is both male and female, and from their union arises the human community. Man is essentially a social being; he cannot flourish or even survive without the support of other human beings (Gn 1:26–30; 2:21–24).

Genesis also inculcates the unity of the human race in that all men and women are descended from the same pair who were made in the divine image. Still, Genesis recognizes the diversity of human beings (Gn 10), a diversity that is a consequence of the divine command to fill the earth. After the sin of Adam and Eve, however, this diversity divided individuals and nations. Cain, a tiller of the soil, killed his brother, Abel, a keeper of flocks, out of jealousy (Gn 4:1–6). After the Noachian flood, the nations of the earth tried to raise a tower to heaven out of pride, but God scrambled their language so that they could no longer cooperate with each other (Gn 11:1–9). The remaining books of the Old Testament contain many accounts of disputes and wars that divided the Israelites among themselves and alienated them from other nations. Nevertheless, the conception of a human race as one family of essentially equal members is to be found in the Book of Genesis. The seeds of internationalism had been planted.

There is a second reference to internationalism in the Old Testament. It has to do with the "nations" or, in Hebrew, *goyim*. Israel was ultimately distinguished from other nations because it worshiped Yahweh, the God of Israel, while the others did not. The other nations were a threat to Israel because of their arms and corrosive ideas, and there are many passages in the prophetic books where the spokesmen of God thunder against the nations that menace or oppress Israel. Yet Yahweh is the Lord of history, and the pagans played a role in the historical process governed by Yahweh. At one time, the nations chastised Israel as the instruments of God's wrath (Is 8:6 ff; Jer 27); at another, they were the instruments of God's mercy to Israel (Is 45:1–6). Later, however, the nations came to be seen in a new light. The universal lordship of Yahweh requires that all nations recognize him as God alone, and this recognition will enable them to share the blessings of Israel. Indeed, the function of Israel is to mediate this knowledge to the nations.

Accordingly, the prophets foresee a time when the nations will enter God's kingdom and there will be universal peace, for "one nation shall not raise the sword against another, nor shall they train for war again" (Is 2:1–4). Yahweh, the God of Israel, will summon the nations into his kingdom, and some of them will proclaim his glory to far distant lands (Is 66:18–21). Psalm 47 calls upon the nations to acknowledge the God of Israel as the only true God; and when the Lord manifests himself as King of all, the whole earth will proclaim his dominion. Psalm 87 extols the holy city of Zion as the spiritual home of all the nations of the earth. The Servant of the Lord, about whom we read in Deutero-Isaiah, is a light not only to the Israelites, but also to the nations (Is 42:6). We understand, therefore, from the prophets of Israel that on the final day the nations of the earth will come together in peace and the primeval unity of mankind will be restored.

Therefore, in the Old Testament we find several ideas that support the conception of the human race as one family, as a single community, despite profound differences among individuals. These ideas are the essential dignity and equality of all human beings who are made in the image and likeness of God, the unity of the human race on the basis of its origin, and the common vocation of all nations to share in the blessings of God's kingdom.

The New Testament

Further evidence of human solidarity is found in the teaching and actions of Jesus that were directed to every member of the human race without exception. It is true that at the outset Jesus and his apostles preached only to the Jewish nation (Mt 10:5–6; 15:24), but on many occasions Jesus revealed his universal vision. Jesus said that the Gentiles, or non-Jews, would also find a place at the banquet in the kingdom of God (Mt 8:11). Jesus anticipated the gathering of his chosen ones from the four winds (Mk 13:27). Jesus clearly taught all human beings to treat one another as brothers and sisters (Mt 25:31–46; Lk 10:25–37). As the Redeemer of all, he offered himself for all (Mk 10:45; 14:24). Finally, at the end of his earthly life, Jesus sent his representatives to proclaim his message to every nation and generation (Mt 28:18–20). Jesus' teaching and actions were directed to all because he was convinced that God is the Father of all.

After some initial hesitation about the precise moment to go to the Gentiles, the primitive Church soon welcomed Gentiles to its bosom. The apostle Paul particularly traveled around the northern and eastern shores of the Mediterranean preaching the new faith to the indigenous peoples. So successful were he and other missionaries that Gentile converts soon outnumbered converts from Judaism. According to Paul, all nations have a common origin, for as he put it, from one stock God has made every nation of mankind to dwell on the face of the earth (Ac 17:26). Paul maintained that all nations are called to share in the blessings promised to Abraham (Gal 3:8). God wishes all to be saved and come to the knowledge of the truth (1 Tm 2:4). Everything in heaven and on earth was created in Christ, it is he who sustains everything in being (Col 1:16–17), and he is the Lord of all (Phil 2:9–11). Finally, according to John's Book of Revelation, the elect from every nation shall walk on the streets of the heavenly Jerusalem ablaze with the splendor of God (Rev 21:22–24).

Reflection upon these and other passages in the New Testament compels us to recognize the solidarity of the human race: its members are one in origin and vocation; they are essentially equal in their human dignity; they have the same rights and duties; there is only one Redeemer and Father of all. Because these ideas are derived from the Bible and its own tradition, the Catholic Church responds favorably to international organizations that reflect and implement human solidarity understood by the Church in this way.

The Church and the Roman Empire

Christianity first saw the light of day in Palestine, a remote province of the eastern Roman Empire. The new religion spread slowly but steadily under the favorable conditions created by the empire. The strength of the empire lay in its administration and legal system and the might of its arms. The empire ruled and guided many peoples of diverse cultures without demanding any uniformity. Under the protection of the Pax Romana, merchants, soldiers, and preachers carried the Christian message along the imperial roads to distant lands. In the first two or three centuries, the Christian faith reached Syria, Asia Minor, Greece, Armenia, Persia, and Egypt in the eastern half of the empire and Italy, Gaul (France), North Africa, Spain, and Britain in the western half.

For their part, the early Christians asked only for freedom to profess their faith and preach it without fear of persecution from the political authorities, but Christians were confronted with the problem of survival. The

Roman Empire was authoritarian, often tyrannical, and compelled its people to worship the Emperor and the goddess Roma. Christians regarded such worship as incompatible with their belief in God and Jesus Christ and refused to offer it. In turn, the state regarded Christians as atheists and dangerous to the political order. The state subjected them to persecution, sometimes sporadic, sometimes systematic, but generally terrible when it occurred.

How did Christians think of the Roman state? From the very beginning there were two schools of thought. The Book of Revelation speaks of the Roman state with abhorrence: it is the beast (13:1–8), Babylon the Great, the mother of harlots and all the world's abominations (17:1–6), which is destined for fearful punishment (Rev 18). On the other hand, several passages in the New Testament inculcate obedience to Roman authority, which, even if the state abuses it, comes from God (Rom 13:1–7; Ti 3:1–2; 1 Pt 2:13–15). This respect for the authority of the state is found also in the writings of Clement of Rome, Polycarp, and the Christian Apologists.

By the Edict of Milan (313), the Emperor Constantine, who had declared his belief in the God of the Christians, and his Co-Emperor, Licinius, who remained a pagan, granted freedom of worship to all in the empire. Paganism ceased to be the official religion and, along with Christianity, became a tolerated religion. Although he was baptized only on his deathbed, Constantine showed increasing friendliness to the Christian Church and showered favors on it. Eventually Christianity superseded paganism as the prevailing religion and was officially adopted by the empire under the Emperors Gratian (375–83) and Theodosius I (379–95).

The implications of the ensuing alliance between church and state were viewed somewhat differently by the parties concerned. Ambrose (340–97), Bishop of Milan, looked upon church and state as two independent authorities, each autonomous in its own domain, but lending assistance to the other. The church prays for the state, and the state is the secular arm of the church that puts the decisions of the church into effect. In matters of faith, bishops judge Emperors, but Emperors do not judge bishops. Ambrose noted that "the Emperor is within the Church, not above it."[2] Pope Gelasius I (492–96) spoke of the two powers that rule the world: the sacred authority of the Popes and the royal power of kings. While the Emperor is supreme in human affairs, he must submit to those in charge of spiritual things and seek from them the means of salvation.[3]

From the beginning of the alliance between church and state, the Emperor, too, believed that it was his duty to assist the Church in carrying out its mission to the world. However, the step between assistance and domination was a short one. The Emperor tended to think of himself as the ruler of a Christendom to which the priesthood gave spiritual care and nourishment. Not infrequently he intervened in matters properly ecclesiastical. A prime example was the Emperor Zeno, who drew up and tried to impose a creed called the Henoticon (484) in the midst of the Monophysite heresy. Eventually the empire died out in the West, the last western Emperor abdicating in 475. In the East, however, the empire carried on until 1453, the eastern Emperor dominating every aspect of religious and civil life.

The Church and the Holy Roman Empire

When Constantine transferred his capital from Rome to Byzantium on the Bosporus in 330, the move presaged the end of the Roman Empire in the West. By the end of the fifth century, the whole of Western Europe was ruled by barbarian kings. Subsequently, the Franks hammered out an empire that included France, Germany, and northern Italy until the tenth century. In 800, Charlemagne, who reigned as King of the Franks from 768 to 814, was crowned on Christmas Day as Emperor of the Romans by Pope Leo III in the St. Peter's Basilica in Rome. Some historians maintain that the Holy Roman Empire, as it came to be known, was born on that occasion.

During the Middle Ages, the Holy Roman Empire represented the quest of men, clerical and lay, for peace and unity in western Christendom. There were two cooperating and complementary powers: church and empire. In theory, the two powers, while distinct, were to collaborate for the good of the peoples subject to both. The last word in religious matters was reserved to the Church and, through it, to the Pope as the visible head of the Church. The final word in political and civil affairs belonged to the Emperor. Still, it was not always easy or even possible to define the limits of ecclesiastical and imperial jurisdiction; and the difficulty, aggravated by human shortcomings, sometimes gave rise to serious disputes between Pope and Emperor.

Under the weak successors of Charlemagne, his empire disintegrated, but it was infused with new life in 962 when the Saxon King of Germany, Otto the Great (936–73), was crowned Roman Emperor by Pope John

XII. Like Constantine and Charlemagne before him, Otto regarded himself as the protector of the Church and responsible for its well-being. He looked upon Christianity and the nationally unified empire over which he ruled as one, but he continued to acknowledge the double authority of papacy and state. Under the Emperor Henry III (1039–56), the empire reached the summit of its power, with Germany at its core. There were few changes in its borders on the east and south, but in the west most of France had been lost to feudal princes, as the French monarchy was evolving under the early Capetians.

In the eleventh century, there were several important attempts to free the Church from lay domination. In 1059, Pope Nicholas II determined that the Pope was to be elected solely by the Cardinals and not, for example, by the Roman aristocracy or the Emperor. Then Pope Gregory VII (1073–85) forbade lay investiture—that is to say, the appointment of persons to ecclesiastical offices by laymen who also gave them the symbols of their office. When the Emperor Henry IV (1056–1106) violated this prohibition, Gregory excommunicated him (in 1076) and absolved his subjects from their oath of allegiance. Subsequently, Henry did penance for his sins and was reinstated, but he continued to be a thorn in the side of the Church.

The strongest Emperor of the twelfth century was the Hohenstaufen Frederick I (1152–90), called Barbarossa. He claimed for himself the authority of Constantine and Charlemagne over Christendom. He was resisted by Pope Alexander III (1159–81). The conflict gave rise to the appointment of several anti-Popes by the Emperor, to wars, bloodshed, and much suffering for the affected peoples until peace was restored in 1177. The thirteenth century opened with the reign of Pope Innocent III (1198–1216). In a unique set of circumstances—for one thing, he was the guardian of the future Emperor Frederick II (1212–50)—Innocent exercised a political sovereignty over Europe greater than that of any of his predecessors or successors. If Innocent involved himself in secular affairs, he did so because he believed that the state existed to serve the higher spiritual power of the Church.

In 1268, at Tagliacozzo in Italy, the last of the Hohenstaufen dynasty, Conradin, the grandson of Frederick II, was defeated in battle and beheaded by Charles of Anjou, the brother of the King of France, Saint Louis IX. The effect of this battle was to cut Italy loose from the empire and limit the imperial borders of Germany. Subsequently, in his famous statement *Unam Sanctam* (1302), Pope Boniface VIII (1294–1303) tried once more to assert the primacy of the papacy in both spiritual and temporal matters, but he met resistance everywhere. Shortly after the death of Boniface VIII and the removal of the papal residence to Avignon in southern France (1305–76), the papacy came increasingly under French domination.

To replace the defunct Hohenstaufen dynasty, the German princes elected the Hapsburg Rudolph I as Emperor in 1273. As Emperor, Rudolph gained control of the lands around Austria, which was an eastern borderland or march of the Holy Roman Empire. After the fifteenth century, the Emperors were chosen almost automatically from the house of Hapsburg. Through dynastic marriages the Hapsburgs extended their hegemony over a large part of Western Europe. Charles V, the Holy Roman Emperor from 1519 to 1556, also ruled Spain (with its vast possessions in the New World), the Netherlands, Burgundy, Austria, Bohemia, Hungary, Naples, and Sicily. However, the Protestant Reformation with its religious and political upheavals led to the decline of the empire. After the terrible Thirty Years War (1618–48) and the Treaty of Westphalia (1648), which ended it, the empire became little more that a federation of principalities over which the Hapsburg Emperor presided without any power. The empire finally gave up the ghost in 1806 when the Emperor Francis II of Austria renounced the imperial crown after the battle of Austerlitz (1805).

Thus perished the empire that had existed for a millennium. It was an attempt to restore the grandeur of ancient Rome animated by the spiritual force of the Roman Church. For the most part, the attempt failed. Nevertheless, at its best the empire embodied the ideal of a civilization in which the loyalty of individuals was defined not so much by nationality as by the vision of a universal Christendom one and undivided.

Nationalism

We can get at the notion of nationalism by speaking first about nationality. Nationality is possessed by a people having a common language and common historical traditions. A nationality may or may not have political unity and independence; the Irish and Polish, for example, did not always have political independence. There is, however, a tendency for each nationality to strive for an independent national state of its own. When the people become conscious of their nationality and feel loyalty and devotion to it, then we have nationalism. Accordingly, we can speak of French, German, Italian, and Spanish nationalism, but nationalism is an almost universal phenomenon. In a pejorative sense, nationalism refers to the tendency, overt or latent, to exalt one nationality over another.

Already at the end of the fourteenth century, nationalism had begun to assert itself in Europe. Nations began to regard themselves as separate political entities and jettison the universal vision of Christendom that looked beyond vaguely defined national boundaries. In the late Middle Ages and early modern times a number of developments encouraged the rise of national feeling. Increasingly, modern languages rather than Latin became the vehicle of literature. Dante, for example, wrote his *Divine Comedy* (1306–21) and Machiavelli his *Prince* (1513) in Italian. Then there was the growth of large centralized states ruled by absolute monarchs, as in the case of England and Spain under the Tudors and Hapsburgs respectively. They were definitely independent states. In the third place, every national government in Western Europe strove to foster and protect its own commercial interests, and to this end it took various measures, such as restricting foreign imports, subsidizing domestic production, acquiring colonies, and building navies to protect shipping. All these measures had the attendant effect of enhancing national patriotism. Finally, loyalty to the Catholic or Protestant religion and identification of these religions with one's country—say, Catholicism with France and Spain and Protestantism with England and Sweden—led to a heightened nationalism.

Possibly modern nationalism originated in sixteenth-century England under the Tudors, of whom Henry VII was the first and Elizabeth I the last. The Tudors gave the country a strong and very patriotic national monarchy. The nationalistic sense was strengthened in the seventeenth century by English Puritans such as Milton and Cromwell, who thought of their countrymen, at least the God-fearing English Puritans, as God's "chosen people," comparable to the Israelites of old. In the eighteenth century, the American Revolution (1775–81) resulted in the creation of a nation different in both origins and character from the nations of the Old World. The liberal and humanitarian nationalism of the new American state was rooted in the idea, expressed in the American Declaration of Independence, that "all men are created equal; that they are endowed by their Creator with certain inalienable rights; that among these are life, liberty, and the pursuit of happiness . . . "

The American Revolution had a powerful impact upon the French Revolution (1789–99). Out of the French Revolution came the famous slogan proclaiming individual liberty, human equality, and the fraternity of all peoples. There was a nationalistic leveling process that deprived the higher classes of the special privileges they had long enjoyed in French society. The republicans of the revolution, following upon Jean-Jacques Rousseau (1712–78), believed that nations should be guided by the popular will. Authoritarianism as exercised by absolute monarchs, they held, had no rightful place in revolutionary France, or elsewhere, for that matter. Subsequently, the principles of the French Revolution were carried throughout Europe by the armies of Napoléon.

German nationalism was fanned by Napoléon's defeat of Prussia at Jena in 1806. German patriots such as Johann Fichte (1762–1814) and Friedrich Schleiermacher (1768–1834) became bitter foes of the French and advocates of German unity, and they stressed the historical differences between nations rather than their common aspirations. Opposition to the French and Napoléon also produced nationalist reactions among the Italians and Spanish.

After the defeat of Napoléon at Waterloo (1815), the Congress of Vienna (1814–15) tried to restore the old despotic order; however, the idea of national self-determination, which was a vital part of the French Revolution, could not be suppressed. In 1848, liberal and nationalistic revolutions broke out in almost every capital of Europe, but they failed for lack of popular support. In 1870, Italy finally became a united kingdom under Victor Emmanuel II (1861–78). About the same time (1871), the loose confederation of German states became the German Empire with Otto von Bismarck (1815–98) as its first chancellor. Thus two new states came into existence, a fact fraught with serious consequences for the future.

Nationalism also took hold in Latin America. Portugal and Spain had created great empires there in the sixteenth century, but in the first half of the nineteenth century these empires disintegrated. The revolutions of 1808–26 resulted in political independence for thirteen nations. A number of explanations have been offered for the revolutionary upheaval: the distance of the colonies from the mother countries, the impact of events in Europe and North America, the growing political and economic maturity of Latin Americans, and, proximately, Napoléon's invasion of the Iberian Peninsula (1808), which drove out the royal families of Portugal and Spain. In certain respects independence made little difference to the people as a whole—the liberator Simon Bolívar (1783–1830) said that he had only "plowed the sea"—but the range of choices for the new countries was greatly expanded.

At the conclusion of World War I (1914–18), with its

great destruction of life and property, four great European empires were dismembered: the Austrian-Hungarian, the Ottoman, the Russian, and the German. The Paris Peace Conference of 1919–20 redrew the map of Europe according to the principle of nationality. Austria, Hungary, Czechoslovakia, Poland, Yugoslavia, and Romania emerged as nation-states. Germany and Turkey were reduced from imperial to national states. Russia was reorganized as a federation of national states: the Union of Soviet Socialist Republics. A relatively few years later, there appeared in the countries that had been defeated or bitterly disappointed in World War I particularly virulent forms of nationalism: the fascism of Benito Mussolini in Italy, the Nazism of Adolf Hitler in Germany, and the communism or Marxian Socialism of Lenin and Stalin in Russia. Eventually these types of nationalism led to World War II (1939–45).

Toward the end of the nineteenth century and at the beginning of the twentieth, there was a new wave of European (and American and Japanese) imperialism. The imperialists believed that only by overseas expansion could their country's future be assured. By the outbreak of World War I (1914), almost all of Africa and most of Asia, with its teeming millions, had been divided among the European powers as outright possessions, protectorates, or "spheres of influence." In Africa, only Ethiopia and Liberia were not ruled by Europeans—that is to say, by the French, British, Portugese, Belgians, Germans, Spanish, or Italians.

Several factors, however, encouraged the growth of the independence movements after World War II: the example of non-African countries that had secured their independence on other continents; the formation of nationalist parties, often led by small cadres of educated persons; the decline of economic benefits from colonization; and the willingness of the colonizers to grant concessions. At the United Nations, 1960 was called the Year of Africa because fourteen French colonies, the Belgian Congo, Somalia, and Nigeria all achieved independence and admission to the United Nations that year. Unfortunately, the independent African states have found the going rough (political stability, social cohesion, and economic growth have proved elusive), but a greater sense of realism has been achieved.

After World War II (1939–45) and even before, nationalism was a powerful force in Asia, too. Some former colonies achieved independence peacefully, while others had to struggle for it. Britain granted independence to India (1947), Pakistan (1947), Ceylon (1948), Burma (1948), and Malaysia (1957), and the United States did the same for the Philippines (1946). The Dutch withdrew from Indonesia in 1949 and the French from Indochina in 1954. Immediately after the war, China became a communist state and Korea was arbitrarily divided into two countries. Japan, devastated and stripped of its empire, quickly recovered economically. The struggle of the Jews for a national state in Palestine (Zionism) was won when Israel was founded in 1948. In Asia, however, as in Africa, there has been a considerable gap in many places between aspirations and accomplishments.

The last decade of the twentieth century witnessed the emergence of a number of new nations in Eastern Europe. In 1991 the astonishing and relatively peaceful dissolution of the Soviet empire was followed by the formation of the Commonwealth of Independent States (CIS). It is made up of eleven of the twelve former Soviet republics, Georgia declining to join. In 1991 and 1992 the breakup of Yugoslavia into several independent states was accompanied by internecine fighting fueled by ethnic antagonisms. Finally, the peaceful division of Czechoslovakia into two independent states took effect in 1993.

A partial response of the Church to the rise of new nations has been to make concordats with some of them. A concordat is an agreement between the Holy See and a sovereign or government about matters of mutual concern. Concordats have to do with such matters as the freedom of the Church to pursue its mission, Catholic schools and education, the support of the Church's ministers, and regulations pertaining to marriage. The first concordat was probably the Concordat of Worms (1122), made by Pope Calistus II and the Emperor Henry V, which settled the so-called investiture conflict.

Other famous concordats were the ones made by Pius VII and Napoléon I of France in 1801 and by Pius XI and the Italian government in 1929, which was part of the Lateran Treaty settling the "Roman Question" and setting up Vatican City as an independent state. In the twentieth century, the Church has made concordats with other states, too, for example, with Colombia in South America and with Latvia, Poland, Portugal, Romania, Germany, Yugoslavia, and Spain in Europe.

4

The Catholic Church and the International Organization (II)

With the decline of the Holy Roman Empire and the rise of nationalism, churchmen began to reflect upon the implications of the developing situation.

Philosophers, Theologians, and Canonists

Already in the thirteenth century, Saint Thomas Aquinas (1225–74), perhaps the most influential theologian of the Catholic Church, began to formulate principles that would profoundly affect Catholic political thought to today. As a matter of fact, Aquinas had accepted and developed the thought of Aristotle (384–322 B.C.) in this regard. In his little treatise on *Kingship,* Aquinas explained the need and role of civil government. Human beings, he wrote, have to live together for their mutual support and protection; however, living together in society requires some means by which they can be governed: "For where there are many men together and each one is looking after his own interest, the multitude would be broken up and scattered unless there were an agency to take care of what appertains to the commonweal." Aquinas goes on to cite the words of the Book of Proverbs

(11:14): "Where there is no governor, the people shall fall." Aquinas concludes that a monarchy is the best form of government because an individual, like the captain of a ship, can more easily provide that unity of direction and government necessary for the welfare of civil society. Unfortunately, however, that portion of the treatise that tells how to prevent a king from becoming a tyrant has been lost.[1]

The teaching of Aristotle and Aquinas on this matter would not be lost upon succeeding generations of Catholic thinkers. True, the teaching of Aristotle and Aquinas grounded the need for government among those who are citizens of a kingdom, citizens who live together and are mutually dependent upon one another, but the principles Aristotle and Aquinas enunciated apply also to citizens of modern nations who live in proximity to each other and are mutually dependent. They, too, need some agency "to take care of what appertains to the commonweal."

The contemporary of Saint Thomas Aquinas Dante Alighieri (1265–1321), the Italian poet, wrote his essay on *Monarchy* (1309) just at the moment when the Holy Roman Empire had begun to decline. Dante wished to support its existence, for he believed the absolute independence of states would destroy the unity and peace of Europe. He believed in the necessity of a single empire (or monarchy) in which each nation preserved its individuality but over which there was a supreme ruler and arbiter to regulate international affairs. The empire was thus an international organization for coordination and unification.

According to Dante, the proper function of the human race, taken as a whole, is to develop the capacity of the intellect to the fullest, for the intellect is the highest faculty of human beings. The human race can do this only when it enjoys universal peace; hence universal peace is the greatest of blessings. Dante goes on: Since the whole human race is ordained to a single end, it ought to have a single form of government, so that it is not a house divided. Therefore, a universal monarchy and monarch are necessary for the well-being of the world.

Dante adduces additional reasons for the organization of all humanity under a single authority. Perfect unity among human beings under a single prince reflects the unity of God, who is himself one and indivisible. Moreover, when a conflict arises between two princes, there must be someone superior to both—a monarch or Emperor—who can render judgment. A monarch who is supreme has nothing to gain; hence, he can be absolutely just in his dealings with others, and the result will be peace, which is the fruit of justice. Finally, Dante remarks that never since the fall of our first parents was the world everywhere at peace until the perfect monarchy of Augustus, when, in the fullness of time, the Son of God was born.[2]

The attentive reader will note that the reasons given by Dante for a single world authority are more cogent than those he offers for the rule of an individual. In the latter case he was swayed by the political system he knew best.

Two centuries after Dante, Francis de Vitoria (1483–1546), a Spanish Dominican who was a professor of theology at the University of Salamanca, Spain, became the Catholic pioneer in the field of international relations. The European world had changed radically: the national states of Europe had achieved an advanced state of development, the New World had just been discovered, and the relationship between Spain and its new colonies had raised many questions. Vitoria expressed his thought

49

on these matters in a series of annual lectures on topics such as civil power (1528), the power of the Church (1532), and the law of war (1539).[3]

For Vitoria, the world as a whole was, in a sense, a single state. We were all members of the world-state because we were all human beings and inhabited the same planet. Human beings were social entities, and they needed to live together in order to develop their many potentialities and satisfy all their needs. For this reason, families, tribes, cities, and eventually national states came into existence. Nations differed accidentally from each other by reason of race, history, territory, character, language, and religion. However, the accidental differences between nations need not prejudice the substantial unity of the human race as a whole. Just as the differences between individuals in a nation complemented each other, so the differences between sovereign nations complemented each other.

Vitoria went on to teach that just as there must be a juridical norm to regulate relations between the citizens of a national state, so there must be a juridical norm to regulate relations between states, and this norm is constituted by international law.[4] Moreover, the world community has the right to create an organ to act in its name with the authority to impose its will, settle disputes, and punish offenders, not because of a treaty or pact, but because of an international need. Such an organ would render war unnecessary, but in the absence of this means each nation has a right to go to war to secure justice. Still, a war is just only if it benefits the whole world, and not otherwise. What is more, just as the majority of citizens might lawfully act to set up a king over the whole state despite the opposition of some, so the majority of nations might act to set up an authority over all despite the opposition of some. Accordingly, Vitoria envisioned an organization of nations with greater power than the League of Nations after World War I or the United Nations after World War II.

Another Spaniard, the Jesuit Francis Suarez (1548–1617), professor at Coimbra, further developed Catholic teaching about the need for an organized political community in his monumental *Tractatus de Legibus ac Deo Legislatore* (Treatise on laws and God as lawgiver), published in 1612. With others, he recognized that the medieval empire had fulfilled its function and was no longer viable, especially since Christendom had broken up into separate kingdoms, each one claiming autonomy. Suarez did not think that it was necessary for the common good of the human race that it should be organized into a single political community. Such a universal community or state was scarcely possible and, indeed, hardly expedient. Aristotle had noted the difficulty of governing rightly a very large city (6 *Polit.*, 4); all the more so, it would be difficult to govern rightly the whole world.[5]

Nevertheless, Suarez recognized a kind of unity, imperfect but real, among the nations of the earth. He put it in this way: "However divided into different peoples and realms, mankind maintains a certain degree of unity, not only specific but also, as it were, political and moral, as is stressed by the natural precept of mutual love and compassion."[6] In other words, each nation, though perfectly independent, is also a member of the world community. Each nation is tied (or should be tied) to the others in virtue of a common humanity and mutual need. The mutual relations between nations are governed by what Suarez and others have called the *jus gentium,* or law of peoples. The law of peoples is ultimately based on human nature, but it arises from international traditions and

customs that enable the nations of the earth to live together in justice and peace.

An American scholar has pointed out the essential
difference between the Vitorian and Suarezian concep-
tions of the international community. He wrote:

> There was, however, an essential difference between the
> international community of Suarez and that of Vitoria.
> To the former, the community of states was inorganic. It
> existed because the states existed and had need of rela-
> tions, one with the other, of "mutual assistance and inter-
> course." But the community which he had in mind was
> not an organized community, with law-making and law-
> enforcing powers. The laws of the international commu-
> nity of Vitoria were created because the community had
> "the power to create" them, just as it had the power,
> backed by the authority of the world, to enforce them. The
> international community of Suarez was governed by laws
> introduced slowly, unconsciously, by custom, in his own
> words, "by the habitual conduct of nations."[7]

The same scholar maintained that the organized
community of Vitoria was exemplified by the vast and
complicated machinery of the League of Nations, while
the inorganic community of Suarez, growing out of the
mere coexistence of states, was exemplified by the International Court set up at The Hague.

A younger contemporary of Suarez, Émeric Crucé
(1590–1648), a French Carmelite and pedagogue, also offered a plan for the organization of international society.
He published his *Le Nouveau Cynée* (The new Cyneas) in
Paris in 1623. In this work Crucé professed to assume
the peacemaking role of the counselor Cyneas at the court
of King Pyrrhus (319–272 B.C.) of Macedonia. Crucé
wished to prevent war; there was no reason for it. To the

objection that the diversity of states causes quarrels and wars Crucé responded:

> Why should I, a Frenchman, wish to harm an Englishman, a Spaniard, or a Hindoo? I cannot wish it when I consider that they are men like me, that I am subject to error and sin and that all nations are bound together by a natural and consequently indestructible tie which ensures that a man cannot consider another a stranger, unless he follows the common and inveterate opinion that he had received from his predecessors.[8]

If the diversity of nations was not a cause for war, neither was religion a cause for war, because all religion tends to the same end: the glorification of God. There must also be between states, for their common good, increased commerce and communication.

To achieve these worthy objectives, Crucé called for a permanent international assembly made up of the representatives of all the nations of Asia and Africa as well as the nations of Europe. In this assembly, the Pope or his legate would have the first place and the Sultan of the Turks would have the second place, because of the "majesty, power and happiness" of his empire. The function of the assembly was to exercise legislative, judicial, and conciliatory authority, and it might arbitrate all international disputes. The assembly might impose sanctions and even use force upon recalcitrant parties "if gentle means are unsuccessful." However, Crucé's work was overshadowed by the more famous work of Hugo Grotius (1583–1645), *De jure belli et pacis* (or The law of war and peace), published two years later, in 1625.

In the nineteenth century, Louis Taparelli D'Azeglio (1793–1862), a Jesuit philosopher and pioneer sociologist, published his *Saggio teoretico di diritto naturale* (or

Theoretical study of natural law) at Palermo in 1840–43). According to Taparelli, every state should desire and promote the well-being of every other state. That well-being consists in the preservation of its political independence and the happiness of its citizens. One state should come to the assistance of another that has been unjustly attacked, for rendering assistance is a matter of friendship and enlightened self-interest. It is the noble duty of a friendly government to admonish a sovereign who has gone astray in his own domain; indeed, it is permissible for one state to intervene in the affairs of another, for fear that the disorders in the latter will spread to itself.

Taparelli goes on to say that one nation ought not to exclude another from what it needs for its own welfare. To meet their needs, the nations of the earth engage in commerce and establish relations with the most distant peoples. It is commerce that brings peoples together and produces material, intellectual, and moral advantages for all. Thus common needs and interests lead nations to form an international society that enables each of them to function well for the benefit of its own citizens. Such a society, of course, must be regulated according to the principles of order and justice.

Taparelli takes a closer look at the international society he was discussing. When intelligent individuals work together to achieve a common goal, they form a society. When states work together to achieve a common goal, which is the well-being of all, they form what may be called a society of societies. However, if a society is to function properly, it has need of an authority to direct its activity. Assuming the free consent of the nations involved, an international society naturally takes the form of a polyarchy—that is to say, an authority vested in the many. The associated nations must agree upon the form—monarchy, parliament, committee, or other—that this authority is to assume. In their common interest nations cannot refuse to acknowledge this authority without breaking the social bonds that unite them. What is more, this authority must have the resources to maintain order and justice and protect the weak against the strong.

Can a nation preserve its independence if it is subject to an international authority? Taparelli answers, "Yes." Just as a family retains its domestic liberty even though it is part of civil society, so a nation can retain its political liberty even when it becomes part of an international society. An international authority does not have the right to change at will the respective boundaries of different nations. If boundaries are to be changed, this can be done only by agreement between the sovereigns concerned. Of course, an international authority ought to obtain complete information about the needs of people. Then it ought to deliberate upon the information that it has gathered and make laws. All the member-nations should collaborate on an equal footing in framing the laws. A code of laws, carefully prepared and universally adopted, would contribute greatly to the security and happiness of all.[9]

Modern Popes

In this section we begin to examine the teaching of modern Popes who, along with many others and with increasing clarity, have seen the need for a worldwide organization of nations and continue to specify the principles that should guide it. International cooperation, centered in one or more international organizations, is necessary, the Popes teach, for many reasons: to settle disputes among nations, preserve the peace, guarantee the territorial integrity and independence of smaller nations, promote the economic development of poorer nations, and safeguard human rights. Such cooperation is appropriate and even demanded in view of the essential unity of the human race under the fatherhood of God. In this section we are concerned with the teaching of the Popes from Leo XIII, at the end of the nineteenth century, to Pius XI, who led the Church prior to the formation of the United Nations in 1945. In the next chapter we shall review papal support of the United Nations, the most recent and comprehensive organization of the nations of the world.

Leo XIII (1878–1903) was one of the greatest Popes of modern times as he led the Church into the twentieth century. Disturbed by the restrictions imposed on the Church by anti-Catholic governments in Germany, France, and Italy, in 1885 he wrote an encyclical letter, *Immortale Dei* (or The Christian constitution of states). In this letter he deplored the exclusion of the Church from the public life of states and called for the cooperation of church and state in seeking the common good. According to the Pope, human beings must live together with other human beings to supply all their needs. Every community of human beings needs a ruling authority for the good order of society. This authority ultimately comes from God because he is the author of human nature. Indeed, all public authority comes from God, the true and supreme Lord of the world.[10] The Pope did not explicitly apply these ideas to the international community of nations, but he might have done so, since the relationship between modern states, the citizens of one world, resembles the relationship between the citizens of a particular state.

Benedict XV (1914–22), who succeeded Pius X (1903–14), witnessed the tragedy of World War I. In 1917, he wrote a letter to the heads of the warring states in which he offered a seven-point plan for ending the war and securing peace. Among other things, he called for a peace based on right rather than might, mutual disarmament, international arbitration of grievances, and evacuation of occupied territories.[11] Initially, the Pope's letter seemed to make little impression upon the recipients, but similar proposals were adopted later by the League of Nations as a matter of common sense and justice.

Then in his encyclical letter *Pacem Dei Munus* (or Peace the gift of God), published in 1920, the Pope seemed to give his approval to the newly founded League of Nations when he wrote:

> It is much to be desired, Venerable Brethren, that all states, putting aside mutual suspicion, should unite in one league, or rather a sort of family of nations, calculated both to maintain their own independence and safeguard the order of human society. What especially, among other reasons, calls for such an association of nations is the need, generally recognized, to make every effort to abolish or reduce the enormous burden of the military expenditures which states can no longer bear, in order to prevent these disastrous wars or at least to remove the danger of them as far as possible. So would each nation be assured not only of its independence, but also of the integrity of its territory within its just frontiers.[12]

The Holy See never became a member of the League of Nations. In 1923, Mr. John Eppstein, a British official of the league, wrote to the papal Secretary of State suggesting formal relations between the Vatican and the league. Pietro Cardinal Gasparri, the Secretary of State, declined the suggestion, undoubtedly at the direction of the Pope, Pius XI. Cardinal Gasparri wrote, however, that the Holy See was available to the league in matters where it was competent—that is to say, in elucidating principles of morality and international law and in assisting the league in its efforts to relieve suffering peoples.[13]

We may speculate about the reasons for the reluctance of the Holy See to join the League of Nations. Perhaps the Holy See feared a strongly negative reaction to its membership from the Italian government, which believed that the Vatican might use the league to press its claim to the Papal States; perhaps the Holy See had little confidence in the capacity of the league to achieve its objectives; perhaps the Holy See viewed the league as largely an instrument of the victorious powers of World War I to safeguard their interests; or perhaps the Holy See considered the league to be primarily an organization with temporal interests beyond the competence of the papacy.

Pius XI (1922–39) succeeded Benedict XV. His first encyclical, *Ubi Arcano Dei* (1922), dealt with the serious problems left behind by World War I and with the peace that only Christ could bring to the nations. The Pope was quite gloomy about the condition of the world after World War I. The old hatreds and clashes of interest continued to assert themselves. The Pope held that true peace among nations had to be grounded on the teachings, precepts, and example of Jesus Christ. No merely human institution could bring peace, and previous attempts along this line had been unsuccessful, especially when nations had bitterly disagreed.[14] Was the Pope expressing his initial disappointment with the League of Nations? Possibly.

Pius XI's encyclical *Mortalium Animos* (1928) was concerned primarily with the promotion of true religious unity, but at the very beginning of the letter the Pope noted the ever-increasing sense of universal brotherhood, and so it was easy to understand the desire of a great many people for an ever-closer union between nations, all the more so because all acknowledge the unity of the human race.[15]

Then in *Quadragesimo Anno* (1931) (or The fortieth year after Leo XIII's *Rerum Novarum*) the Pope wrote that it would be a good thing if the nations of the world, who are so closely linked by solidarity and interdependence, would promote international economic collaboration by means of wisely framed treaties and institutions.[16]

5

Papal Support of the United Nations

In this chapter, we wish to review the support given by modern Popes to a very specific international organization: the United Nations. The support has been explicit and vigorous, and it is grounded upon certain principles: the unity of the human race, whose members have a common origin, nature, and destiny; the need of human beings to live together in peace on this earth and to share its resources for their common good; and, to this end, the necessity of some form of authoritative direction centered in one or more international organizations.

Pius XII

Pius XII (1939–58) was elected Pope on March 2, 1939, a few months before the outbreak of World War II on September 1, 1939, when Germany invaded Poland. On August 24, 1939, just before the outbreak of the war, he appealed for peace in the face of the gathering storm. "Nothing is lost by peace," he said, "but everything is lost by war."

In November of the same year (1939), in an address to Haiti's Minister to the Vatican, the Pope began to speak about a new international organization. He said:

The world will enjoy peace and order only if the leaders of nations renounce the use of force against what is right; if, recognizing the insufficiency of a purely human morality, they accept the supreme authority of the Creator as the basis of individual and collective morality; and if they render to the heavenly Father the homage he desires, that is to say, the homage of fraternal union among his children of every country and language.

Only then will those leaders be able to realize and perfect a stable and useful organization, such as is desired by all men of good will, an organization which, because it respects the rights of God, can assure the mutual independence of nations great and small, impose fidelity to treaties and safeguard the sound liberty and dignity of the human person.[1]

Again in 1939, in the first of a long series of Christmas messages, the Pope proposed his famous five-point plan for peace. The third point declared, in effect, that some juridical institution was needed to avoid arbitrary breaches and unilateral interpretations of treaties. Such an institution would guarantee the faithful observance of the conditions agreed upon and facilitate the revisions and correction of them when necessary.[2] The Pope returned to this idea in his Christmas message of 1941.

Then, from August to October 1944, delegates from the United States, Great Britain, the Soviet Union, and China met at Dumbarton Oaks, Washington, D.C., to draft plans for a new international organization. Referring to their work in an address on the fifth anniversary of the beginning of the war, September 1, 1944, the Pope said:

Already in our Christmas message of 1939, we looked forward to the creation of international organizations which would avoid the pitfalls of the past and really preserve the peace against every possible threat in the future according to the principles of justice and equity. Today, in view of the terrible experience of the past, statesmen and peoples are devoting ever-increasing attention and concern to a new international peace institution. We are truly pleased and genuinely hope that the concrete realization of this project will correspond in large measure to its lofty goal which is the maintenance of peace and security throughout the world with benefit to all.[3]

When the Dumbarton Oaks Conference published its tentative proposals for the new peace organization, the Pope took cognizance of them. He said:

The proposals already published by international commissions permit one to conclude that an essential element for international good order in the future would be the creation of an organ to maintain peace. By common consent this organ would be invested with supreme authority and be responsible for suppressing in the very beginning every threat of isolated or collective aggression. No one could greet this development with greater joy than he who for a long time has defended the principle that war as a solution to international conflicts is now obsolete.[4]

While the Charter of the United Nations was being debated at San Francisco from April 25 to June 26, 1945, on the basis of the Dumbarton Oaks proposals, the Pope commented:

The idea of a new peace organization has been prompted, as no one can doubt, by the best of intentions. The whole of humanity eagerly follows the progress of such a noble enterprise. What a bitter disappointment it would be if it were to fail, if so many years of suffering and hardship were to come to naught, allowing that spirit of oppression to triumph anew from which the world hoped finally to be delivered. O unhappy world! Its final state, as Jesus said, would be worse than the first from which it had so painfully emerged.[5]

In his Christmas message of 1948, Pope Pius XII restated the doctrinal reasons for his support of the United Nations:

The Catholic doctrine about the state and civil society has always been based upon the principle that, according to the will of God, the nations of the earth form a community with a common goal and duties. Even when the proclamation of this principle and its practical consequences have been vigorously contested, the Church has rejected the erroneous idea of a sovereignty which is absolutely autonomous and without social obligations. The Catholic is convinced that every man is his neighbor, that every people is a member, with equal rights, of the family of nations. The Catholic cooperates wholeheartedly in those generous efforts which initially may have only modest results and encounter fierce opposition, which, however, are designed to draw individual states out of their narrow-minded and egocentric mentality.[6]

On the same occasion, the Pope expressed the hope that "the United Nations might become the full and faultless expression of universal solidarity for peace, purging from its institutions and its statutes every vestige of its origin which was of necessity a solidarity in war."[7]

Pope Pius XII returned to the doctrinal basis of his support for the United Nations in his Christmas message of 1951. He saw in the development of an organized international community a response to an underlying law. He spoke of the societal institutions that are necessary for the good of human beings. The most important of these are the family, the state, and also the international society of states, because the common good, which is the essential purpose of every state, can neither exist nor even be imagined without reference to the human race as a whole. In this way, the union of states is something natural; and when states recognize and accept it as such, they are responding to the voice of nature. It is right that this natural union of states should express itself in an external, stable organization. Such an organization represents the "tranquillity of order" that, according to Augustine, is the nature of peace.[8]

The pontificate of Pius XII coincided with the formative years of the United Nations. The Pope greeted the establishment of the United Nations with hearty approval. The members of the human race, by reason of their common origin and end, constitute a family. The nations of the earth form a community: they are united by common interests and a common aim, they depend upon one another, they need to live in peace for the common good, and the common good cannot be achieved or even conceived without reference to the human race as a whole. If the community of nations is to function properly, there must be an international authority that, without suppressing the independence of individual states, is invested with legislative and judicial authority to determine a common course of action and settle disputes.

At the same time, the Pope was fully aware of the shortcomings of the United Nations. It did not recognize the supreme authority of the Creator as the basis of individual and collective morality. In the face of excessive nationalism, it could not exercise the authority that was necessary to guarantee the peace. Not unexpectedly, according to the mind of the Pope, the initial years of the United Nations produced only meager results. Unfortunately, significant disarmament remained only a dream, the "hot" war of World War II had become a "cold" war, and a large part of the human race continued to live in misery.

John XXIII

The pontificate of Pope John XXIII (1958–63), who succeeded Pope Pius XII, was short but memorable. He was almost seventy-seven years old when he was elected Pope. A man of humble origins (his parents were share-croppers in northern Italy) with a warm personality, he was one of the most beloved Popes of modern times. As Pope, he wrote a number of widely read encyclical letters, including *Mater et Magistra* (1961), on Christianity and social progress, and *Pacem in Terris* (1963), on establishing peace throughout the world. His diary, *Journey of a Soul,* published posthumously, revealed a spiritual life of great depth. In order to "open some windows" in the Church, Pope John summoned the Second Vatican Council, which met between 1962 and 1965 and completed its work only after his death. It is difficult to exaggerate the significance of this council for the Church in the twenty-first century.

In his encyclical *Pacem in Terris,* Pope John devoted a major section to the relationship of individuals and nations with the world community. He began by speaking of the growing interdependence of political communities: ideas, persons, and goods circulate freely between countries; national economies are becoming integral parts of one world economy; and political conditions in one country affect political conditions in other countries, too.

The human race is one family, the Pope continued; all its members are equal by virtue of their natural dignity, and so there is an objective duty to provide for the common good of the entire human family. The far-reaching changes and complex problems confronting the human race, especially the preservation of peace and security, cannot be solved by the diplomatic means employed by public authorities in the past. Today the common good of all nations requires the efforts of public authorities who are in a position to act in an effective manner on a worldwide basis.

The international authority, which the Pope believed was necessary, must be set up by common accord and not imposed by force. If this international authority is to avoid even the appearance of partiality and safeguard the juridical equality and moral dignity of all nations, then all its members must join it freely and submit to its decisions by a conscious and free choice.

The primary duty of an international authority, the Pope said, is to recognize, respect, safeguard, and promote the rights of the human person. Moreover, it is the duty of an international authority to deal with economic, social, political, and cultural matters on a worldwide scale. However, the world authority is not to supplant the public authorities of individual states, but to enable them to fulfill their duties with greater ease and security.

The Pope then addressed himself specifically to the United Nations and its intergovernmental agencies. They exist to maintain and consolidate peace among nations and to encourage friendly relations among them on the basis of equality, mutual respect, and cooperation in every sector of society. The Pope concluded:

We earnestly hope that the United Nations may increasingly adapt itself—in its structure and in its means—to the magnitude and nobility of its tasks. As soon as possible, may it become the effective guardian of human rights. These rights, we say, flow directly from the dignity of the human person, and for this reason they are universal, inviolable and inalienable. All this is the more desirable because today the men of every nation take a more active part in the public life of their countries, they follow the affairs of the whole world with greater interest, and they are becoming more conscious of an international community.[9]

The Second Vatican Council

The Second Vatican Council was summoned by Pope John XXIII, and it met in the fall of each year from 1962 to 1965. The council was called to complete the work of the First Vatican Council (1869–70), which had been interrupted by the outbreak of the Franco-Prussian War. Moreover, the profound and complex changes that had overtaken the Church and the world in the first half of the twentieth century demanded the attention and consultation of all the bishops of the Catholic world. Some sessions of the council were attended by more than twenty-five hundred bishops representing the largest part of the Catholic episcopacy. Pope John died in 1963, before the council had completed its work; but his successor, Pope Paul VI, maintained the council in existence, lending it warm support.

One of the major documents published by Vatican II begins with the Latin words *Gaudium et Spes*. This document is concerned with the situation and role of the Church in the modern world. Having described in some detail the effects of change on the world, the document reaffirms at the outset the dignity of the human person and the right of every person to lead a life that is truly human. Although there are striking physical, intellectual, and moral differences among individuals, they are basically equal with respect to their fundamental human rights. True, the purpose of the Church can be realized fully only in the next world, but the Church serves as a leaven in this world by proclaiming the dignity of human beings. The Church encourages its members to meet their responsibilities in this world, for the Christian who neglects his temporal duties neglects his duties to his neighbor and his God.[10]

In its discussion of the place of the Church in the modern world, Vatican II turned its attention to peace and the community of nations. According to the council:

> Peace on earth cannot be obtained unless personal well-being is safeguarded and men freely and trustingly share with one another the riches of their inner spirits and their talents. A firm determination to respect other men and peoples and their dignity, as well as the studied practice of brotherhood, is absolutely necessary for the establishment of peace. Hence, peace is likewise the fruit of love, which goes beyond what justice can provide.[11]

Then, speaking in general terms, the council noted that relations between states are becoming increasingly close, and the common good of all must be pursued intelligently and effectively. Agencies of the international community need to do their part to meet the essential needs of human beings. The international agencies that already exist—the council did not mention any of them by name—deserve well of the human race. These represent the first attempts to provide a solid basis for solving the critical problems of our age.[12]

Paul VI

Perhaps the most ringing endorsement of the United Nations came from Pope Paul VI (1963–78), the successor of Pope John XXIII. On July 11, 1963, only two weeks after his election, Pope Paul received an official visit from U Thant, the Secretary-General of the United Nations. In his remarks on that occasion, the Pope said to his distinguished visitor:

The Holy See holds a very high conception of that international organism; it considers it to be the fruit of a civilization to which the Catholic religion, with its driving center in the Holy See, gave the vital principles; it considers it an instrument of brotherhood between nations, which the Holy See has always desired and promoted, and hence a brotherhood intended to favor progress and peace among men; it considers the United Nations as the steadily developing and improving form of the balanced and unified life of all humanity in its historical and earthly order. . . .

The ideologies of those who belong to the United Nations are certainly multiple and diverse, and the Catholic Church regards them with due attention; but the convergence of so many peoples, so many races, so many states in a single organization, intended to avert the evils of war and to favor the good things of peace, is a fact which the Holy See considers as corresponding to its concept of humanity, and included within the area of its spiritual mission in the world.[13]

Of even greater significance was the address of the Pope to the General Assembly of the United Nations in New York on October 4, 1965. The United Nations was about to observe its twentieth anniversary. For the Pope, his appearance before the General Assembly and his message expressed his solemn approval of the United Nations and its work, an approval shared by his recent predecessors and the whole Catholic episcopacy. The Pope was convinced that the United Nations represents *le chemin obligé de la civilization moderne et de la Paix mondiale,* the obligatory path of modern civilization and world peace. Never again must the organization that the nations have established be allowed to fail; rather, it must be continually improved and adapted to historical conditions. The United Nations marks a stage in the progress of humanity.

The nations of the world can no longer afford to ignore each other, the Pope said, and the United Nations offers a form of coexistence that is at once simple and fruitful. By admitting individual states to membership, the United Nations recognizes them as national entities worthy of the respect of all. In doing so, the United Nations promotes an orderly and stable international life and sanctions the important principle that relationships among nations must be governed by reason, justice, law, and negotiation and not by violence, fear, and deceit.

The Pope went on to say to the members of the General Assembly:

You exist and you work together to unite nations, to bring them together with each other. You are an association, a bridge between peoples, a network of relations between states. We are tempted to say that in a way you are in the temporal order what the Catholic Church wishes to be in the spiritual order: one and universal. On the natural level there can be no loftier conception of humanity. Your vocation is to bring together as brothers not only some peoples, but all peoples. A difficult undertaking? Undoubtedly. But such is the nature of your undertaking, an exceedingly noble one. Who does not see the corresponding necessity of gradually establishing a world authority capable of acting effectively on the juridical and political planes?

The Pope urged the members of the Assembly not to lord it over one another, but to regard themselves as equals. Not that they are all equal, but at the United Nations they make themselves equal for the sake of brotherhood. Never again, the Pope said—and here he reached the high point of his address—never again must one be against another. There must be no more war. As John F. Kennedy said, "Mankind must put an end to war or war will put an end to mankind." It is peace that must guide the destiny of peoples and humanity as a whole. All thanks and honor to the United Nations for the conflicts that it has prevented or settled.

How can international peace be achieved? The Pope answered by saying that peace is achieved with the mind, with ideas, and with the works of peace. If the nations of the earth wish to live in peace, let the arms fall from their hands. Modern weapons of destruction cause bad dreams and evil thoughts, demand enormous expenditures that might be used for better purposes, and warp the mental outlook of human beings. Alas, defensive weapons are still necessary in the present historical context, but surely the international community can find the means to guarantee peace and security without recourse to arms. Here is a goal worthy of the United Nations, which will deliver all from the nightmare of ever-threatening war.

However, the United Nations is working not only to achieve peace, but also to promote collaboration among nations of the earth for the good of one and all. This is the best side of the United Nations, and it reflects the plan of God for the human race. The United Nations proclaims the basic rights and duties of human beings, their essential dignity, and their liberty, especially their religious liberty. Here it is really a question of human life, and that life is sacred. Human life should find its staunchest defense at the United Nations. The task of the world body is to provide sufficient bread at the table of mankind and not to reduce the number of those at the banquet of life.

The Pope concluded his address by saying that it is not enough to feed the hungry. What is more, each person should be assured a manner of life in keeping with his dignity. That was what the United Nations was trying to do. Moreover, it was helping governments speed social and economic progress, overcome illiteracy, improve the health of peoples, and place science and technology at the service of all. All this was splendid and deserved everyone's praise and support. However, the structure the United Nations was building should not rest on a purely earthly foundation; rather, it should be supported by an appeal to the consciences of individuals and ultimately to spiritual principles stemming from faith in God.[14]

Then, five years later, on the twenty-fifth anniversary of the United Nations, in 1970, the Pope sent a letter to U Thant, the Secretary-General, commemorating the occasion. The Pope repeated his words to the General Assembly in 1965: the United Nations is "the obligatory path of modern civilization and world peace." To be sure, the Pope continued, the United Nations had not yet been able to fulfill the high hopes and expectations cherished by many when it was founded, but it remained the privileged forum where all people came together to pursue peace and justice, where all men and women rediscovered what they had in common—their humanity.

It was the judgment of the Pope that the Charter of Human Rights, proclaimed by the United Nations in 1948, remained one of its greatest accomplishments. To no one's surprise, because of its huge size and complexity the United Nations had encountered many obstacles and endured many reverses. Still, it must use its voice and influence on behalf of those who cannot be heard—the oppressed, the weak, and the humiliated. Once more, the Pope spoke out against exaggerated nationalism and called for reciprocal, controlled disarmament and hoped that the work of the living might never be used against life.

Further, the Pope noted, technological progress did not of itself ensure a moral way of acting; indeed, such progress made even greater demands upon the conscience of mankind. It was the vocation of the United Nations to foster the common good of all men and women, and this included religious freedom so widely restricted in so many countries. The vocation of the United Nations was to fortify states against the selfish temptations that assailed them, to give consistency to the efforts of persons of goodwill, and to help nations build a society in which individuals could achieve an authentic personal development. May the United Nations apply itself resolutely to this task, the Pope said, and he invoked the blessing of Almighty God upon it.[15]

Subsequently, Pope Paul received Mr. Kurt Waldheim, the successor of U Thant, at the Vatican on two separate occasions: February 5, 1972, and July 9, 1977.[16] In his meetings with the Secretary-General, the Pope reaffirmed a number of important ideas that he had expressed previously. His position vis-à-vis the United

Nations and its important role had not changed over the years.

John Paul II

Pope Paul VI died August 6, 1978. Pope John Paul I was elected almost three weeks later on August 26, 1978; however, the Pope died thirty-four days later, on September 28, 1978—one of the shortest pontificates in centuries. Pope John Paul II succeeded the deceased Pontiff on October 16, 1978.

Less than a year after his election, John Paul II addressed the General Assembly of the United Nations in New York on October 2, 1979. He did so at the invitation of the Secretary-General, Dr. Kurt Waldheim. Speaking in English, the Pope explained the reasons for his appearance before the General Assembly:

The formal reason for my intervention is, without any question, the special bond of cooperation which links the Apostolic See with the United Nations Organization, as is shown by the presence of the Holy See's Permanent Observer to this organization. The existence of this bond, which is held in high esteem by the Holy See, rests on the sovereignty with which the Holy See has been endowed for centuries. . . . Of course, the nature and aims of the spiritual mission of the Apostolic See and the Church make their participation in the tasks and activities of the United Nations very different from that of the states which are communities in the temporal sense.

Besides attaching great importance to its collaboration with the United Nations Organization, the Apostolic See has always, since the foundation of your organization, expressed its esteem for and its agreement with the historic significance of this supreme forum for the international life of humanity today. Also it never ceases to support your organization's functions and initiatives, which are aimed at the peaceful coexistence and collaboration between nations . . . The Church is deeply interested in the existence and activities of the organization whose very name tells us that it unites and associates nations and states. It unites and associates; it does not divide and oppose. It seeks out ways for understanding and peaceful collaboration, and endeavors with the means at its disposal and the methods in its power to exclude war, division and mutual destruction within the great family of humanity today. . . ."[17]

The balance of the Pope's address had to do with the important subject of human rights, and we shall examine it in the next chapter.

As his predecessors did, Pope John Paul II also received the Secretary-General of the United Nations at the Vatican. On April 6, 1982, the Pope received Mr. Javier Pérez de Cuéllar, the successor of Mr. Kurt Waldhein. During their meeting, the Pope spoke of his high regard for the institutional principles and basic goals of the United Nations. He recalled the words of Pope Paul VI that the United Nations represents "the obligatory path of modern civilization and world peace." The need for a world organization had become ever more pressing for several reasons: the growing interdependence of peoples living ever more closely together, the threat of nuclear warfare, the proliferation of arms, and the dire straits of two-thirds of the world's population. All these problems required an international solution and a world organization to seek it.[18]

75

Then in 1985, to commemorate the fortieth anniversary of the Charter of the United Nations, the Pope sent a congratulatory message to Mr. Jaime de Pinies, President of the General Assembly at that time. Again the Pope expressed his support for the United Nations and its objectives. The presence of Permanent Observers representing the Holy See at UN organizations in New York, Geneva, Rome, Paris, and Vienna attested to that support. The Holy See contributes to the goals of the United Nations by appealing to the consciences of individuals to overcome the forces that divide them and follow new paths to peace, understanding, and cooperation.

A number of obstacles impede the progress of the United Nations, the Pope wrote. Those obstacles are excessive nationalism, ideological rigidity, bypassing international bodies in times of crisis, and the attempt to use these bodies for the purpose of propaganda. Still, failure must not turn the United Nations aside from pursuing its goals; rather, failure reveals the areas where improvement is necessary. During the previous forty years, the world would have been much poorer without the United Nations. With the threat of nuclear warfare, the United Nations must continue to press for solutions to international problems through law and justice and not through force.

The United Nations has made important progress in defining and protecting fundamental human rights. The events of the last forty years seemed to confirm the need for an international authority with the juridical and political means to promote the welfare of all nations. Such an authority would make the recourse to arms unnecessary as a solution to conflicts. The Pope was also concerned with the backbreaking debt of the Third World. The economic, social, and human costs of this debt had brought many nations, especially in South America, to the brink of disaster. This is a situation that cannot be tolerated.

In conclusion, the Pope noted what he considered to be the most important priorities of the moment: disarmament that was general, balanced, and controlled; strengthening the moral and juridical authority of the United Nations, so that it could safeguard peace and foster the development of all peoples; implementation of the agreements that nations had signed; and practical recognition of the Charter of the United Nations and Universal Declaration of Human Rights as well as other international juridical instruments.[19]

In 1989, to commemorate the twenty-fifth anniversary of the establishment of the Permanent Mission of the Holy See to the United Nations, Pope John Paul sent a written message to Dr. Javier Pérez de Cuéllar, Secretary-General of the United Nations. The Pope wished not only to commemorate that important date in 1964 when Pope Paul VI chose to send an ad hoc mission to the United Nations, but also to reaffirm the importance that the Holy See and the Catholic Church attribute to the United Nations. The establishment of a permanent office and mission rendered the presence of the Holy See at the United Nations more stable and significant. The representative has the status of an observer. This status allows the Holy See an active presence while safeguarding its ability to preserve the universality that its very nature demands. In conclusion, the Pope recalled once again the words of Pope Paul VI as he addressed the General Assembly in 1965: The United Nations was "the obligatory path of modern civilization and world peace."[20]

In his final meeting with Mr. Pérez de Cuéllar at the Vatican, just prior to the latter's retirement from his office at the United Nations, the Pope again assured the Secretary-General of the confidence that the Holy See places in the world organization. The Pope believed that after a difficult period of financial crisis and many tensions, the United Nations could now attempt to accomplish its mission with greater hope of success. The Pope took the occasion to express his gratitude to the Secretary-General for his diligent work on behalf of peace. The Pope said:

We have seen you promoting peace on all continents. Your wise, tenacious diplomatic activity obtained a cease-fire accord which put an end to the conflict between Iran and Iraq. To you Namibia owes the fact that it gained independence. You contributed to the accords in regard to Afghanistan. Your mediation has allowed the progress of freedom in several Central American countries which for a long time had been torn apart by deadly conflicts. You have not ceased to turn your attention to the worrisome situation in Cyprus. Most recently, thanks to your patient, discreet involvement, people who have been held hostage for years in the Near East have regained their freedom. At this very moment, the United Nations is accompanying the Cambodian people on the path of peace and rebirth. I cannot mention all the areas in which you personally participated in the United Nations' positive activity, not even in the change of relations between East and West. For all this, I wish to express the gratitude of peoples in whose service you have placed all your capacities and devotion.[21]

Then, on October 5, 1995, after some sixteen years, Pope John Paul II addressed the General Assembly of the United Nations in New York for the second time to commemorate the fiftieth anniversary of its foundation. He did so at the invitation of Dr. Boutros Boutros-Ghali, the Secretary-General of the world organization. Speaking successively in several modern languages, the Pope said that his presence and words were meant to be a sign of the interest and esteem of the Holy See and the Catholic Church for the world body today. Although their respective purposes and approaches are obviously different, the Church and the United Nations find wide areas of cooperation on the basis of their common concern for the human family.

According to the Pope, the quest for human freedom had become a powerful force on the threshold of the new millennium. On his previous visit to the General Assembly in 1979, the Pope noted that the quest for freedom had its basis in those universal rights that human beings enjoyed by the very fact of their humanity. One of the highest expressions of fundamental human rights is the United Nations' own Universal Declaration of Human Rights, which it adopted in 1948. There are indeed universal human rights, rooted in the nature of the person, rights that reflect the objective and inviolable demands of a universal moral law. This universal moral law is written on the human heart, and it makes a politics of persuasion rather than of coercion possible.

According to the Pope, the nonviolent revolutions of 1989 demonstrated that the quest for freedom cannot be suppressed. The quest arises from a recognition of the inestimable dignity and value of the human person. A decisive factor in the success of those nonviolent revolutions was the experience of social solidarity. That solidarity was the moral core of the "power of the powerless," a beacon of hope and an enduring reminder that it is possible for man's historical journey to follow a path that is true to the finest aspirations of the human spirit.

The Pope noted that the quest for freedom in the second half of the twentieth century has engaged not only individuals, but nations as well. World War II was fought because of violations of the rights of nations. Many of those nations suffered grievously because they were considered "other" or "inferior." Even after the end of World War II, the rights of nations continued to be violated. The result was the "Cold War," in which the threat of nuclear holocaust hung over humanity. While the Universal Declaration of Human Rights spoke eloquently of the rights of persons, no similar international agreement has adequately expressed the rights of nations. This situation must be considered carefully if freedom and justice are to be fully realized.

Looking more closely at the rights of nations, the Pope said that the old problem of nationalities has emerged anew. Yes, by sharing in the same human nature, people automatically feel that they are members of one great family, as in fact they are. But as the result of the historical conditioning of this same human nature, people are bound in a more intense way to a particular human group, beginning with the family and ending with the state and nation. However, the tension between the universal and the particular can be singularly fruitful if they are lived in a calm and balanced way.

A presupposition of the rights of a nation is certainly its right to exist. Its right to exist naturally implies that every nation enjoys the right to its own language and culture. Moreover, every nation has a right to build its own future by providing an appropriate education for the younger generation. At the same time, each nation has the duty to live in peace, respect, and solidarity with other nations.

The Pope observed that in his travels throughout the world he has come into contact with a rich diversity of nations and cultures in every part of the world. Unhappily, the world has not yet learned to live with diversity. The fear of "difference," especially when it expresses itself in a narrow and exclusive nationalism that denies any rights to the "other," can lead to violence and terror.

And yet if we make the effort to look at matters objectively, we can see that, transcending all the differences between individuals and peoples, there is a fundamental commonality. Different cultures are but different ways of facing the question of personal existence. Thus the differences between cultures, which some find so threatening, can, through respectful dialogue, become the source of a deeper understanding of the mystery of human existence.

Then the Pope turned his attention to the relationship between freedom and moral truth. Freedom, he maintained, is the measure of man's dignity and greatness. Freedom is not simply the absence of tyranny or oppression. Nor is it license to do whatever we like. Freedom is related to truth and is fulfilled in the human quest for truth and in living in the truth. Detached from the truth about the human person, freedom deteriorates into license in the lives of individuals; and, in political life, it becomes the caprice and arrogance of the most powerful.

Against this background, the Pope believed, it is clear that utilitarianism, which defines morality not in terms of what is good but what is advantageous, obstructs the building of a true culture of freedom. Utilitarianism often has devastating consequences because it inspires political and economic aggression on the part of stronger nations against weaker ones. Instead of political and economic aggression, the international economic scene needs an ethic of solidarity, if participation, economic growth, and a just distribution of goods are to characterize the future of humanity. We must recommit ourselves to that solidarity that enables others to live out, in the actual circumstances of their economic and personal lives, that creativity that is a distinguishing mark of the human person.

The United Nations needs to rise more and more above the cold status of an administrative institution and to become the moral center where all nations of the world feel at home, where they can develop a shared awareness of being, as it were, a "family of nations." Being a family of nations, the United Nations has the task of advancing national relationships from simple "existence with" others to "existence for" others in a fruitful exchange of gifts. The idea of "united nations" bespeaks mutual trust, security, and solidarity. Fortunately, the threat of nuclear warfare with which the second half of the twentieth century began seems to have receded.

We must learn not to be afraid, the Pope advised; we must rediscover a spirit of hope and trust. Hope and trust are the premise of responsible activity and are nurtured in the inner sanctuary of conscience where a human being is alone with God. In order to recover our hope and trust at the end of this century of sorrows, we must regain sight of that transcendent horizon of possibility to which the souls of human beings aspire.

As a Christian, the Pope's hope and trust are centered on Jesus Christ. The new millennium will mark the two thousandth anniversary of his birth. Christians believe that his birth and resurrection revealed God's love for all of creation. For Christians, Jesus Christ is God made man and a part of human history. Precisely for this reason, Christian hope for the world and its future extends to every human person. Commitment to Christ does not distract Christians from interest in others but, rather, invites them to be responsible for others, especially the weakest and the suffering, to the exclusion of no one.

The Pope concluded his address by saying that he came before the General Assembly as a witness: a witness to human dignity, a witness to hope, and a witness to the conviction that the destiny of all nations lies in the hands of a merciful Providence. However, mankind must overcome its fear of the future, but we will not overcome it completely unless we do so together. The answer to the fear that darkens human existence at the end of the twentieth century is the common effort to build a civilization of love, founded on the universal values of peace, solidarity, justice, and liberty. The "soul" of the civilization of love is the culture of freedom: the freedom of individuals and nations. With God's grace and human creativity we can build such a civilization; and in doing so, we shall see that the tears of this century have prepared the ground for a new springtime of the human spirit.[22]

6

Human Rights (I)

According to article 1 of the UN charter, one of the basic purposes of the world organization is to promote and encourage respect for human rights and fundamental freedoms for all without regard to race, sex, language, or religion. According to article 62 of the charter, the Economic and Social Council is empowered to make recommendations, prepare draft conventions for submission to the General Assembly, convene international conferences, and set up commissions in the interest of human rights. The Economic and Social Council set up the Commission on Human Rights in 1946, and this commission is the major UN body working for the preservation and extension of human rights. It meets for a period of several weeks each year at Geneva to devise ways and means of achieving its goals. Other commissions and subcommissions have also been set up to deal with such matters as the status of women, discrimination, and minorities.

The Universal Declaration of Human Rights

On December 10, 1948, only three years after the United Nations had come into existence, the General Assembly adopted the Universal Declaration of Human

Rights. The assembly proclaimed the declaration as "a common standard of achievement for all peoples and nations," and it called upon all member-states to recognize and observe the human rights set forth in the declaration. In 1950, the General Assembly decided that December 10 of each year should be observed as Human Rights Day all over the world.

Article 1 of the declaration states that "all human beings are born free and equal in dignity and rights. They are endowed with reason and conscience and should act towards one another in a spirit of brotherhood." Article 2 states that "everyone is entitled to all the rights and freedoms set forth in this Declaration, without distinction of any kind, such as race, color, sex, language, religion, political or other opinion, national or social origin, property, birth or other status. . . . "

Articles 3–21 enumerate the civil and political rights and freedoms to which all human beings are entitled. These include the right to life, liberty, and security of person; freedom from slavery, torture, and inhuman treatment; the right to recognition everywhere as a person before the law; the right to equal protection of the law; freedom from arbitrary arrest, detention, or exile; the right to presumption of innocence until proved guilty; freedom from interference with one's privacy, family, home, or correspondence; and the right to freedom of movement, to asylum from persecution, and to a nationality.

Moreover, men and women of full age have the right to marry and to found a family. Indeed, the declaration states that "the family is the natural and fundamental group unit of society and entitled to protection by society and the state." Everyone has the right to own property, to practice freedom of thought, conscience, and religion, and to manifest his religion or belief in teaching, practice, worship, and observance. Everyone has the right to freedom of opinion and expression, to peaceful assembly and association, and to take part in the government of his country, either directly or through freely chosen representatives. The will of the people shall be the basis of governmental authority, and this shall be expressed in periodic and genuine elections. There should be universal and equal suffrage.

Articles 22–27 of the declaration set forth the economic, social, and cultural rights to which all human beings are entitled. These rights include the right to social security, to work, to favorable working conditions, and to protection against unemployment. Everyone has a right to rest and leisure and to a standard of living adequate for the well-being of himself and his family. Motherhood and childhood are entitled to special care and assistance. Everyone has a right to education, and parents have a prior right to choose the kind of education that shall be given to their children. Everyone has the right freely to participate in the cultural life of the community, to enjoy the arts, and to share in scientific advancement and its benefits.

The concluding articles, 28–30, recognize that everyone is entitled to a social and international order in which these rights may be fully realized; however, the rights of each are limited by the rights of others and by the just requirements of morality, public order, and the general welfare in a democratic society.

The International Covenants on Human Rights

Following the adoption of the Universal Declaration of Human Rights in 1948, work began on drafting two international covenants on human rights—one on economic, social, and cultural rights and the other on civil and political rights—designed to express in binding *legal* form the rights proclaimed in the declaration. On December 16, 1966, the General Assembly unanimously adopted the International Covenant on Economic, Social and Cultural Rights and the International Covenant on Civil and Political Rights together with the latter's Optional Protocol. Another decade went by before the covenants were ratified by a sufficient number of countries (thirty-five) to bring them into force. A second Optional Protocol was adopted in 1989.

The two covenants are based on the Universal Declaration of Human Rights, and they specify in greater detail the rights recognized therein. However, a significant right regulated in the covenants but omitted from the declaration is the right of peoples to self-determination, including the right freely to dispose of their natural wealth and resources. The First Optional Protocol provides a means by which individuals can complain to the United Nations about violations of civil and political rights. The Second Optional Protocol aims at abolishing the death penalty.

States ratifying the Covenant on Economic, Social and Cultural Rights make periodic reports to the Economic and Social Council on the measures taken toward realizing these rights. The council may make general recommendations and promote appropriate international action to assist signatory states. States ratifying the Covenant on Civil and Political Rights report to a special Human Rights Committee composed of persons of high moral character and recognized competence in the field of human rights. This committee acts in accordance with provisions laid down in the covenant itself and in the optional protocols.

The Work of the United Nations on Behalf of Human Rights

The United Nations is deeply involved in the struggle for human rights:

> In addition to setting standards for and monitoring observance of human rights, the United Nations also strives to promote respect for human rights through research, information and publicity activities, and through advising governments that seek help in this area.
>
> Many studies of specific human rights issues have been ordered by the General Assembly and the Economic and Social Council. Some have been carried out by the Center for Human Rights or the Advancement of Women Branch, some by specialized agencies, some by expert committees and some by special rapporteurs. In most cases, the studies are based on data obtained from governments, intergovernmental bodies and concerned nongovernmental organizations.
>
> United Nations studies have provided the basis for the elaboration of international conventions against genocide, slavery, racial discrimination in education, and forced labor; a declaration against religious intolerance; principles of medical ethics by which health-care personnel are bound to protect prisoners from torture; and draft principles of nondiscrimination towards persons born out of wedlock.[1]

In 1968, the twentieth anniversary of the adoption of the Universal Declaration of Human Rights by the General Assembly, the United Nations sponsored an International Conference on Human Rights, held at Teheran from April 22 to May 13. This was the only worldwide governmental conference ever devoted exclusively to that subject. The Teheran conference reviewed progress made since the universal declaration, evaluated the effectiveness of the United Nations' human rights activities, and adopted a program of action and a proclamation.

The United Nations also works on behalf of human rights by combating violations. Each year the Commission on Human Rights holds public meetings on alleged violations, nongovernmental organizations and other qualified parties can present information on situations of concern to them wherever they occur in the world, and the governments involved are able to reply. Further investigations may be launched, discussions with governments may be pursued, assistance may be rendered, and, in some cases, condemnations may be issued. The Human Rights Commission keeps certain situations under constant review.

Each year the United Nations receives tens of thousands of complaints from groups and individuals who claim their rights have been violated. Copies of the complaints are sent to member-states, which then have the opportunity to reply. If "a consistent pattern of gross and reliably attested violations of human rights" is discovered, the Commission on Human Rights may investigate further and then submit a report to the Economic and Social Council. However, the work of the United Nations on behalf of human rights goes much further—a subject to be taken up later.

In December 1993, the General Assembly established the post of United Nations High Commissioner for Human Rights, with principal responsibility for UN human rights activities.

The Catholic Church, Natural Law, and Human Rights

Reference has already been made in chapter 3 to certain biblical ideas relevant to our discussion. These ideas include the fundamental dignity and equality of all human beings, who are made in the image and likeness of God, the unity of the human race on the basis of its origin, the common vocation of all nations to share in the blessings of God's kingdom, the efficacy of Christ's death and resurrection on behalf of all men and women, and the universal fatherhood of God. All these ideas compel us to reverence every individual and treat him or her as a brother or sister. Because these ideas are derived from the Bible and its own tradition, the Catholic Church tries, with varying degrees of success, to inculcate and implement the human rights consistent with this view of mankind.

Ever since the time of Saint Thomas Aquinas (1225–74), however, there has been another reason for the stance of the Catholic Church with respect to human rights. The reason is the Church's greater consciousness of the natural law as a support for human rights. The natural law is recognized by an analysis of human nature and its basic tendencies. Human beings are rational animals with the tendencies that are characteristic of animals and rational beings. Endowed with intelligence, men and women can perceive their essential nature and identify those tendencies that must be satisfied to achieve personal fulfillment. The result is a natural dictate or command of reason to act in a specific way to achieve a specific goal, and this is the natural law. For example, my nature inclines me to preserve my life; I can preserve my life only by eating and drinking; hence, the natural law, the command or dictate of reason, obliges me to eat and drink.

In accordance with this view of the matter, that is good that is in harmony with human nature and satisfies its tendencies, while that is evil that is not. (Needless to say, not all the proclivities that we experience are in harmony with human nature. It is the function of reason to determine which are harmonious and which are not.) The natural law obliges us to do what is good and avoid what is evil understood in this sense. Among the natural tendencies we have, some we have in common with all creatures, such as preserving one's life and being; others we have in common with all animals, such as the tendency to propagate and care for offspring; still others are proper to human nature, such as the tendencies to learn the truth, live in society, and so on. We comply with natural law when, under the direction of reason, we act to fulfill these tendencies for personal completion.

We may speak of the precepts of the natural law. These are dictates of human reason obliging us to do something or avoid something in view of the makeup and tendencies of human nature. The precepts of the natural law are universal in the sense that they are derived from human nature, which is the same in all men and women and does not change radically. Human nature is basically the same throughout the world, and we of the twentieth and twenty-first centuries are still the same rational animals that the ancient Chinese, Israelites, and Greeks were. Proponents of the natural law often point to the famous Ten Commandments of the Mosaic law as precepts of the natural law that have been recognized and accepted by peoples everywhere. Such, for example, is the fourth commandment: "Honor thy father and thy mother," which obliges us to do something good, and such

91

is the seventh commandment: "Thou shalt not steal," which obliges us to avoid something evil. It is true, of course, that some precepts of the natural law have been forgotten or denied by a debased family, tribe, or nation.

Every law has its sanction. For example, a traffic law forbids us to drive an auto at an excessive speed. In many countries, violating this traffic law brings with it a monetary fine. So, too, the natural law is not without its sanction. Those who live in conformity with nature and thereby achieve fulfillment are happy, while those who thwart nature are necessarily unhappy. As a Chinese proverb has it, "there is no happiness like that of doing good." Herein lies the intrinsic sanction of the natural law. Experience teaches that those who violate the law of nature, even unwittingly, can experience inner turmoil, endanger their health, diminish the quality of family life, impair social relationships, and—where nations are concerned—endanger the peace. Believers would add that those who comply with the natural law fulfill God's plan for human beings and are rewarded by him, while those who knowingly violate the natural law oppose God's plan for human beings and are punished.

All of which brings us to the subject of human rights. Those who understand natural law as we have explained it in the preceding paragraphs say that natural law confers rights on those who are bound by it. If nature obliges a man to support himself and his family by his work, then he is entitled to a job and a living wage. If a woman needs an education to fulfill her role in the modern world, then she has a right to go to school. If a nation needs certain raw materials to care for its people, then it has a right to those materials even if they are monopolized by a neighbor. In other words, the very reason for a right is to allow a person to fulfill an obligation. If the natural law imposes an obligation upon an individual, then he has the right to fulfill that obligation. The natural law, which is rooted in humanity, begets the right. Moreover, the existence of the right in one person implies an obligation in others to respect that right.

What rights flow from the natural law? Those who agree with the preceding explanation of the natural law would say that the Universal Declaration of Human Rights proclaimed by the United Nations is an excellent summary of the rights flowing from the natural law. The preamble of the declaration deduces these rights from the inherent dignity of the human person and from the need to preserve freedom, justice, and peace in the world. While the preamble to the declaration does not explicitly appeal to the natural law to ground these rights, the proponents of natural law would say that in effect it is doing so. In any case, modern Popes dealing with the subject of human rights have often pointed to the natural law to defend them.

Pius XII and John XXIII

Contemporary Popes did not lag behind the United Nations in defense of human rights. Pius XII (1939–58) published his first encyclical letter, beginning with the Latin words "Summi Pontificatus," on October 20, 1939. World War II had just broken out on September 1 of the same year. The Pope grieved that men had lost sight of that kinship and love that ought to bind them together. Such love was called for by their common human origin, by their common possession of intellect, and by that sacrifice of redemption that Christ had offered to his eternal Father for the salvation of souls. Were not men and women brothers and sisters, sons and daughters, of the same Father? Were they not redeemed by the same divine blood?

Writing in the same encyclical, the Pope identified a leading reason for the confusion and disorder that plagued modern states:

> One leading mistake we may single out as the fountain-head, deeply hidden, from which the evils of the modern state derive their origin. Both in private life and in the state itself and, moreover, in the mutual relations of race with race, of country with country, the one universal standard of morality is set aside. By which we mean the natural law, now buried away under a mass of destructive criticism and of neglect. This natural law reposes, as upon its foundation, on the notion of God, the almighty Creator and Father of us all, the supreme and perfect Lawgiver, the wise and just Rewarder of human conduct.
>
> When the willing acceptance of that will is withdrawn, such willfulness undermines every principle of just action. The voice of nature, which instructs the uninstructed and even those to whom civilization has never penetrated about the difference between right and wrong, becomes fainter and fainter until it dies away. Nothing is left to remind us that we shall one day have to give an account of what we have done, well or ill, before a Judge from whom there is no appeal.[2]

Pius XII often spoke of individual human rights in various contexts—in his annual Christmas messages, for example—but it was his successor, John XXIII (1958–63), who drew up a comprehensive list of them in his encyclical letter of 1963, *Pacem in Terris* (or Peace on earth). For Pope John, human rights flowed directly and simultaneously from human nature and were, therefore, universal, inviolable, and inalienable. The dignity of human nature was enhanced by the fact of Christ's redemptive action on behalf of all and by the presence of grace in the soul.

According to Pope John, every person has a right to life and a decent standard of living even in cases of sickness, old age, and unemployment. Every individual has a right to personal respect, to a good reputation, to a knowledge of the truth, and to freedom of expression. Every person has a right to share in the benefits of culture and to secure an education commensurate with his ability. Every human being has a right to worship God publicly and privately, to choose freely a state of life, and to marry and set up a family.

Economic rights include the right to work and to work in a safe environment, to receive a wage sufficient for oneself and one's family, and to own private property. Everyone has a right to freedom of assembly and association, to freedom of movement within one's own country, and to juridical protection and the right to immigrate to other countries and to participate in public affairs. Along with Pius XII, Pope John also appealed to the natural law to defend these rights.[3]

In the same encyclical, *Pacem in Terris,* Pope John made a significant comment about the United Nations' Universal Declaration of Human Rights. The Pope wrote:

On December 10, 1948, the General Assembly of the United Nations published a document of the highest importance, the Universal Declaration of Human Rights. In the Preamble of the Declaration, the General Assembly expressed the fervent hope that all the rights and freedoms proclaimed therein would be recognized and respected by all peoples and nations. To be sure, some statements in the Declaration do not please all—and rightly so.

Nevertheless we think that the Declaration must be regarded as an initial stage in setting up a juridical-political organization embracing all peoples. Indeed, the Declaration solemnly acknowledges the dignity of the human person before all nations; it asserts the right of every individual freely to seek the truth, to follow the norms of rectitude, to fulfill the demands of justice, to live a life worthy of a human being and to enjoy the other rights connected with those mentioned.[4]

The Second Vatican Council

The Second Vatican Council, that great gathering of Catholic bishops from all over the world, specified the nature of human rights in several important documents. In its statement about the status of the Church in the modern world, *Gaudium et Spes,* the council repeated in effect the list of human rights drawn up by Pope John XXIII in *Pacem in Terris*. The council noted that more people are becoming aware of human dignity and of the universality and inviolability of human rights and duties. It is necessary, therefore, that every individual should have whatever he needs to live a truly human life—namely, food, clothing, and shelter. He should also have the right freely to choose a state of life, to found a family, and to receive an education. Further, every person has a right to his good name, to respect, to suitable information, to freedom of conscience and religion, and to protection of his life.[5]

The bishops of the Council went on to say:

Since all persons are endowed with a rational soul and have been created in the image of God, since they have the same nature and the same origin, since they have been redeemed by Christ and have the same divine calling and destiny, the fundamental equality of all should be increasingly recognized. Surely, all men and women are not equally physically, intellectually or morally. Nevertheless, with respect to the fundamental rights of the person, every form of discrimination, whether social or cultural, whether based on sex, race, color, social condition, language or religion, is to be overcome and removed as something contrary to the will of God.[6]

However, the bishops of the council insisted that only the recognition of God and his divine law can fully ensure respect for the individual and human rights. They wrote:

The Church, therefore, in virtue of the gospel committed to her, proclaims the rights of men and women and accepts and esteems the powerful movements of the present moment by which these rights are fostered on all sides. Yet these movements must be penetrated by the spirit of the gospel and protected against every kind of false autonomy. For we are tempted to think that our personal rights are fully preserved only when we are free from every norm of the divine law; but in this way the dignity of the human person is lost rather than preserved.[7]

In another important document on religious freedom, *Dignitatis Humanae,* the bishops of the council specified in greater detail the nature and implications of human rights in this regard. Vatican II declared that the human person has a right to religious freedom. This freedom means that all men and women should be protected from coercion on the part of individuals or social groups or any human power, so that no one is to be forced to act in a manner contrary to his beliefs, whether publicly or privately, whether alone or in association with others.

Needless to say, however, religious freedom is circumscribed by certain limits, such as the rights of others and public order.[8]

The right to religious freedom is based on the dignity of the human person. Because human persons are endowed with reason and free will and are, therefore, responsible moral agents, they have the obligation to seek and embrace truth, especially religious truth. However, they cannot discharge this obligation as free and responsible agents unless they are free from all external coercion. A person is bound to follow his conscience, and he is not to be forced to act in opposition to the dictates of conscience.

From these principles the bishops drew the appropriate conclusions. Individuals also have a right to religious freedom when they act in concert. It is natural for persons to band together to give expression to their religious convictions. Hence religious communities rightfully claim freedom to worship the Supreme Being publicly, to select and train their own ministers, to erect buildings for religious purposes, to give public witness to their beliefs, and to establish educational, cultural, charitable, and social organizations.

Parents have a right to determine the form of religious education that their children receive. The state, therefore, should not penalize parents directly or indirectly when they choose a particular school or means of education for their children.

Religious freedom, however, is not unlimited. This caution was expressed above. The bishops of the council noted that we exercise religious freedom in human society; hence religious freedom must be regulated by personal and social responsibility, which entails respect for the rights of other and the welfare of all. Justice and civility may not be abandoned in the name of religious freedom. It follows that society has the right to defend itself against possible abuses committed on the pretext of freedom of religion; but human freedom should not be restricted except and insofar as restrictions are necessary.

The freedom of the Church is the fundamental principle regulating its relationship to the state.

Paul VI

In 1968, the twentieth anniversary of the adoption of the Universal Declaration of Human Rights by the General Assembly, the United Nations sponsored an International Conference on Human Rights at Teheran from April 22 to May 13. At the invitation of the President of the conference, Pope Paul sent a delegation headed by the Reverend Theodore Hesburgh, President of the University of Notre Dame. The Pope also sent a message on April 15, a week before the conference opened.

Pope Paul acknowledged that the Universal Declaration of Human Rights had provoked justifiable criticism, as Pope John XXIII had noted in his encyclical *Pacem in Terris;* but as Pope John had also noted, the declaration marked an important step in the formation of a juridical-political organization embracing all peoples. Indeed, the declaration solemnly recognizes the dignity of the human person, and it asserts the right of every individual to seek the truth, follow the norms of morality, fulfill the demands of justice, live a life worthy of human beings, and enjoy other related rights. In his encyclical *Pacem in Terris,* Pope John had also expressed the hope that the declaration might soon become an effective safeguard of the rights of the human person, which flow directly from one's natural dignity, rights that are, therefore, universal, inviolate, and inalienable.

In all this, Pope Paul was recalling the thoughts of his predecessor, Pope John XXIII. For his part, Pope Paul spoke of the ideal and hope of humanity—namely, the realization of the fundamental rights and duties of human beings, of their liberty, dignity, and, above all, their religious liberty. The Church resolutely seeks, he said, the elimination of every form of discrimination.

Who does not see, the Pope asked, how far the human race must still travel to give effect to the rights justly proclaimed "universal, inviolate and inalienable"? In the Pope's encyclical *Populorum Progressio,* he had appealed to all men and women to live as brothers and sisters because all are sons and daughters of the living God. Racial discrimination begets so many evils—social injustice, economic misery, and ideological oppression as well as revolution—and great is the temptation to resist such injuries to human dignity with violence. Would that the magnificent principles proclaimed by the United Nations might find practical application. Ways and means must be devised so that these principles are respected by all in all places for the benefit of all.

To speak of human rights, the Pope wrote, is to speak of what is good for everyone. There is a golden rule: "Do unto others what you would have them do unto you." The Church wishes to reaffirm at this time the rights of all human beings, and it wishes to work with all men and women of goodwill to construct a world where every human person, without exception, can live a life that is fully human, where *liberty* is not an empty word.[9]

Five years later, in 1973, Pope Paul sent a message

to the General Assembly of the United Nations as that body prepared to commemorate the twenty-fifth anniversary of the Universal Declaration of Human Rights. Once again the Pope expressed his high regard for the declaration as one of the United Nations' highest achievements. Just as the promotion of human rights leads to peace, so peace in turn leads to the realization of human rights. There is an urgent need, the Pope wrote, to construct a human community that guarantees to all, especially to minorities, the right to life, personal and social dignity, a protected and improved environment, and an equitable distribution of the world's resources. The Church feels injured when the rights of individuals are violated anywhere in the world, and the Holy See gives its full moral support to the Universal Declaration.

The Pope noted that the collaboration of states for the promotion of human rights does not constitute interference in the internal affairs of a state; indeed, the promotion of these rights is the best guarantee of avoiding external interference. Moreover, it would be deplorable if the declaration remained only an abstract recognition of rights without being put into practice. In many places, however, these rights are still flaunted, as in cases of racial and ethnic discrimination, the existence of obstacles to the self-determination of peoples, violations of religious liberty, the inhumane treatment of prisoners, the elimination of political opponents, attacks on human life, even in the mother's womb, and other forms of violence. The Pope was encouraged, however, by the growing awareness and commitment to the fundamental values contained in the Universal Declaration.

The Pope also expressed his approval of the two International Covenants on Human Rights. These covenants reflect the spirit of the Universal Declaration. The implementation of these covenants will surely promote and safeguard the rights in question.[10]

John Paul II

When Pope John Paul II (1978–) addressed the General Assembly of the United Nations on October 2, 1979, he devoted the major part of his address to the subject of human rights. According to the Pope, the Universal Declaration of Human Rights "has been placed as the basic inspiration and cornerstone of the United Nations Organization." He went on to say:

This Declaration—with its train of many declarations and conventions on highly important aspects of human rights, in favor of children, of women, of equality between races, and especially the two International Covenants on Economic, Social and Cultural Rights and on Civil and Political Rights—must remain the basic value in the United Nations Organization with which the consciences of its members must be confronted and from which they must draw inspiration. If the truths and principles of this document were to be forgotten or ignored . . . , then the noble purpose of the United Nations Organization could be faced with the threat of a new destruction. This is what would happen if the simple yet powerful eloquence of the Universal Declaration of Human Rights were decisively subjugated by that which is wrongly called political interest.

Pope John Paul II repeated the words of Pope Paul VI to the General Assembly: "No more war! War never again!" Yet there were crises threatening the peace—the Palestinian conflict, Lebanon, more powerful weaponry, resistance to disarmament, and so on. Yet the Universal Declaration has struck a real blow against the roots of war, since war springs up where human rights are violated. The Pope went on to enumerate some of the more important human rights:

> The right to life, liberty and security of person; the right to food, clothing, and housing, sufficient health care, rest and leisure; the right to freedom of expression, education and culture; the right to freedom of thought, conscience and religion, and the right to manifest one's religion either individually or in community, in public or in private.
>
> The right to choose a state of life, to found a family and to enjoy all the conditions necessary for family life; the right to property and work, to adequate working conditions and a just wage; the right to assembly and association; the right to freedom of movement, to internal and external migration; the right to nationality and residence; the right to political participation and the right to participate in the free choice of the political system of the people to which one belongs. All these human rights, taken together, are in keeping with the substance of the dignity of the human being, understood in its entirety, and not as reduced to one dimension only.

As a matter of fact, the Pope said, human beings live at the same time in both the world of material values and that of spiritual values. The preeminence of spiritual values defines the proper sense of earthly, material goods and the proper way to use them. Men and women should have full access to the truth, to moral development, and to the complete possibility of enjoying the goods of culture that they have inherited. However, in the last one hundred years, the Pope believed, sensitivity to the spiritual dimension of human existence has been diminished in favor of material and economic factors. Peace will come, though, only when people unite around what is most fully and profoundly human—the spiritual dimension of human existence.

Pope John Paul went on to identify two main situations in which human rights are threatened or violated in the modern world. The first situation has to do with the grossly unequal distribution of material goods both within individual nations and among nations themselves. The immense inequalities between rich and poor have come about for many reasons, but the terribly unfortunate fact is that vast numbers of people suffer from hunger, malnutrition, destitution, underdevelopment, disease, and illiteracy. The only way to overcome this disparity, with its intolerable consequences, is through the concerted and coordinated cooperation of all countries.

The second main situation in which human rights are threatened or violated has to do with the various forms of injustice in the realm of the spirit. Men and women can be wounded in their relationship with truth, in their consciences, in their most personal beliefs, in their view of the world, in their religious faith, and in their civil liberties. Regrettably, we still see in the realm of the spirit recurring threats and violations, often with no possibility of appealing to a higher authority or obtaining an effective remedy. Furthermore, there are social structures that often condemn many people to second- or third-class citizenship without a real chance for social advancement or a professional career or access to positions of responsibility or an opportunity to educate one's children freely. The Pope also recalled the teaching of Vatican II about religious freedom as an essential right of human beings, a right that is so frequently ignored or violated.

In conclusion, the Pope expressed his joy because the United Nations had proclaimed 1979 as the Year of the Child. Concern for the child, even before birth and from the first moment of conception, the Pope said, "is the primary fundamental test of the relationship of one human being to another." May children have a better future, in which respect for human rights will become a complete reality and in which the fear of a nuclear holocaust will not hang over their heads! May the United Nations ever remain the supreme forum of peace and justice, the authentic seat of freedom of peoples and individuals in their longing for a better future![11]

Then in 1980, as a kind of follow-up to his address before the General Assembly of the United Nations the previous year, Pope John Paul II sent a letter to the heads of the nations that had signed the so-called Helsinki Final Act in 1975. At the beginning of the final act, adopted by the thirty-five-nation Conference on Security and Cooperation in Europe, the participating governments, including the United States and the Soviet Union, drew up a Declaration on Principles Guiding Relations between Participating States. According to this declaration, the signatories solemnly declared "their determination to respect and put into practice," alongside other "guiding" principles, "human rights and fundamental freedoms including freedom of thought, conscience, religion or belief, for all without distinction as to race, sex, language or religion." Further:

> They [the signatories] will promote and encourage the effective exercise of civil, political, economic, social, cultural and other rights and freedoms all of which derive

from the inherent dignity of the human person and are essential for his free and full development.

Within this framework the participating states will recognize and respect the freedom of the individual to profess and practice, alone or in community with others, religion or belief acting in accord with the dictates of his own conscience.

[There follows a paragraph about protection for minorities. Then it is said:]

The participating states recognize the universal significance of human rights and fundamental freedoms, respect for which is an essential factor for the peace, justice and well-being necessary to ensure the development of friendly relations and cooperation among themselves as among all states. . . .

In the field of human rights and fundamental freedoms, the participating states will act in conformity with the purposes and principles of the Charter of the United Nations and with the Universal Declaration of Human Rights.

Writing to the heads of the nations that had signed the Helsinki Final Act, Pope John Paul referred with satisfaction to the protection of human rights specified in the United Nations' Universal Declaration of Human Rights of 1948, in the two International Covenants on Human Rights of 1966, and in the Helsinki Final Act of 1975. Moreover, he noted that most state constitutions of the present day provided for freedom of conscience and religion. What was the basis of freedom of conscience and religion? According to the Pope, there were two fundamental elements: the dignity of the human person who experiences the need to act freely in accordance with his conscience and the human need to express one's personal religious sentiments openly, publicly, and in communion with others.

Then the Pope listed the requisites for religious freedom at the *personal* level: freedom to worship privately and publicly, freedom for parents to educate their children in accordance with their religious convictions without direct or indirect penalty, freedom to receive religious assistance in public institutions such as hospitals and prisons, and freedom from coercion of any kind in all aspects of public and economic life. According to the Pope, the requisites for religious liberty at the *community* level include the freedom of religious bodies to choose their own leaders, the freedom of religious leaders to communicate with their people at the local and international levels, the freedom to maintain institutions for religious training and theological studies, the freedom to proclaim one's faith by the spoken and printed word, the freedom of access to the press, radio, and television, and the freedom to exercise a ministry of charitable works.

The Pope went on to speak about the suffering and bitterness caused by the suppression or violation of religious freedom, and even today millions of people endure these evils. On the other hand, religious liberty brings peace to individuals and communities, strengthens a nation's moral cohesion, fosters the common good, helps create good citizens, and contributes to international peace, which is threatened by any violation of human rights.[12]

Over the years, at the behest of Pope John Paul II, the Holy See has continued to monitor the observance or nonobservance of human rights throughout the world. The Pope's representatives have reported their conclusions to the appropriate agencies of the United Nations. From a negative point of view, all parts of society and of the world have witnessed massive violations of human rights. Religious freedom has been particularly vulnerable. There have been dangerous outbursts of nationalism, and tribal claims and conquests have proved extremely deadly. Grinding poverty continues to oppress a great part of the world. From a positive point of view, religious freedom has been advanced, especially in Central and Eastern Europe. The political future of Cambodia seems brighter. Apartheid has been abolished in South Africa, and peace has been extended in the Near East.[13] At the beginning of the third millennium, the prospects for a greater implementation of human rights are not without hope.

7

Human Rights (II)

In this chapter we are concerned with the struggle of the Holy See and the United Nations for human rights in specific areas.

The Elimination of Racial Discrimination and Torture

From its inception, the United Nations has affirmed the principles of equality and nondiscrimination among individuals and nations. In 1963, however, the United Nations wished to reaffirm its position on this matter, and so the General Assembly adopted the United Nations Declaration on the Elimination of All Forms of Racial Discrimination, which states that discrimination between human beings on the grounds of race, color, or ethnic origin is an offense to human dignity, a denial of charter principles, a violation of the rights proclaimed in the Universal Declaration of Human Rights, and an obstacle to friendly and peaceful relations among peoples.

Two years later, in 1965, the assembly adopted the International Convention on the Elimination of All Forms of Racial Discrimination. This convention contains more detailed provisions for eliminating discrimination in all its forms, and it set up a Committee on the Elimination of Racial Discrimination to further the implementation of the convention. In 1973, the General Assembly adopted the International Convention on the Suppression and Punishment of the Crime of Apartheid, which entered into force in 1976. The convention declared apartheid, the system of required racial separation, to be a crime against humanity and that inhuman acts resulting from such a policy were crimes that violated the principles of international law and the UN charter. Subsequently, in April 1994, South Africa conducted its first universal-suffrage election. Blacks participated in the election in great numbers. In the following month, May 1994, Nelson Mandela was inaugurated as the first black president of South Africa. Blacks also held a majority in the new parliament, and apartheid ceased to exist.

In 1973, on the twenty-fifth anniversary of the Universal Declaration of Human Rights, the assembly inaugurated a Decade for Action to Combat Racism and Racial Discrimination. The goals of the decade were to promote human rights, especially by eradicating racism and racial discrimination, to identify and dispel fallacious beliefs that contribute to racism, to arrest the expansion of racist policies, and to put an end to racist regimes. In 1983, the assembly proclaimed a Second Decade to continue the struggle.

The United Nations also continued its struggle against torture. Both the Universal Declaration of Human Rights and the International Covenant on Civil and Political Rights prohibit torture and cruel, inhuman, or degrading treatment or punishment. In 1975, the General Assembly adopted the Declaration on the Protection of All Persons from Being Subject to Torture and Other Cruel, Inhuman or Degrading Treatment or Punishment, which states that such acts are an offense to human dignity and a violation of human rights and fundamental freedoms. The Convention against Torture and Other Cruel, Inhuman or Degrading Treatment or Punishment of 1984 obliges states to make torture a crime and prosecute and punish those guilty of it.

Just when the General Assembly of the United Nations was proclaiming anew its opposition to racial discrimination, the Second Vatican Council issued its statement on the status of the Catholic Church in the modern world, *Gaudium et Spes,* in 1965. In that statement, the bishops of the council taught that "with respect to the fundamental rights of the person, every type of discrimination, whether social or cultural, whether based on sex, race, color, social condition, language or religion, must be overcome and removed as something contrary to the will of God." In their statement on missions, *Ad Gentes,* the bishops exhorted the Christian faithful to avoid altogether racial prejudice and bitter nationalism. And in their statement on the relationship of the Church to non-Christians, *Nostra Aetate,* the bishops rejected "as something foreign to the mind of Christ, any discrimination against human beings or harassment of them because of their race, color, condition of life or religion."[1]

When the United Nations sponsored a Second World Conference to Combat Racism and Racial Discrimination in Geneva in 1983 (the first such conference was held in Geneva in 1978), the head of the delegation of the Holy See, Msgr. Giuseppe Bertello, once again expressed the official attitude of the Catholic Church. After recalling earlier efforts of the Catholic Church to eliminate racial discrimination, Monsignor Bertello pointed out that the Catholic Church cannot offer practical solutions to complex historical problems, but it can speak up about the rights and values of the human condition. Unfortunately, various forms of discrimination against human beings continue to fester and racial discrimination is quite rampant. Such discrimination is ruled out by a conception of humanity that asserts the basic unity of the human race and the basic equality of all human beings and nations. As Pope Paul VI said at the beginning of 1978, "The Church cannot be silent concerning its teaching that all racist theories are contrary to faith and Christian love."

Monsignor Bertello added that the theme of a World Day of Peace, "Every man is my brother," must become more than just a slogan. Surely armed struggle is not the best way to resolve international problems; rather, collaboration and honest negotiations are the way to go. This does not mean, however, that we may ignore the cultural differences of each nation; on the contrary, we must respect them. In any event, the struggle against racial discrimination finds the Holy See and the United Nations working together again to protect the freedom of individuals and groups.[2]

Women

The Preamble of the Charter of the United Nations proclaimed the determination of member-states to reaffirm faith in fundamental human rights, in the dignity and worth of the human person, and in the equal rights of men and women. This is the mandate for the United Nations to advance the status of women. In article 55, the charter gives the Economic and Social Council responsibility for promoting human rights and fundamental freedoms for all without distinction as to race, sex, language, or religion.

In 1946, the Economic and Social Council established the Commission on the Status of Women to prepare recommendations for promoting the rights of women in the political, economic, social, and educational fields. In 1952, the General Assembly adopted the Convention on the Political Rights of Women, which states that women shall be entitled to vote in all elections, hold public office, and exercise all political functions established by national law on equal terms with men. The culmination of the United Nations' work in this area was the Convention on the Elimination of All Forms of Discrimination against Women, which was adopted by the General Assembly in 1979 and came into force in 1981. The convention covers measures to be taken by states to eliminate discrimination against women in various fields, including political and public life, nationality, education, employment, health, marriage, and family life.

The year 1975 was observed as International Women's Year. Its focal point was the world conference held in Mexico City, which adopted a World Plan of Action subsequently endorsed by the General Assembly. Minimum objectives of the World Plan of Action included a marked increase in literacy and civic education of women, extension of coeducational training in industry and agriculture, equal access to education, increased employment opportunities, reduction of unemployment and discrimination in the terms and conditions of employment, equal eligibility to vote and seek elected office, a greater participation in policy-making conditions, increased welfare service, parity of social and political rights, and recognition of the value of women's work in the home and in other nonremunerated activities. To implement the World Plan of Action the General Assembly proclaimed the period 1976–85 as the United Nations Decade for

Women with the theme: "Equality, Development, and Peace."

A world conference was held at Copenhagen in 1980 to assess the progress that had been made up that point during the Decade for Women. Then in 1985, at Nairobi, the General Assembly convened a World Conference to Review and Appraise the Achievements of the United Nations Decade for Women. This conference adopted Forward-looking Strategies for the Advancement of Women to the Year 2000, a document dealing with ways and means to overcome obstacles to the progress of women. In addition, emerging areas of concern were addressed, such as the economic value of underpaid work of women and their greater participation in decision making; violence against women; data banks on women's issues; and family planning. The document also identified particularly vulnerable groups of women in need of special consideration. The review and appraisal of implementation of the strategies is to be done on a five-year basis.

In 1982, the General Assembly adopted a Declaration on the Participation of Women in Promoting International Peace and Cooperation, so that women can contribute, on a equal basis with men, to national and international efforts to secure world peace, economic and social progress, and international cooperation.

The Holy See took careful note of the United Nations' work on behalf of women. On two different occasions, Pope Paul VI received Mrs. H. Sipila, Secretary-General of the 1975 World Conference of the International Women's Year, at the Vatican. During their first meeting, in 1974, the Pope spoke of the advancement of women as a "sign of the times" and a call of the Spirit. The equality of men and women must be grounded in the dignity of the human person and in their relationship to God as sons and daughters. The Pope expressed the conviction that in the family, the fundamental unit of society, women will continue to exercise, in full coresponsibility with men, their task of welcoming, giving, and raising life. The figure of the Virgin Mary, the disciple of the Lord, remains a solid point of reference in this regard.[3]

In his second meeting with Mrs. Sipila, in 1975, the Pope noted that the theme of the International Women's Year—"Equality, Development, and Peace"—expressed a vast network of problems confronting the contemporary world. How humanity would benefit if all women placed their gifts of mind and heart at the service of these goals! In his encyclical *Pacem in Terris,* Pope John XXIII had hailed as "a sign of the times" the fact that women were becoming more aware of their natural dignity and demanding both in public and private life their rights as human persons.

Pope Paul went on to mention one effort he had particularly at heart—the campaign against illiteracy. Illiteracy prevents women, especially in rural areas, from achieving their essential rights, for as he wrote in his encyclical *Populorum Progressio,* "an illiterate is a person with an undernourished mind." The Pope encouraged local Catholic churches to examine themselves with regard to the effective participation of women in the Church's life, and he asked the blessing of Almighty God upon the work of the world conference.[4]

The Holy See was represented by a delegation at the World Conference of the International Women's Year held at Mexico City in 1975. The head of the delegation, Msgr. Ramon Torrella Cascante, Vice President of the Pontifical Commission for Justice and Peace, made a statement in which he underscored the deep interest of the Church in the International Women's Year. The Holy

See asked the members of the conference to be truly themselves—that is to say, to be truly the voices of the persons, cultures, and situations they represented in all their rich diversity. What kind of society should the delegates strive for? They should strive for a society focused on the human person, who has been created in the image of God, a society that sees the family as its natural and basic unit. A society of this kind will recognize in woman, as in man, the dignity and value of the human person.

To be sure, the head of the Vatican delegation continued, the fundamental equality of persons must not obscure the diversity of men and women. In fact, men and women complement each other, and "unisex" stereotypes would be an impoverishment of the human race, but the complementarity of men and women will be expressed differently in different cultures. It was hoped that the Catholic Church could contribute to this expression on the basis of its age-old experience and evangelical principles. Unquestionably, the Church has been subject to cultural conditioning that has led to discrimination against women, but it, too, shares modern hopes for the equality of women.

For women, as for men, the family and home remain of primary importance. Not all means of regulating the size of one's family are legitimate, and the Church categorically condemns abortion. Moreover, provisions relating to maternity protection should not be regarded as unequal protection of the sexes. Women in rural districts of developing countries need special help, as do women who are illiterate and the wives of migrant workers. As Pope Paul wrote in *Populorum Progressio,* literacy is "a fundamental factor of social integration as well as of personal enrichment," while "for society, it is a privileged instrument of economic progress and development." UN-ESCO and congregations of religious women have worked valiantly to help women learn to read. New horizons opened to women through literacy would enable them to make a real contribution to peace.

In conclusion, the spokesman of the papal delegation noted that woman is not automatically a peacemaker or a paragon of sweetness, devotion, patience, and love. She, too, must learn to overcome egoism, aggression, a desire to dominate, and even hatred. She, too, must develop qualities of strength, creativity, and breadth of vision. But what splendid results the world might expect if both branches of the human race would contribute to a world of justice, peace, and love![5]

The Holy See was represented at the world conference held at Copenhagen in 1980 to assess the progress being made during the Decade for Women. The Holy See was also represented at the world conference held at Nairobi in 1985 to review the final results of the decade. Msgr. Paul J. Cordes, Vice President of the Pontifical Council for the Laity, spoke for the papal delegation. The Decade for Women had achieved some notable results, such as new formulations of civil law in many countries fostering the equality of men and men, the advancement of women on all levels of society, greater educational opportunities for women, and the dismantling of some crippling social structures. However, women were still among the principal victims of war, poverty, hunger, forced immigration, refugee status, organized prostitution, and other social evils. Much, very much, remains to be done.

With respect to the material needs of humanity, the gospel commits every Christian to combat poverty and misery. At that moment, more than two hundred thousand women religious of the Catholic Church, to say nothing of men religious and lay volunteers, were working to improve material conditions in the Third World. Their work has been supported by the generous financial contributions of other Catholics, and it shows that the Catholic Church takes the material needs of humanity very seriously.

Without doubt, the spokesman continued, men and women are members of the animal kingdom with all the attendant circumstances, but at the same time they are gifted with intelligence and freedom and can realize what is just, good and true. In this capacity lies human dignity, and out of this capacity is born a duty to combat those conditions in which human dignity is impaired and reduced to one dimension. In some cases, women have preserved, more successfully than men, certain essential human values, such as the free offering of oneself to another, an attitude characteristic of the mother of a child.

The mother of a child needs the help and support of her culture and community. During pregnancy, she has a right to a loving and stable relationship with her husband that is guaranteed by law. She has a right to protection from attacks on feminine sexuality and her unborn child. She has a right to complete knowledge of her body and its biological functions so that she can control her fertility in a rational manner. She has a right to work without taking her away from her family responsibilities. She has a right to an income that allows her to devote herself completely to her family when the need arises. A woman should not have to give up the experience of motherhood in order to achieve genuine emancipation. For many Christians and Muslims, Mary, the Mother of Jesus, is the highest expression of womanhood. Women need to commit themselves more and more to action, and they must have the freedom to find their own way.[6]

The Holy See was represented at the Fourth World Conference on Women, convened at Beijing from September 4 to 15, 1995. The delegation of the Holy See was headed by a woman, Mrs. Mary Ann Glendon, and was composed mainly of women. Mrs. Glendon began her remarks to the conference by saying that it was the task of all to move from aspiration to action. The historical oppression of women had deprived the human race of untold resources. The delegation of the Holy See applauded the purpose of the draft Platform of Action, which aimed at freeing women from the cultural conditioning that has so often prevented them from becoming conscious of their own dignity. Needless to say, however, there were also some areas where the delegation of the Holy See disagreed with the Platform of Action.

Mrs. Glendon then turned her attention to specific issues of particular concern to women. The Beijing conference rightly placed a high priority on the rights of women to enjoy equal opportunities and conditions with men in the workplace as well as in the decision-making structures of society. However, many women face exceptional difficulties as they seek to balance greater participation in economic and social life with family responsibilities.

Justice for women in the workplace requires, in the first place, the removal of all forms of exploitation of women and girls as cheap labor. Justice requires equal compensation and equal opportunities for advancement while addressing the added responsibilities women may bear as working mothers and single parents.

Furthermore, effective action on behalf of working mothers requires recognition of the priority of human

119

over economic values. Our societies offer far too little concrete assistance to those women who are struggling to do a decent job of raising children in economically trying circumstances. Women should be guaranteed means of economic and social security that reflect their equal dignity and their equal rights to ownership of property and access to credit and resources. The effective contribution of women's work to economic security and social well-being is often greater than that of men.

Then the speaker addressed another issue of particular concern to women, that of illiteracy and education. In today's world, a scandalously high number of persons are illiterate, and over two-thirds of them are women. The Catholic Church is doing something about the problem. On August 29, 1995, Pope John Paul II recommitted all of the over three hundred thousand social, caring, and educational institutions of the Catholic Church to positive and energetic action on behalf of girls and young women, especially the poorest. The action is directed at ensuring them equality of status, welfare, and opportunity with men, especially with regard to literacy and education, health and nutrition, and the possibility of completing their education. More and more it is being recognized that investment in the education of girls is fundamental to the advancement of women later on.

The question of education is closely linked with the question of poverty and with the fact that the majority of those who today live in poverty are women and children. The "feminization of poverty" must be of concern to all women. Women themselves must lead the fight through solidarity with the poorest among them. In this respect, the speaker drew attention to the work of religious sisters. In their communities they have developed new and effective forms of solidarity, caring, and leadership on behalf of women. These religious sisters show how religious principles are for so many women a source of inspiration and perseverance in the service and advancement of women.

The speaker addressed still another issue of particular concern to women: the urgent need of health care. The delegation of the Holy See supported the special emphasis of the conference on expanding and improving health care for women. So many women in today's world do not have access to a basic health care center. Connected with this problem are problems of poor nutrition, unsafe water, and those diseases that afflict millions of women each year.

The delegation of the Holy See concurred with the Platform of Action in dealing with questions of sexuality and reproduction. The documents of the conference were not bold enough in acknowledging the threat to women's health from widespread attitudes of sexual permissiveness. Moreover, the international community has consistently stressed that the decision of parents concerning the number of their children and the spacing of births must be made freely and responsibly by them. Responsible procreation also requires the equal participation and sharing of responsibility by husbands.

The delegation of the Holy See joined with all participants in the conference in the condemnation of coercion in population policies. Couples need to be provided with clear information about all possible health risks associated with family planning methods. The speaker noted that there is a clear consensus within the international community that abortion should not be promoted as a means of family planning and all efforts must be made to eliminate those factors that lead women to seek abortions. Once again concerned women must take the lead in the fight against societal practices favoring abortion.

According to the speaker, the conference rendered a great service by casting a spotlight on violence toward women and girls, violence that may be physical, sexual, psychological, or moral. Much more needs to be done in our societies to identify the range and causes of violence against women. Much more must be done to eliminate the practice of female genital mutilation and other deplorable practices such as child prostitution, trafficking in children and their organs, and child marriages. The violence experienced by women is also linked to those factors that reduce women to the role of sex objects. Finally, greater attention should be paid to the needs of elderly women, who experience special problems in all our societies.

We must now look to the future. The freer women are to share their gifts with society and assume roles of leadership, the better are the prospects for the entire human community to advance in wisdom, justice, and dignified living. May Almighty God accompany us and sustain us in our task![7]

Children

The UN agency particularly concerned with the rights and welfare of children is the United Nations International Children's Emergency Fund (UNICEF). In 1946, the General Assembly created UNICEF to alleviate the emergency needs of children in postwar Europe and China for food, drugs, and clothing. In 1953, the General

Assembly gave UNICEF a widened and permanent mandate to continue its work on behalf of children in developing countries, so that they can realize their full potential and be delivered from malnutrition, disease, and illiteracy. (Meanwhile, the name of the agency was changed to the United Nations Children's Fund, but the well-know acronym, *UNICEF,* was retained.) UNICEF also seeks to ensure for every child the basic rights and privileges embodied in the Declaration of the Rights of the Child, adopted by the General Assembly in 1959. The agency was awarded the Nobel Prize for Peace in 1965. Its headquarters are in New York.

To deal with the problems of children on the spot, the Children's Fund maintains country and regional offices in more than one hundred developing countries. It cooperates with developing countries in several ways:

> The Children's Fund provides a framework for advocacy on behalf of children and works to increase both decision-making and public awareness of the special needs of children. It undertakes analyses of national development plans, relates those plans to the well-being of children, and the rates of disease and death among children. The Children's Fund helps plan and design services; it also delivers supplies and equipment, and provides funds to train teachers, nutritionists, health and sanitation workers, and social workers particularly for work at the community level.[8]

In recent years, UNICEF has made great progress in child survival and development by emphasizing immunization, breast-feeding, growth monitoring, and a simple oral rehydration method. The organization has been actively involved in emergency relief efforts to bring food and relief supplies to African countries stricken by drought. UNICEF continues to be responsible for coordinating the follow-up activities of the International Year of the Child observed in 1979.

This UN agency is supported entirely by voluntary contributions. Governments contribute more than three-quarters of its income while the rest comes from organizations and individuals through greeting-card sales and various fund-raising campaigns.

The 1959 Declaration of the Rights of the Child was consolidated into a legally binding Convention on the Rights of the Child adopted by the General Assembly in 1989 and subsequently ratified by more than one hundred nations. The Holy See was one of the signatories. The convention defines a child as "every human being below the age of eighteen years." The convention sets minimum standards for the survival, health, and education of children, while offering protection against exploitation and abuse.

A new UN Committee on the Rights of the Child has been set up to monitor compliance with the provisions of the convention. The tasks of the committee and UNICEF are clear. The sad plight of children in underdeveloped nations was, once again, highlighted by UNICEF's 1992 report. One in three children in the Third World are malnourished. More than 100 million children of primary age die annually from diseases that could be prevented by immunization.

The rights and needs of children were also of great concern to the Holy See. In 1978, Pope Paul VI received Mr. Henry Labuisse, the Executive Director of the United Nations Children's Fund, at the Vatican. The Pope expressed his appreciation for the great good that UNICEF has done over the years for the children of the world, but at the same time he noted how he had repeatedly dissociated himself from projects that might directly or indirectly favor contraception, abortion, or any other practice that does not respect the supreme value of life. The International Year of the Child (1979) was approaching, and the interest of the Church in that event reflected the attitude of Christ himself, who identified himself with the child (Mk 9:37). Service to the child is not a transitory goal, but rather a permanent task invested with dignity and enduring priority.

The Pope continued:

A renewed concern for the real needs of children everywhere is dictated by a realistic awareness of the present situation in the world. Despite technological progress, children still suffer and die from a lack of basic nourishment, or as victims of violence and armed conflicts that they do not even understand. Others are victims of emotional neglect. There are people who poison the minds of the young by passing on to them prejudices and empty ideologies. And today, children are exploited even to the point of being used to satisfy the lowest depravities of adults. A despicable aspect of this exploitation is the fact that it is often controlled by powerful forces motivated by financial gain.

Every child has the God-given right to be born, the right to a mother and father united in marriage, and the right to be born into a normal family. The Pope also said:

In order to fulfill its aim, the International Year of the Child is called to promote the inestimable value of the child in today's world: the child as a child, as a human person, and not simply as a potential adult. Childhood is an essential phase of human life, and every child has the right to live childhood to the full and to make an original contribution to the humanizing of society and to its development and renewal. All of us personally know this contribution of children to the world. Who has not been struck by children's simple, direct and innocent perception of situations, their open and loving generosity, their lack of prejudice and discrimination, their infectious joy and spontaneous sense of brotherhood, and also their capacity for remarkable sacrifice and idealism?

The Church stresses that every child is a human person and has the right to the integral development of his personality. The role of the family is irreplaceable in attaining this end, since the child cannot be understood and assisted apart from the family, which is the first educator toward physical, psychological, intellectual, moral, and religious development. The Pope expressed the hope that new, revitalized projects would flourish to help needy children everywhere, and he was pleased to note that many individual Catholics, Catholic organizations, and local churches were taking part in preparation for the International Year of the Child.[9]

In 1984, Pope John Paul II welcomed Mr. James Grant, Executive Director, and the Executive Council of the United Nations Children's Fund to the Vatican, where he addressed them. The Pope praised UNICEF's concern for all the children of the world. Children are a most precious treasure deserving of the utmost love and respect, and they are given to each generation as a challenge to its wisdom and humanity. Every child is in some way a sign of hope for the parents and the nation. Indeed, Christ has identified himself with every child (Mt 18:5).

However, the Pope said, there is a dark side. The plight of so many children in the world is critical. The scandalous imbalances that exist in society are reflected in a particular way among our children. While in one sector of the world children are suffering from the lack of the most elementary human necessities, in other sectors children from the earliest years are being introduced into a society based on consumerism, possession, and even waste. Such a situation is a challenge to the conscience of every man and woman in the world.

The Pope recalled the teaching of the Church that human life must be respected and protected from the first moment of conception. Is there not a certain fear of the child in our society, a fear of the demands of love and generosity that the procreation and education of children require? The Church is convinced that one of the most vital answers to the situation of the child in today's world will come through reinforcing and strengthening the family. A healthy family life will ensure that the child attains well-rounded personal development. An essential element of any program that seeks to benefit the child is that of providing for the presence of the mother alongside her young children and of ensuring that mothers are trained to carry out effectively their role in the areas of nutrition and health education. Mothers deserve adequate recognition for their work in the home because of its value to the family and society.

The Pope concluded his remarks by speaking of those children who do not know the joy of a true family:

> Precisely because the Church realizes what a great value the family is, she feels particularly close to all those children who have not had the joy of growing up in a healthy and complete family. As I said in *Familaris Consortio,* "There exist in the world countless people who unfortunately cannot in any sense claim membership in what can be called in the proper sense a family. Large sections of

humanity live in conditions of extreme poverty in which promiscuity, lack of housing, the irregular nature and instability of relationships, and the extreme lack of an education make it impossible in practice to speak of a true family. There exist others who, for various reasons, have been left alone in the world."

Alongside all the efforts which we must make to see that families are helped to carry out their role more effectively, it is important to dedicate urgent and immediate attention to those children who are deprived of family life. In particular I make an appeal to other families to respond to their vocation to hospitality and to open their doors to children who need temporary or permanent care.[10]

In 1990, on the occasion of the World Summit for Children sponsored by the United Nations, Pope John Paul II addressed a message to Mr. Javier Pérez de Cuéllar, Secretary-General of the United Nations. The Pope said he applauded the World Summit for Children as an important expression of public and governmental concern for the welfare and rights of children. In the Child of Bethlehem, the Pope said, Christians contemplate the uniqueness, dignity, and need of every child for love. In the Christian view, the treatment of children is a measure of fidelity to the Lord himself.

However, the plight of millions of children on every continent is a heart-breaking reality. Children are the most vulnerable of all because they are least able to make their voices heard. The Pope wished to speak on their behalf. The children of the world appeal for love. In this case, love stands for the real concern of one human being for another; and the good that each one owes the other is the bond of our common humanity. The well-being of the world's children depends greatly on the measures taken by states to support and help families fulfill their natural life-giving and formative functions.

The inalienable dignity of each child and his right to life from the first moment of conception, even in the face of difficult circumstances or personal handicaps, cry out for greater respect. The International Convention on the Rights of the Child is a statement of priorities and obligations that can serve as a reference point and stimulus for action on behalf of children everywhere. The Pope noted the Holy See's prompt acceptance and signing of the convention with the hope that the goals stemming from it would respect the moral and religious convictions of all concerned.

In conclusion, Pope John Paul recalled the words that he addressed to the General Assembly in New York in 1979: "What better wish can I express for every nation and for the whole of mankind and for all the children of the world than a better future in which respect for human rights will become a complete reality."[11]

Subsequently, the Holy See continued to express its support of the family as the basic unit of society. On October 25, 1993, Archbishop Renato R. Martino, the Holy See's Permanent Observer to the United Nations, addressed the Third Committee of the Forty-eighth Session of the General Assembly. "Peace," the Observer said, "is built on truth, justice, freedom and love, and the family is the privileged place for learning to live these values."[12]

Then, on October 19, 1994, Cardinal Alfonso López Trujillo, President of the Pontifical Council for the Family, spoke to the International Conference on the Family organized in New York by the General Assembly of the United Nations. The Cardinal asked, "Are not the strength of the family and its protection the best guarantee for respecting children in agreement with the United

Nations Convention on the Rights of Children?" The Cardinal also said, "An adequate family policy requires that the family be recognized and helped as a social subject, one that integrates each and every one of its members, the man and woman, the husband and wife, sons and daughters, babies, youth, the elderly, the healthy and the sick."[13]

Youth

In general, here we are speaking of young people between fifteen and twenty-four years of age.

In 1965, the General Assembly adopted the Declaration on the Promotion among Youth of the Ideals of Peace, Mutual Respect and Understanding among Peoples. The declaration stressed the importance of young people in today's world with their potential contribution to development and international cooperation.

Accordingly, activities of the United Nations and its member-states have focused on: the preparation of youth, through education, for full participation in all aspects of life and development; health policies and programs which would ensure that young people are able to take advantage of opportunities open to them; the adoption of all possible means to increase employment for youth; the opening of channels of communication between the United Nations and youth organizations; and the promotion of human rights and their enjoyment by youth.[14]

In 1970, the United Nations sponsored its first World Youth Assembly at its headquarters in New York. In

1979, the General Assembly designated 1985 as International Youth Year with the theme: "Participation, Development, and Peace." The assembly wished to focus attention on the situation of young people and their aspirations and problems with a view to engaging young people in the development process. Problems facing young people included unemployment and their migration from rural to urban settings. In 1981, the General Assembly put forward a comprehensive program for observing the International Youth Year in 1985. This program was to be carried out in conjunction with regional and national plans of action.

Then, in November 1985, the General Assembly held a series of plenary meetings called the United Nations World Conference for the International Youth Year. Out of the conference came guidelines for further planning and follow-up beyond the youth year. The United Nations is now actively involved in the implementation of these guidelines. The United Nations Youth Fund has been operating since 1985 to involve young people in the development of their countries.

A notable feature of the International Youth Year was the address of Pope John Paul II to young Muslims at Casablanca on August 19, 1985. At the request of the Permanent Mission of the Kingdom of Morocco, the address was subsequently published as a document of the General Assembly of the United Nations. The King of Morocco, visiting the Pope in Rome a few years earlier, had invited him to speak to the young people of his country during the International Youth Year. The Pope began his address by noting that Christians and Muslims have many things in common both as believers and as human beings. The thoughts of the Pope turned first to God, the Creator, who expects of us obedience to his holy will. God is the just judge who grants mercy to the repentant sinner. The responsibility of believers is to foster unity and peace among the peoples and nations who form a single community on this earth. They all have the same origin and the same final destiny in God.

According to the Pope, today more than ever before, all believers must bear witness to their faith in God, because the world is becoming increasingly secularized. They must bear witness to their humble efforts to ascertain the will of God. Christians and Muslims wish that all may arrive at the fullness of God's truth, but the search will be successful only when it is free from all external constraints of mind and heart in accordance with human dignity. It was the Pope's conviction that we cannot invoke God the Father of all if we refuse to act kindly toward all men and women who have been made in the image of God, if we refuse to respect their rights, which are the expression of God's will.

Young people look forward to the future, the Pope said, and they aspire to a more just and humane world. Wisdom teaches us that self-discipline and love are the only instruments for achieving the desired renewal. Young people themselves must undertake initiatives and not expect everything from their parents and the authorities but should cooperate with adults. Young people need adults just as adults need young people. The world of the future will depend on the youth of all countries. Unfortunately, however, our world is torn apart by many conflicts because human beings do not accept their differences and do not know each other. Yet God created all men and women equal in dignity, although they differ in gifts and talents. Each one has something to give and something to receive from others.

If we are to have peace with justice, the Pope continued, everyone should have enough to live on. God gave the earth to the entire human race so that all peoples and nations might derive their livelihood from it. But men and women do not live on bread alone; they need to develop their minds and consciences; they need to study in order to know and understand the world God has given them; and, what is far more important, they need to cultivate the spiritual dimension of life. Christians and Muslims ought joyfully to acknowledge the religious values they have in common: belief in one God; belief in the importance of prayer, fasting, and almsgiving and in the need for repentance and pardon; and belief in judgment, the resurrection, and eternal life.

Of course, a fundamental difference between Christians and Muslims is the Christian regard for Jesus as Lord and Savior. Surely Christians and Muslims have often misunderstood and even fought with each other in the past, but now, according to the Pope, God is calling them to change their old habits and respect and cooperate with each other. The Pope concluded his message by thanking the King of Morocco for his invitation to speak to the young people of his country and by thanking God even more for making the Pope's visit possible.[15]

The same year, 1985, Miss Mary Reiner, a young member of the delegation of the Holy See, read a statement on its behalf to the United Nations World Conference for the International Youth Year at the Fortieth Session of the General Assembly in New York. The speaker addressed three related topics: the importance of the International Youth Year, the situation of modern youth, and some major concerns of contemporary youth.

The International Youth Year, according to the speaker, was a time to think about young people as they prepare themselves for the world of tomorrow. The world depends upon the action of adults for and with the young people of today. The International Youth Year should mark the beginning of long-term programs designed to confront the problems arising out of unemployment, the erosion of spiritual values, and threats to the environment. Efforts to help young people should help them deepen and broaden their concept of human freedom. The International Youth Year is a challenge to adults and young people to construct a new civilization of truth and love.

The United Nations, the speaker continued, deserves much credit for the amount of research it has undertaken to determine the status of modern youth. Now, more than ever, we are better informed about their situation, but the results of the research are alarming. The research tells us about the poor health and education of many young people; about their inability to find work; about the perilous condition of many young women, refugees, migrants, and prisoners; about so-called street and abandoned youth; about young prostitutes, male and female; and about young victims of violence. The plight of many young people is particularly sad and unjust in view of the vast attention, talent, and money devoted to armaments.

According to the speaker, the youth of today want to live and not die in war. They want to participate in decisions affecting them and their future. Modern youth are very demanding, sometimes falling into exaggeration and succumbing to personal selfishness. However, like the youth of every age, they are searching for truth, ideals, responsible participation, moral beauty, and innocent joy. Modern youth are questioning and they ask: What is the meaning of life? Is there hope for the future? They sense the necessity of finding a reality that gives ultimate meaning to our fragmented existence. Finally, the youth of today are fearful about survival in an atomic age, about the destruction of the environment, and about national problems that remain unsolved.

Then the young speaker related some of the concerns of her generation. One concern has to do with the meaning of life in the future. That meaning, the speaker said, will be found in truth—truth in thought and truth in action—for it is truth that sets one free. A second concern has to do with goodness. A young person ought to find goodness in the family; indeed, a stable family can teach its young members love, trust, and sharing. However, a family that encourages its younger members to persevere in the face of difficulty must itself be supported by society and not hindered by it. A third concern of youth is to explain to the world why they are filled with hope. The reason is that young people have a vision of life where love, beauty, strength, enthusiasm, courage, and resilience flourish. May the adults of today commit themselves to young people for the transformation of society into a better world for tomorrow![16]

8

Human Rights (III)

Again in this chapter we are concerned with the struggle of the Holy See and the United Nations for human rights among specific groups of people.

The Aging and the Elderly

In many countries the proportion of the population aged sixty or older will increase because of the gradual decline in the birthrate and the rising life expectancy. The United Nations is committed to helping countries meet the needs of the elderly and maximize their contribution to development.

In 1973, the Secretary-General of the United Nations presented a comprehensive report to the General Assembly on the question of aging. The assembly responded by recommending to governments a variety of programs designed to benefit older people. In 1978, the General Assembly decided to convene a World Assembly on Aging at Vienna in 1982. The World Assembly adopted the Vienna International Plan of Action on Aging. The plan aims at maintaining the elderly in their own families and communities, furnishing them with a choice of health care opportunities, enabling families to care for elderly relatives, and providing social security, employment, and adequate housing. The plan of action also includes recommendations for meeting the needs of particularly vulnerable groups, such as elderly refugees and migrant workers.

There is a Commission for Social Development that reviews the implementation of the Vienna Plan of Action every four years. In 1988, an International Institute on Aging was established at Valetta, Malta. The United Nations Trust Fund for Aging has also been established to help developing countries implement the Vienna Plan of Action.

In 1982, Pope John Paul II sent a message to the World Assembly on Aging convened at Vienna. The Pope greeted with interest and hope the initiative of the United Nations in taking up the problems of the aging, for their number was increasing. The United Nations was not dealing simply with abstract or technical problems but much more with the destiny of human beings and their particular and personal history. As the Pope said in 1980 when he met with the elderly in Munich, aging is a natural stage of human existence and its crowning and fulfillment. It is from this point of view that the Bible speaks of the elderly with respect and admiration. Of course, life is precious in all its stages, and no person is authorized to suppress the life of an innocent human being, whether it be a fetus or embryo, child or adult, old person, incurably sick, or dying. Still, death is a part of our human condition and gives it its true and mysterious dimension.

What are the characteristics of old age? On the one hand, the Pope said, there are the negative aspects that are sad and difficult to accept, especially for the person who is alone. These aspects include a certain weakening of one's physical and spiritual powers, a progressive separation from one's usual activities, sickness, and the separation linked with death. However, faith can transform these aspects. For believers, it is as though one is walking along the way of the cross toward the radiant dawn of Easter. On the other hand, there are the positive aspects of old age:

It is a time when men and women can gather the harvest of experience of their entire lives, making the choice between what is accidental and essential, and achieving a level of great witness and profound serenity. It is a period of life when men and women dispose of a great deal of time, even of all their time, by loving their habitual or occasional companions with a disinterest, a patience and a discreet joy of which the elderly act as admirable examples. Further, for believers, old age offers the happy possibility to meditate on the splendors of the faith and pray in a deeper manner.

To reap this harvest, the Pope said, two things are necessary. The first is that the elderly themselves accept their age and appreciate its possible resources, and the second is that society recognize the values of the elderly and integrate them into its ranks. The elderly have a right to expect support from their families. This may mean inviting the elderly into the homes of their children or, when such a course is impossible, maintaining warm and regular ties with the one who has had to go to a home for the elderly. The Pope added:

Having said this, it is also certain that, living with their own flesh and blood, the elderly can, with the appropriateness and discretion that this will always require, bring to their relatives that affection and wisdom, that understanding and indulgence, that advice and comfort, that faith and prayer which are, for the most part, the charisma of the twilight of life. Living in this manner, the elderly will equally contribute to giving their due place, especially by example, to attitudes which are often undervalued today, like listening, self-effacement, serenity, self-giving, interiority, and discreet and radiant joy.

It is worth noting also that the habitual or occasional presence of the elderly among their relatives is often a precious factor in linking and creating mutual understanding between the generations which are necessarily diverse and complementary. Indeed, this strengthening of the family, along with the lines I have just recalled, and according to its possible manner, can be a source of balance and vitality, of humanity and spirituality for that fundamental cell of all society which bears the most expressive name that exists in all the languages of the world: "the family."

Aging generations, the Pope continued, sometimes ask themselves if they have a place in current society. However, society has a duty to respond to the aspirations of aged persons. This response cannot be of a single type. It is well if the elderly can continue to live with their families and in their own environment. If they cannot, then there must be institutions that, ideally, provide the warmth of a family, a certain autonomy compatible with the necessities of community life, and activities that correspond to the physical and professional capacities of the elderly.

According to the Pope, there was another service that society can render to the elderly. It can encourage the creation of associations of the elderly and support those associations in existence. These associations are already doing much good by combating isolation and the feeling of uselessness, which often accompany retirement and old age. Television and radio can help in this regard by presenting a picture of human life that develops and expands until the end of one's earthly existence.[1]

Disabled Persons

In 1971, the General Assembly adopted the Declaration on the Rights of the Mentally Retarded, which states, in effect, that such individuals, as far as feasible, have the same rights as other human beings, including the right to medical care, to economic security, and to live with their family or with foster parents.

In 1975, the General Assembly adopted the Declaration on the Rights of Disabled Persons, which proclaims that disabled persons—those with a physical or mental deficiency—have the same civil and political rights as their fellow citizens. According to the declaration, disabled persons have a right to those treatments and services that will make them as self-reliant as possible. They also have a right to economic and social security and to employment or a useful and remunerative occupation.

The General Assembly proclaimed 1981 as International Year of Disabled Persons with the theme: "Full Participation and Equality." By the end of the year, national committees had been set up in more than one hundred countries and a special trust fund had been established by the assembly to finance projects for the disabled.

As a follow-up to the Year of Disabled Persons, the General Assembly, in 1982, adopted the World Program of Action concerning Disabled Persons. The World Program initiated a global strategy to prevent disability, rehabilitate disabled persons, and secure their full and equal participation in social life and development. On behalf of disabled persons, the World Program addresses issues of legislation, physical environment, income maintenance and social security, education and training, employment, recreation, culture, religion, and sports. To implement the World Program, the General Assembly proclaimed the United Nations Decade of Disabled Persons (1983–92); and in 1988, the Secretary-General appointed a Special Representative to further the goals of the decade.

In 1981, the Holy See published a statement for the International Year of Disabled Persons being observed at that time. In the statement, the Holy See asserted that disabled persons deserve the practical concern of the world community both because of their numbers and especially because of their condition. Following the example of its Founder, the Christian community, too, must be concerned for the disabled. Certain basic principles have application in this regard. A first principle is that the disabled person (whatever the nature, origin, and severity of his disability) is a fully human subject whose rights are innate, sacred, and inviolable. A second principle is that the disabled person has a right to enjoy a decent life, as normal and full as possible. A third principle is that a disabled person, insofar as his condition permits, should be rehabilitated and integrated in the life of society without at any time losing sight of his personal dignity.

The statement of the Holy See asserted that the respect, the dedication, the time, and the means required for the care of disabled persons are the price that a society must pay in order to remain truly human. Society should undertake even more extensive research to overcome the causes of disabilities, both physical and mental. It would be best if disabled persons lived with their families or foster parents. It is in the home, surrounded by loved ones, that a disabled person finds the surroundings most natural and conducive to his development. There needs to be support for parents when they discover that one of their children is handicapped. Handicapped children and young people have a right to instruction, whether in an ordinary or specialized school. A disabled person needs particular understanding and encouragement when he passes from school to placement in society or professional life. Obviously, the disabled person possesses all the civil and political rights that other citizens have. On the other hand, a handicapped person should not be content merely to receive from others but should also make an active contribution to society insofar as that is possible.

The statement of the Holy See went on to note that those who work with the handicapped need not only technical and professional competence, but also a rich, human sensitivity by which they can respond to the handicapped's needs. The professional help given the handicapped needs to be augmented by material and moral support from public authorities. Education will be needed to counteract the defensive mechanisms established by the general public, consciously or unconsciously, against the presence of the disabled and handicapped in their midst.

Christians have an indispensable role to carry out in this regard. As followers of Christ, they should adopt his attitude toward suffering people. He affirmed love of neighbor as one of the two great commandments of God. During the International Year of Disabled Persons,

Christians would stand with others dedicated to the service of the disabled and make their contribution in personnel and resources. Celebrating the Day of Peace in St. Peter's at the beginning of 1981, Pope John Paul mentioned publicly the Year of the Disabled Persons and called for special attention to their problems. He noted that a small part of the vast sums spent on armaments could be used more profitably for the handicapped.[2]

Labor

The ILO was established in 1919, under the Treaty of Versailles, as an autonomous organization associated with the League of Nations. In 1946, the ILO became the first specialized agency associated with the United Nations. According to its constitution, the ILO seeks to establish universal and lasting peace through the promotion of social justice. The ILO's tripartite structure is unique among UN agencies in that it includes representatives of workers, employers, and governments who have an equal voice in determining its policies. The ILO works through an International Labor Conference, which is its official policy-making body; a Governing Body, which is the executive council of the ILO; and an International Labor Office headed by a Director-General. The headquarters of the ILO are in Geneva. In 1969, the agency was awarded the Nobel Peace Prize.

Among the concerns of the ILO on behalf of workers are human rights, freedom of association, adequate wages, hours of work, minimum ages for employment, conditions of work for various classes of workers, workmen's compensation, social insurance, vacation with pay, industrial safety, employment services, and labor inspection. The ILO recommends international minimum standards and drafts international labor conventions having to do with these matters. Recommendations provide guidance for national policy, legislation, and practice, while conventions create binding obligations—for states that ratify them—to put their provisions into effect. Since the ILO was founded, more than three hundred and fifty recommendations and conventions have been adopted.

The fight against unemployment and poverty has been a central preoccupation of the ILO since its foundation in 1919; indeed, its motto is: "Poverty anywhere constitutes a danger to prosperity everywhere." In 1969, the ILO launched its World Employment Program to assist national and international efforts aimed at providing jobs for the world's rapidly expanding population.

The ILO carries out an extensive program of technical cooperation, and its experts are assigned all over the world to help in such fields as vocational training, management techniques, manpower planning, employment policies, occupational safety and health, social security systems, cooperatives, and small-scale handicraft industries. Opportunities for study and training are offered at the ILO's International Center for Advanced Technical and Vocational Training in Turin, Italy.

In 1954, Pope Pius XII welcomed representatives of the ILO to the Vatican. The organization might be justly proud, the Pope said, because for more than thirty years it had promoted the collaboration of governments, employers, and workers. It had encouraged them to rise above personal feelings and acknowledge unavoidable change, and it had enabled many workers to extricate themselves from inhuman working conditions. Pope Leo XIII and other recent Popes were quite explicit in their approval of efforts to improve the condition of the working classes.

According to Pope Pius XII, the ILO, founded in 1919, has responded ever more effectively to the needs of workers. Those needs include the limitation of working hours; regulation of the work of women and adolescents; protective measures against illness, unemployment, and accidents; and measures aimed at social security and full employment. Fortunately, the ILO does not pit one social class against another; rather, it fosters everything that contributes to the good of society as a whole. The labor movement should continue to strive for a social order in which all collaborate for the common good. May the Master of all, the Pope concluded, the One who became a worker himself, bless the efforts of the ILO.[3]

In 1969, Pope Paul VI traveled to Geneva to address the ILO on the occasion of its fiftieth anniversary. The Pope did so at the invitation of the Director-General. The Pope noted that work is viewed in the pages of the Bible as an essential element of the human condition. Jesus, the Son of God, became a worker. The Pope recalled the work of pioneers, both Catholic and Protestant, in the labor movement. As evidence of the Church's sympathy for the ILO and the labor movement in general, he cited relatively recent documents of the magisterium: *Rerum Novarum, Quadragesimo Anno, Mater et Magistra, Gaudium et Spes,* and *Populorum Progressio.* With all his heart, the Pope rejoiced at the vitality of the fifty-year-old, but still young, organization, that was founded by the Peace Treaty of Versailles in 1919. Up to the time of the Pope's address, the ILO had concluded 128 conventions and made 132 recommendations.

According to the Pope, it is man who must come first in labor: it is man who works, and it is for man that he works. However, work is still ambivalent: it can be truly creative, yet it can be dehumanizing if the one who performs it becomes its slave, if he gives up his intelligence and freedom and loses his dignity. The goal of the ILO is to defend the freedom of workers and the ideal of brotherhood among men. The ILO has a single aim—not money, not power, but the good of man. The organization is ever learning more fully what the good of man requires and translates it into new rules of social conduct and norms of law. The ILO strives to bring together the three forces at work in the human dynamics of modern labor: government, employers, and workers.

Pope Paul quoted with approval the words of Albert Thomas, the first Director of the ILO: "The social factor must take precedence over the economic factor; it must regulate and guide it in the highest cause of justice." The ILO contributes to universal peace by striving for social justice. Daily the task of the ILO becomes more urgent. How many evils, abuses, injustices, and cries of pain still afflict the world of labor! The organization must courageously and untiringly work against them. Man must be protected against himself—that is to say, man carried away by the formidable forces he has unleashed, swept along by the irresistible current of his inventions, and stunned by the disparity between the prodigious goods at his disposal and their unequal distribution.

For fifty years, Pope Paul said, the ILO has striven to ensure the proper remuneration for the labor of men, women, and young people. Now it must try to ensure the participation of workers not only in the fruits of their labors, but also in the economic and social responsibilities upon which their future and the future of their children depend. The ILO must try to regulate the rights of strong nations and favor the development of weak ones by working for appropriate laws and conventions. Like each man, so, too, each people must be able by their own work to develop themselves, grow in humanity, and progress from less humane conditions to more humane ones. The Pope spoke of the need of young people for training and jobs if they are to build up the world of tomorrow, and he concluded by appealing to the Spirit to animate and strengthen the children of the same Father.[4]

In 1982, Pope John Paul II traveled to Geneva to address the sixth-eighth session of the ILO. By addressing the ILO, the Pope said, he wished to pay tribute to all who work in any way. Work in any of its forms deserves particular respect because it represents the output of a human being from which it derives its value and dignity. The ILO occupies an important place in international life because of its age and lofty objectives, which includes the preservation of peace through the cultivation of social justice. According to the Pope, he mentioned the ILO in his encyclical on human work, *Laborem Exercens* (published in 1981), to draw attention to its many achievements and encourage its activities aimed at making work more human. The appointment of a Permanent Observer to the ILO in 1967 is evidence of the Holy See's esteem for, and desire to collaborate with, the organization.

The message of the Holy Father did not differ substantially from the ones he had delivered in the past to the General Assembly of the United Nations and several of its agencies. That message is a simple one: it has to do with the cause of man, his dignity, and the inalienable rights flowing therefrom. As Pope Paul had noted in 1969 when he addressed the ILO, the organization aims at bringing together men of government, employers, and employees for the good of man and his work. The structure and objectives of the ILO reflect the reality of work, for all work is a necessity, a duty, and a task: it is a way of assuring a livelihood together with family life and certain fundamental values; it unites men and enables them to realize their humanity; and it was given to them so that they might subdue the earth and dominate it.

There is an essential link, John Paul continued, between work and human existence. We must always ask: Does his work serve man? Is it compatible with his dignity? Does it tend to eliminate unjust inequalities and promote a peaceful future for the world? The blatant injustices of the last century led workers, especially industrial workers, to unite in a great burst of solidarity. Despite improved conditions in many countries, flagrant injustices persist elsewhere. However, the solidarity of workers, which derives its strength from the primacy of the human person over things, will create the machinery of dialogue and cooperation. It is not utopian to assert that the world of labor can also be a world of justice.

The problems of modern workers must be viewed and solved on a worldwide scale. Indeed, all the major societal problems are now world problems. A new world of conscience must be created; each of us, without denying his origins and his membership in his family, his people, and his nation, must regard himself as a member of a great family, which is the world community. As each nation tries to develop its own spiritual and material resources, it must at the same time be outward-looking and respond to the needs of all.

Unemployment has become a major problem of our present society, with harsh consequences for workers that are often overlooked. One cause of unemployment lies in the improvement of the means of production so that fewer workers are needed in the process, but we may not sacrifice the individual for the requirements of production or economic laws. The Pope recalled his words in *Laborem Exercens:* Unemployment "in all cases is an evil; and when it reaches a certain level, it can become a social disaster. It is particularly painful when it affects young people especially." Solidarity is the key to the employment problem: all must be prepared to make the necessary adjustments and sacrifices. Solidarity among human beings is built up by creating and then preserving the conditions upon which the free participation of all in the common effort depends. The right to associate freely is a fundamental one for all who are part of the work community; unfortunately, however, this right is frequently flouted.

The Pope concluded his remarks by praising the many accomplishments of the ILO and by offering a prayer that it might successfully pursue the awesome adventure of making work more human.[5]

On June 13, 1995, Archbishop Paul F. Tabet, the Permanent Observer of the Holy See at the ILO, addressed the eighty-second assembly of the General Conference at Geneva. He noted that unemployment is becoming a very serious problem in industrialized countries as well as in most of the other countries of the world. In *Laborem Exercens* Pope John Paul II had written that it is the task of civil society to see to it that every man, every woman, and especially every young person has the opportunity to work. In the introduction to his report the Director-General of the ILO had also written "that employment must become the absolute priority of the international community."

Monsignor Tabet asked: Is the free market that is developing in today's world really at the service of human beings with a view to their material progress and spiritual development? The ILO is in a unique position to initiate an ethical reflection upon the conditions of workers and effects of contemporary competitiveness upon their lot. The ILO needs to be concerned with all those, including the marginalized, who desire to become active partners in economic and social life.

New and desirable social policies ought to respect man in all his dimensions, including his desire for social integration. Economic life should promote the production of the world's riches for the benefit of the largest possible number. The speaker encouraged the ILO to propose pertinent legal instruments to establish a balance between the laws of international exchange and the social requirements of countries and regions, especially the poorest. All this requires a new mentality whereby some lose some of their advantages that others may live with dignity and humanity.[6]

Refugees

The problem of refugees became particularly acute after World War I (1914–18), when the number of refugees was counted in the millions. In 1921, the League of Nations established the first worldwide agency to help refugees with the appointment of a League of Nations High Commissioner for Refugees. In 1933, the ascendancy of Nazism in Germany started another flood of refugees. In 1943, the United Nations Relief and Rehabilitation Administration (UNRRA) was established to bring aid to war-stricken areas of the world. Through its efforts, some 6 million displaced persons were repatriated at the end of World War II (1939–45). In 1946, by vote of the General Assembly, the International Refugee Organization (IRO) assumed the functions of UNRRA, and it helped to resettle more than a million persons.

In 1951, the IRO gave way to the office of the United Nations High Commissioner for Refugees (UNHCR), which is based in Geneva. While the problems of postwar refugees in Europe were reduced or eliminated, large number of refugees began to appear elsewhere, especially in Africa, Southeast Asia, the Middle East, and Central America.

According to the Statute of the United Nations High Commissioner for Refugees, a refugee is a person who, owing to a well-founded fear of persecution for reasons of race, religion, nationality, membership in a particular social group, or political opinion, is outside the country of his nationality and is unable or, owing to such fear, unwilling to avail himself of the protection of that country.

The basic task of the UNHCR is to ensure the feeding, clothing, and sheltering of refugees and to assist in their repatriation or, if that is impossible, find them asylum in a host country where their rights are safeguarded. An essential element of the refugee's international legal status is the widely accepted principle of *nonrefoulment,* which prohibits the expulsion or forcible repatriation of a person to a country where he may have reason to fear persecution. The legal status of refugees has been defined more specifically in two international instruments—the 1951 Convention relating to the status of Refugees and its 1967 Protocol—that define the rights and duties of refugees. In regard to many matters such as employment, education, and public assistance, signatories have agreed to treat refugees as they treat nationals of their own countries. The reunion of family members has the highest priority.

The UNHCR was awarded the Nobel Peace Prize in 1954 and again in 1981.

By no means has the Holy See been indifferent to the plight of refugees. In 1959, Pope John XXIII delivered a radio message to mark the opening of "World Refugee Year" proclaimed by the United Nations. The Pope expressed his support for the noble initiative, and he recalled the words of Christ: "I was a stranger and you welcomed me, naked and you clothed me, a prisoner and you came to see me" (Mt 25:35). The Pope's heart went out to the thousands of refugees who were fleeing from the many upheavals of the day and were still living in less than human conditions. What a sad situation at a time when remarkable progress was being made in so many other ways! The Pope spoke of the work of his immediate predecessors on behalf of refugees, and he wished to join his efforts to theirs. Finally, he appealed to the faithful, the pastors of souls, and public authorities to continue and even intensify their work, so that many unfortunate people might enjoy their personal and family rights once more.[7]

In 1964, Pope Paul VI addressed the participants in the twelfth session of the Executive Committee that oversees the work of the High Commissioner's Office. The Pope received them at the Vatican and declared himself honored by their visit. He was deeply anguished by the continuing plight of so many refugees, but he was encouraged by all that had been done on their behalf despite the inevitable difficulties. Helping refugees, the Pope said, is an extremely complex undertaking involving legal protection, financial and social support, medical and psychological treatment, and the training of youth and old people. The Office of the High Commissioner was to be commended for its highly successful work in meeting the needs of refugees. The work of the UNHCR was an act of love toward one's neighbor.[8]

In 1977, the Holy See addressed the specific problems of refugees in Southeast Asia. The views of the Holy See were stated by Msgr. Audrys Backis, the head of the papal delegation, at the Meeting on Refugees and Emigrants of Southeast Asia held in Geneva. The refugees in that distant region were looking for a homeland; the countries that received them had exhausted their resources, and few other doors had opened. The Catholic Church was represented in Geneva because, in obedience to her Founder, she was challenged by the cries of those in distress. Indeed, all present at the meeting firmly believed in the principle enunciated in article 13 of the Universal Declaration of Human Rights that "everyone has the right to leave any country, including his own, and to return to his country" and in the principle enunciated in article 14 that "everyone has the right to seek and to enjoy in other countries asylum from persecution."

According to Monsignor Backis, the lot of refugees in Indochina posed a humanitarian problem without precedent. Hundreds of thousands of refugees were facing dangers and risks that threatened their lives. Christians, both in the countries of first asylum and in the countries offering permanent asylum, have been quite generous in their response to the needs of refugees. For the Holy See, a lasting solution to the plight of refugees must be based on their dignity as persons. A "solution" should not discriminate against the aged, the handicapped, and the so-called unproductive. Moreover, something ought to be done to stop the dangerous and confused exodus of refugees without infringing upon their right to migrate and

153

reunify their families. Centers for the reception of refugees should not become places of permanent asylum, for they do not afford normal human living conditions. The Holy See wished to pay homage to the splendid work done by various governments, by the United Nations, and especially by the UNHCR and support them in their efforts.[9]

In 1982, Pope John Paul II received Mr. Paul Hartling, the UNHCR, at the Vatican. The Pope expressed his pleasure at the meeting. According to the Pope, there were at that time 10, perhaps 15, million refugees in the Near East, Southeast Asia, Africa, Central America, and elsewhere. It was a disgrace that so many countries were no longer capable of granting freedom and a decent living to all their citizens The countries of origin could not be absolved of their responsibility for the situation, but here and now something had to be done to alleviate the misery of so many refugees.

In the view of the Pope, the merit of the UNHCR is that he seeks not only short-term but also long-term solutions to the problem. Of course, the cooperation of other agencies is needed and most welcome. The Pope noted that the Bible in general and the gospel in particular constrain us to help displaced persons find asylum. A goodly number of Catholic agencies are actively engaged in this effort. The Pope exhorted those in charge to provide freedom and a dignified life for refugees in their own country, and he also appealed for hospitality and welcome in other countries. All this, to be sure, does not dispense refugees from doing what they can to help themselves.[10]

Two years later, in 1984, Pope John Paul II sent a message to the Second International Conference on Assistance to Refugees in Africa (ICARA II), held in Geneva.

Once again, the Pope expressed his support for the efforts being made on behalf of millions of refugees on the African continent; they were the brothers and sisters of us all. At stake was the dignity of a human person, a gift of God. The heavy financial burden of providing for refugees should be borne not only by the host countries, but also by the international community. Moreover, the Pope urged the conference to bear in mind the individual tragedy of each refugee and the distress of each family. These could be forgotten in the face of the refugee problem as a whole. Holding the conference was already a first response to the problem, offering hope to the millions of refugees and showing them that they are welcome, respected, and loved. In conclusion, the Pope expressed his hope that the refugees would soon be able to return to their own country—an inalienable right—with increased skills acquired during their time of exile.[11]

The forty-fourth session of the Executive Committee of the UNHCR was held in Geneva October 4–8, 1993. Archbishop Paul Tabet, the Apostolic Nuncio, spoke for the delegation of the Holy See. The Holy See, he said, urges states to pool their resources and together find a response that corresponds to the magnitude of the refugee problem. What is needed is a better exchange of information on refugee problems and a greater coordination of the efforts of relief agencies. "Preventive diplomacy" on behalf of refugees includes respect for human rights through a democratic form of government, greater economic balance, and a judicious use of developmental aid. The institution of asylum and the principle of "non-ejection" need to be supported and strengthened. States should not close their borders to real refugees. The principle of family unity should always be taken into consideration. Women and children need special attention, for they are often the first victims of conflicts and can be the objects of the most despicable crimes. Assistance to refugees is a real contribution to peace.[12]

Health

The specialized agency of the United Nations working in the field of health is the WHO. It was founded April 7, 1948, and the anniversary of its foundation is celebrated throughout the world as World Health Day. Headquarters are in Geneva. The work of the organization is carried out by the World Health Assembly, the Executive Board, and the Secretariat. Membership in the WHO is open to all states, and members of the United Nations join the organization by accepting the constitution.

The constitution of the WHO states certain principles upon which its work is based:

Health is a state of complete physical, mental and social well-being and not merely the absence of disease or infirmity. The enjoyment of the highest attainable standard of health is one of the fundamental rights of every human being without distinction of race, religion, political belief, economic or social condition.

The health of all peoples is fundamental to the attainment of peace and security and is dependent upon the fullest cooperation of individuals and states.

The achievement of any state in the promotion and protection of health is of value to all.

Unequal development in different countries in the promotion of health and control of disease, especially communicable disease, is a common danger.

Healthy development of the child is of basic importance; the ability to live harmoniously in a changing total
environment is essential to such development.

The extension to all peoples of the benefits of medical,
psychological and related knowledge is essential to the
fullest attainment of health.

Informed opinion and active cooperation on the part
of the public are of the utmost importance to the improvement of the health of the people.

Governments have a responsibility for the health of
their people which can be fulfilled only by the provision
of adequate health and social measures.

In 1977, the World Health Assembly, the policy-making body of the WHO, set the overriding priority of the
organization as "Health for All by the Year 2000" and
planned a global strategy to achieve this objective. The
implementation of this plan requires the combined efforts
of governments and people using a primary care model.
The eight essential elements of primary health care are:
education on prevailing health problems; proper food
supply and nutrition; safe water and sanitation; maternal and child health, including family planning; immunization against major infectious diseases; prevention and
control of local diseases; appropriate treatment of common diseases and injuries; and provision of essential
drugs.

The WHO helps countries build up their health systems by developing personnel and services, promotes research in all major fields of health, has mounted a
worldwide campaign to provide effective immunization
for all children, provides essential drugs and other supplies and equipment, and directs and coordinates a special program and global strategy to prevent and control

AIDS. In 1967, the WHO began a global program to eradicate smallpox; and in 1980, the World Health Assembly declared that smallpox had been eradicated in all parts of the world.

The Popes have not been slow to praise the work of the WHO. In 1949, Pope Pius XII addressed the World Health Assembly, the governing body of the WHO, at the Vatican. The organization was observing its first anniversary. Despite the persistence of many problems after the end of World War II, the Pope rejoiced because so many nations were working together to improve the health of all. Among many less developed peoples, the level of health and sanitation was well below that in other countries. Periodically, epidemics and endemic diseases threatened to wipe out whole peoples. Meanwhile, other countries were attaining new levels of good health.

Private and particular initiatives in the field of health cannot be praised too highly, the Pope said, but the WHO brings a more universal, a more concerted, and, consequently, a more effective collaboration to bear upon the solution of health problems. Moreover, in our modern world no nation can completely isolate itself from health risks in other nations. Pope Pius noted that health means more than the absence of bodily ailments and mental abnormality; rather, it also encompasses the spiritual and social well-being of humanity; indeed, it goes beyond the bounds of biology and medicine to include spiritual and eternal goods as well.[13]

In 1968, Pope Paul VI addressed a message to Dr. Marcolino Candau, Director-General of the WHO, on the occasion of its twentieth anniversary. The Pope expressed his respect for the organization and those who work so generously for the health of all. As the constitution of the WHO puts it, "health is a state of complete physical, mental and social well-being . . . " The fight against disease in all corners of the world entails difficult, costly efforts. These efforts can bear fruit only through the cooperation of all and through dialogue between the experts and those who wish to serve. Christ's parable of the Good Samaritan should be an inspiration to all. Let it be noted, the Pope said, that any reduction in governmental budgets for public health will adversely affect the most needy, and the training of competent health personnel is a priority in less favored countries and required support from the more favored ones.[14]

In 1973, the same Pope, Paul VI, addressed a message to the same Director-General of the WHO, Dr. Marcelino Candau, on the occasion of its twenty-fifth anniversary. The Pope was anxious to join many others who were paying tribute to the organization. As its constitution states, the purpose of the WHO is bringing all peoples to the highest levels of health possible. The professions dedicated to the health of men and women are among the noblest of them all because they serve human life, which is called to bloom in endless happiness. The programs of the WHO on behalf of the outcasts of society, such as the mentally impaired, the handicapped, and the victims of drug addiction, surely reflect concern for human life. It was the Pope's fervent wish that the WHO would continue to support life in all its forms.[15]

A year later, in 1974, Msgr. Silvio Luoni, the Permanent Observer of the Holy See at the UN agencies in Geneva, made a statement on behalf of the Holy See at the twenty-seventh assembly of the WHO in Geneva. With the WHO, the Holy See believes that health is a fundamental right of all men and women. While basic health protection should be ensured at all levels, there is no one model of health services for all countries. The

159

WHO is right is supporting the initiatives of countries themselves to set up health systems in accordance with their own needs and circumstances.

A second consideration put forward by Monsignor Luoni had to do with abortion. Some countries wish to protect the mother's health by liberalizing abortion laws and making clandestine abortions unnecessary. What a contradiction: to wish to protect the health of the mother while condemning the child in her womb to death! In some countries health personnel are discriminated against when, in accordance with the Hippocratic oath, they refuse to cooperate in the destruction of life. Do we understand the consequences if we distinguish between various forms of life, protecting some and eliminating others? As for the Church, it has always been and always will be on the side of life.

A third reflection put forward by Monsignor Luoni had to do with the WHO's efforts to seek out safe, effective, and acceptable methods for the regulation of human fertility. The Church is concerned with population problems because she is concerned with the integral good, both material and spiritual, of the human person. With regard to population growth, the Church wishes to avoid unjustified optimism and excessive pessimism. The Church asks, first and foremost, that family planning respect the dignity of the human person and the freedom and responsibility of the couple. The solution to population problems must be found in the total context of social justice, development, environment, and human rights.[16]

In the following year, 1975, Monsignor Luoni read another statement at the twenty-eighth assembly of the WHO in Geneva. The Permanent Observer of the Holy See limited himself to reflections on the family. According to article 16 of the Universal Declaration of Human

Rights, "the family is the natural and fundamental group unit of society and is entitled to protection by society and state." It is hardly necessary to stress the importance of health for each member of the family. According to the report of the Director-General to the assembly, the WHO seeks to ensure a lasting balance between human beings and their environment, thus making them less vulnerable to disease and enabling them to lead a more productive and agreeable existence.

Monsignor Luoni went on to ask: Is not the health of the family often jeopardized by the habitat in which it is compelled to live? Indeed, the health of a family is dependent upon a whole complex of economic and social factors. The report of the Director-General noted how important it is to care for the health of expectant mothers and of infants and young children. Still, his report was devoted largely to family planning problems; but the regulation of births should be carried out with respect for human dignity and responsibility. All this is particularly important in developing countries, where programs are carried out in communities handicapped by illiteracy. The Holy See rejects abortion, sterilization, and all non-natural methods as illegitimate means of regulating births. On the other hand, good progress has been made in the field of natural family planning. In regulating births, ethical standards need to be upheld, and the WHO should be active in supporting them.[17]

At the twenty-ninth assembly of the WHO, held in Geneva in 1976, Msgr. Joseph Geraud spoke on behalf of the Holy See. Once again, the speaker reacted to the annual report of the Director-General of the organization. The report merited approval because of its emphasis upon the family as the basic social unit, because of the importance that it attached to the development and

161

growth of the fetus, and because of the fairly extended treatment of natural methods of regulating birth and fertility.

However, the Delegation of the Holy See could not accept certain parts of the Director-General's report. In the report, there was reference to what was called "the struggle against uncontrolled fertility" considered as a defective state of health and a "human waste." Against this background, the report speaks of various methods of family planning without distinguishing between them as to their morality. Methods of family planning need to respect the whole human person with all his rights and values. Is not evil masked by hiding it under the guise of other words, for example, by referring to abortion as the interruption of pregnancy and by speaking of sterilization as health care? The Church has confidence in human beings and in their capacity for love. That is why she defends and proclaims the holiness of marriage and procreation.[18]

9

Culture and Education

In this chapter we are concerned with the efforts of the United Nations and its specialized agency, UNESCO, on behalf of culture and education and with the position of the Holy See on these important matters.

UNESCO

UNESCO is a specialized agency of the United Nations with headquarters in Paris. Its counterpart in the League of Nations was the International Committee for Intellectual Cooperation. The constitution of UNESCO was drawn up by a conference convened in London in 1945, and an agreement between the United Nations and UNESCO was approved by the General Assembly in 1946. UNESCO works through a General Conference, an Executive Board, and a Secretariat. The General Conference, composed of representatives of member-countries, meets every two years to decide the policy, programs, and budget of the Organization. The Executive Board, consisting (in 1995) of fifty-one members elected by the General Conference, meets at least twice a year and is responsible for supervising the programs adopted by the

General Conference. The Secretariat, headed by the Director-General, carries out the programs. National commissions of cooperating bodies of member-states act in liaison between UNESCO and national scientific and cultural organizations.

According to the constitution of UNESCO, it was the belief of the founding nations that the wide diffusion of culture and education is indispensable to human dignity and constitutes a sacred duty. It was also the belief of the founding nations that a lasting and secure peace cannot be based exclusively upon the political and economic arrangements of governments, but it must also be founded upon the intellectual and moral solidarity of mankind. Hence, according to its constitution, UNESCO was founded:

> to contribute to peace and security by promoting collaboration among nations through education, science and culture in order to further universal respect for justice, for the law and for the human rights and fundamental freedoms which are affirmed for the peoples of the world, without distinction of race, sex, language or religion, by the Charter of the United Nations.

To improve and expand education, UNESCO works to overcome illiteracy and make primary education universal. To further scientific progress, UNESCO has acted as a catalyst for regional and international research projects in such areas as the environment, marine science, hydrology, and oceanography. The UN agency also seeks to promote the development of organizations for scientific research and for training science teachers and technical instructors. In the social sciences, UNESCO has produced studies on such subjects as racism, the socioeconomic factors of development, the relationship between humans and their environment, and tensions leading to war.

UNESCO's cultural activities are concentrated chiefly on the stimulation of artistic creativity, the study and development of cultures, and the conservation of the world's inheritance of books, works of art, and monuments, as well as the preservation of cultural identities and oral traditions. After World War II, UNESCO labored for the reconstruction of libraries and museums in war-devastated countries. It has launched successful campaigns to preserve ancient monuments in Egypt, Indonesia, and Pakistan, and it is working to save the city of Venice in Italy and the Acropolis in Athens. The UN agency encourages cultural exchanges between East and West, undertaking translations of important writings and organizing personal exchanges. Under the World Heritage Convention, UNESCO lists sites of exceptional historical importance and/or natural beauty. In this way, all can become aware of their rich cultural and natural heritage.

UNESCO assists in the establishment of schools of journalists, communication research institutes, radio stations, news agencies, and television stations. Training is also provided to communication professionals. This activity is in accordance with the constitution of the agency, which directs it to promote the free flow of ideas by word and image through the mass media and, in so doing, advance the mutual knowledge and understanding of peoples.

Paul VI

In 1970, at the close of the International Year of Education, Pope Paul VI addressed a message to Mr. René

Maheu, the Director-General of UNESCO. The Pope expressed his high regard for UNESCO's work on behalf of education, science, and culture. The Pope quoted a sentence from his own encyclical *Populorum Progressio:* "Hunger for education is no less depressing than hunger for food." Methods of education must be constantly re-evaluated in view of a world constantly changing, and students should learn to pursue their education throughout their lives. The Church has mounted a mighty educational effort over the centuries and will continue to do so, for the Church believes that she can help men and women build a world in which all can live as free and responsible citizens.

Education should aim at a complete humanism, one that is open to the Absolute. Creator and creatures are not rivals for supremacy, since the scientific and technical achievements of humanity are in harmony with the intention of the Creator. According to the Pope, the contemporary generation of youth was seeking knowledge that teaches one how to live rather than knowledge that is constantly evolving. Young people need the example of educators who live in accordance with the truth, educators who are themselves ever alert to the demands of the times and looking to the future.

Education needs to be a joint effort, a community task involving the family, teachers, social and professional groups, and the churches, all working together for the common good of which civil authorities are the guarantors. Parents are the first educators of their children. A successful education complements that which is done in the family. It is of capital importance that all segregation be banished from education so that the young learn to live in harmony with their equals. All over the world diverse groups are coming in close contact with each other. When people discover their differences, they realize how they complement each other.

By developing the mind and molding the will, true education awakens the conscience of a young person and encourages him to act for the benefit of others. Catholic educators wish to work in close collaboration with other educators and overcome every temptation to narrow self-interest or aggressive rivalry. There never will be enough men and women of goodwill to accomplish the goals of education. Wherever Catholics are engaged in educational tasks, the Church asks them to distinguish themselves by working for the good of those entrusted to their care. The lofty mission of all educators, the Pope concluded, is to help men and women achieve their marvelous destiny.[1]

Pope Paul VI addressed a second message to Mr. René Maheu, the Director-General, on the occasion of UNESCO's twenty-fifth anniversary in 1971. The Pope offered his congratulations and recalled that UNESCO was founded to contribute to peace and security by promoting collaboration among peoples and nations through education, science, and culture. The Pope noted that Monsignor Roncalli, who was to be the future Pope John XXIII, was the first Permanent Observer of the Holy See at UNESCO's headquarters in Paris. Many Catholic organizations also maintain ties with the UN agency.

Pope Paul wrote that men and women become fully human only through culture—that is to say, through the cultivation of natural goods and values, as the Second Vatican Council put it.[2] The vocation of UNESCO is to further the universal desire for unity among peoples despite the political and ideological differences that divide them. Education forms men and women, science enables them to act, and culture completes their development.

Culture includes the patrimony of the past, and UN-ESCO's efforts to preserve the monuments of the past merit praise. Everyone should be able to participate in the development of the spirit through culture, and for this purpose the ability to read and write is essential. The Pope repeated a statement he made on another occasion: "An illiterate person is a person with an undernourished mind."

The Pope concluded his message to Mr. Maheu by saying that the aim of education, beyond instruction, is to impart to the young a wisdom rooted in a particular culture, which is deeper than all forms of knowledge that are in constant evolution. Further, the aim of education is to enable the young to act upon the knowledge and wisdom they have acquired, to strengthen their wills and awaken their consciences—in short, to build a world in which all men and women can live as free and responsible persons. The Pope prayed that God might bless the tireless efforts of UNESCO to hasten the advent of a more just and fraternal society.[3]

In 1974, Pope Paul awarded the John XXIII International Peace Prize to UNESCO. Speaking at the Vatican to Mr. Amadou Mahtar M'Bow, a native of Senegal and the new Director-General of the organization, the Pope noted that the prize had greater symbolic than monetary value. The prize spoke of the common journey of the Holy See and UNESCO along the road to peace. The dedication of the Holy See to peace is derived from the Founder of the Catholic Church, Jesus Christ, the Prince of Peace. UNESCO, too, is dedicated to peace. The agency was founded on the principle that "peace must be built on the foundation of the intellectual and moral solidarity of mankind," and it must remain above the political rivalries that trouble other areas of human life.

Encouraged by the achievements of UNESCO in the past, Pope Paul looked forward to the future. UNESCO labors to bring people together through education, science, and culture. It strives to form a brotherhood among peoples, to impart a common thought, to promote a uniform sociology of culture, and to create an identical civil language among men. UNESCO seeks to dissipate the nightmare of a terrible and apocalyptic war, making the world safe for tomorrow. It is natural for the Church and UNESCO, without losing their identities, to work together for the common goal of peace. Pope Paul concluded his message with the words of Pope John XXIII, in whose name he had conferred the International Peace Prize on UNESCO:

There is an immense task incumbent on all men of good will, namely, the task of restoring the relations of the human family in truth, in justice, in love and in freedom: the relations between individual human beings; between citizens and their respective political communities; between political communities themselves; between individuals, families, intermediate associations and political communities on the one hand, and the world community on the other. This is a most exalted task, for it is the task of bringing about true peace in the order established by God.[4]

During the pontificate of Pope Paul VI, the Holy See was represented at sessions of the General Conference of UNESCO at Paris in 1972, again at Paris in 1974, and at Nairobi in 1976. At Paris in 1972, the head of the papal delegation, Msgr. Giuseppe M. Sensi, began his remarks with certain general observations. He spoke of the profound need to invoke eternal verities in the face of all the changes modern men and women experience. Science and technology have achieved many astounding and positive results, but we are also in danger of destroying ourselves by our thoughtless exploitation of nature. Hope for the future lies with the young, who desire fraternity, sharing, and solidarity with others. While UNESCO shows great respect for indigenous cultures, this respect should not lead to the isolation of individual nations. Nor should the more developed nations exercise a cultural domination over the others.

To these general statements Monsignor Sensi added brief comments on three subjects: education, information, and population. It is good that UNESCO seeks the renewal of education. All sectors of society should be encouraged to coordinate their educational resources. The state must play its role without jeopardizing the rights of parents and legitimate pluralism. Education needs to be a lifelong process if the individual is to develop all his potentialities, and it should be not only intellectual but also moral. With respect to information, it, too, is an important concern of UNESCO, and rightly so. The men and women who gather and furnish information have a serious responsibility to convey truth and uphold moral values. The right to information flows from the human desire for truth. With respect to population problems, UNESCO rightly continues its research and collection of data. However, population problems cannot be solved without taking moral principles into account. Questions about the birthrate must be considered in the light of an integral vision of human beings and their vocation.[5]

Again at Paris in 1974, the head of the papal delegation, Msgr. Andre-Jacques Fougerat, addressed the biennial session of the General Conference of UNESCO. The rights and duties of individuals, he said, can be truly affirmed only in the name of that which transcends human beings. For Catholics, this transcendent reality is God. Men and women of learning become increasingly aware of the moral implications of their quest for knowledge. Yes, a vast area of reality can be investigated by experimental methods, but other cases of reality, such as beauty, friendship and love, suffering and death, and God, the Supreme Reality, must be approached in other ways. In any event, the whole of reality should be part and parcel of education.

The papal delegation, its spokesman said, rejoiced over the benefits of technology but feared the misuse of it, and one hoped that it would be more widely used in the service of less developed countries. Moreover, it is right to respect the cultural differences between countries, but at the same time it is needful to recognize what cultures have in common and promote international solidarity on that basis. At that time, international solidarity was progressing too slowly, and nations should adopt a more universal outlook. What is needed is a new kind of humanism that transcends cultural differences while respecting them. Finally, the Holy See's delegation supported efforts to improve the quality of life for all, provided this ideal remains open to the values of the spirit.[6]

The next session of the General Conference of UNESCO was held in Africa for the first time—at Nairobi in 1976. The delegation of the Holy See was led by Msgr. Agostino Cacciavillan, who spoke on its behalf. The spokesman reaffirmed the great interest of the Holy See in the work of the UN agency. In many ways, the work and objectives of UNESCO correspond to those of the Church. There were three matters that merited the attention of the delegates at this time. The first had to do with development and the kind of person that will emerge from the process. The second matter had to do with the glaring inequalities—economic, social, and cultural—within nations themselves and between privileged and less privileged nations. However, true and effective brotherhood, based on the unity of the human race, should inspire greater efforts to solve this problem. The third matter had to do with human rights. UNESCO is charged with the defense and promotion of the right to culture and education, but in many places there is a huge gap between the acknowledgment of rights and their implementation. To deal properly with the aforementioned matters, an exceptional educational effort is required, and those involved must be animated by a spirit of service and not a desire for power.[7]

John Paul II

Pope John Paul II was elected to the Chair of Peter in 1978, and in 1980 he delivered a major address to the General Conference of UNESCO at its headquarters in Paris. The Pope recalled the foundation of UNESCO in 1945 and the universal desire for peace, unity, and reconciliation that led to its establishment. If this noble desire was to be fulfilled, the Pope said, respect for the inalienable rights of human beings and recognition of their spiritual dimension are fundamental. The Pope urged his listeners to rededicate themselves to the ideals and principles that guided the agency at its inception.

The Holy Father then proposed two fundamental considerations that, he said, throw light on the significance of the work and objectives of UNESCO. The first consideration was this: It is through culture that men and women live a truly human life. Culture is a specific manner of existing and being, and it creates a bond with other human beings. Culture has to do primarily with what a person "is" and only secondarily with what a person "has." Human beings are the artisans of their culture. One cannot conceive e culture without human beings; they are the primordial and fundamental elements of culture. In culture, the material is spiritualized by its subjection to the intelligence and will of persons; and in turn, the material incarnates, as it were, the spiritual powers of persons. Culture reflects the whole person, body and soul.

All of which brought the Pope to a second consideration of a very different kind. There is an essential link between culture and religion, of which Europe—from the Atlantic to the Urals—is a prime example. There is a fundamental link between the message of Christ and human beings in their essential humanity, and that link is creative of culture. For a culture to be created, we must affirm the dignity and transcendent value of men and women, and this affirmation lies at the heart of the gospel and the mission of the Church.

From what the Pope said, he concluded that the primary duty of culture is education so that men and women not only "have" more but "are" more, and in the latter case not only "with others" but "for others." There can be no doubt that morality plays a fundamental role in all this. Unfortunately, however, there has been a unilateral movement in culture and education toward "having" and "possessing" rather than toward "being," and as a result human beings have become the object of ideological and political manipulation.

The nation is a broad community of individuals united by many ties, but above all by culture. It is the main educational force ensuring that men and women

173

can "be" more within the community. The Polish nation, of which the Pope is a member, has maintained its national existence not by depending on physical force, but by relying on its culture. The Pope urged the assembled delegates to safeguard the fundamental sovereignty possessed by every nation in virtue of its culture. The mass media ought not to become a means of cultural domination over others. Without yielding to selfish interests, the media should help build a more human existence. Human beings become increasingly human through the possession of truth. UNESCO deserves great credit for working toward this end by promoting literacy and education. In passing, the Pope appealed for the right of Catholic parents to educate their children in schools reflecting their own beliefs.

The Pope went on to praise the institutions devoted to scientific investigation. In these institutions the vital bond between humanity and truth is daily forged anew. The Pope paid tribute to all those who pursue the truth, sometimes at great personal risk. However, there is always the danger that scientific research will be debased and made to serve goals unworthy of it. The Pope recalled that scientists were brought before international courts at the close of World War II for conducting immoral experiments. Even today, research is going forward for purposes that are contrary to the good of humanity and more sophisticated nuclear weapons are being developed and added to the arsenals of an ever-increasing number of countries. Let us do our utmost, the Pope urged, to respect the primacy of ethics in all the spheres of science and preserve the family of man from the terrible prospects of nuclear war.

The Holy Father concluded his remarks with an appeal to the scientific community:

Together you are an enormously powerful force—the force of united intelligences and consciences. Show yourselves more powerful than the most powerful in our contemporary world. Resolve to manifest the most noble form of solidarity with humanity—that which is based on the dignity of the human person. Build up peace on the foundation of respect for the rights of human beings—those which are bound up with the material and economic dimension of their lives and those which are bound up with the spiritual and interior dimension of their existence in this world. May wisdom inspire you![8]

In 1981, on a visit to Hiroshima, Japan, Pope John Paul II addressed scientists and representatives of the United Nations University (UNU). The General Assembly had approved the charter of the university in 1973, and its headquarters were located in Tokyo after Japan had pledged a contribution of $100 million towards the University Endowment Fund. As a new and unique kind of academic institution, the UNU seeks to help solve pressing global problems of human survival, development, and welfare. It addresses these problems through worldwide networks of academic and research institutions, including its own research and training centers, and individual scholars. The UNU has established three research and training centers: one for development economics research, in Finland; one for natural resources, in Côte d'Ivoire; and one for new technologies, in the Netherlands. The university disseminates information gathered from its work and other sources by means of workshops and research seminars all over the world, as well as by publications aimed at policymakers, scientists, and scholars.

At Hiroshima, Pope John Paul expressed his esteem for the UNU, which was founded to promote the lofty ideals of the United Nations through research, advanced training, and the dissemination of knowledge. Then the Pope got into the body of his talk. At Hiroshima the world made the terrible discovery that nuclear energy would henceforth be available as a weapon of destruction. Science and technology have produced many wonderful results, but they can also lead to human suffering and degradation. The future of humanity depends as never before on our collective moral choices. From now on, it is only through a conscious choice and a deliberate policy that humanity can survive. A society will succeed in eliminating some of the causes of war only by pursuing the good of each individual and of humanity as a whole. In this pursuit the scientific world has an important role to play. Surely the Pope was aware that one cannot exclude greed and hate as causes of war, but we shall increase the chances for peace by building a more humane world.

Our future together on this planet, the Pope said, demands that humanity make a moral reversal. He appealed to the men and women of Japan and, through them, to the whole world to work for the social and moral reconstruction of the world so that it becomes "a just world, a world made to man's scale, a world that enables human beings to fulfill their capacities, a world that sustains them in their material, moral and spiritual needs." If rich nations choose to do so, they can assemble an impressive number of specialists for the task of development. Priorities will have to be redefined, less being spent for military purposes and more for human development. Can we remain indifferent when one soldier's equipment costs many times more than a child's education?

The Pope went on to say that three temptations must be resisted: the temptation to pursue technological development for its own sake as if one should always do what is technically possible, the temptation to use technology solely for economic profit without reference to the good of all, and the temptation to use technology in order to dominate others. The survival of the human race is henceforth indissolubly linked with the progress, development, and dignity of all peoples, and scientists need to study more deeply the ethical problems of a technological society.

Finally, the construction of a new social order presupposes, over and above the essential skills, a lofty inspiration, a courageous motivation, and a belief in man's future, dignity, and destiny. Human beings must be loved for themselves. This is the supreme value that all sincere humanists, generous thinkers, and religious persons wish to support. Religious knowledge and science need to be linked together, and we must convince ourselves of the priority of ethics over technology, of the primacy of persons over things.[9]

Then, in 1982, Pope John Paul sent a message to Mr. Amadou Mahtar M'Bow, Director-General of UNESCO, in connection with the World Conference on Cultural Policies held in Mexico City that year. Cultural progress, the Pope wrote, is closely connected with the construction of a more just and fraternal world. The Church follows the work of UNESCO with great interest and wishes to continue its cooperation with the agency. To reflect on UNESCO's work on behalf of culture is to visualize the nations of the world shaking hands across their borders, prizing every culture and collaborating with each other for the betterment of mankind.

Human beings, the Pope said, must be the center and focal point around which all cultural activities revolve. It should never be forgotten that human beings have a spiritual, moral, and religious dimension. Culture needs to respect this dimension so it can serve the real good of individuals and society. As for the future, the Pope looked forward to a culture marked by a disinterested search for truth and human values, a culture that promotes human life and does not destroy it, a culture that assigns technology its proper place so that it serves mankind without rejecting ethical values. The Pope concluded his message by invoking God's blessing on UNESCO and its praiseworthy initiatives.[10]

During the pontificate of Pope John Paul II, the Holy See continued to be represented at sessions of UNESCO's General Conference. At the session of the General Conference at Belgrade in 1980, the delegation of the Holy See was led by Msgr. Ernesto Gallina, who expressed the delegation's gratitude for the warm welcome extended by UNESCO to the Pope earlier in the year at Paris. Monsignor Gallina took the occasion to reaffirm the esteem of the Holy Father for the organization and his intention to collaborate with it in the pursuit of common goals. Getting into the main part of his message, the speaker noted the difficulty of reconciling the rights of individuals with the rights and capabilities of the nation as a whole, and he urged the organization to foster educational opportunities that prepare an individual not only for a productive role in society, but also for family life, responsible citizenship, and leisure activity.

Cultural pluralism, Monsignor Gallina went on to say, presents a problem to be sure: how to reconcile cultural diversity with national unity. Human beings need to recognize how they are united by the progress of science, by their common humanity, by their fundamental equality, and, according to believers, by their common origin in God. UNESCO is to be commended for its efforts to safeguard the great monuments of civilization and the great beauty spots of the world. The good things of this world, including works of art, national resources, and scientific discoveries, should serve all without compromising national sovereignty. Still, it must be said that those who have more should make substantial sacrifices for the benefit of those who have less. Fortunately, the new means of communication can create bridges of thought and speech, and the network of international organizations dedicated to understanding among peoples can also help.[11]

A more recent session of the General Conference of UNESCO, the twenty-seventh, was held at Paris in 1993. Archbishop Lorenzo Antonetti spoke for the Holy See. The Holy See applauded the efforts of UNESCO to adapt to the ongoing changes of the delicate world situation and to face the need to improve its administration. A major problem facing the organization at the moment was the need to implement on a practical level the rights and freedoms already stated in a theoretical way in many charters, treaties, and conventions. Today a great number of people are still deprived of the possibility of full personal development. A great number of people are still excluded from the decision-making process and, because of illiteracy, too easily become the victims of injustice. The solution necessarily depends upon education and culture, which are the objectives of UNESCO.

However, an education that corresponds to the objectives of the organization and one that would be an agent of peace among peoples cannot limit itself merely to transmitting technical knowledge. The spiritual heritage of peoples must also be considered as the basis of a formation that includes human rights and religious tolerance.

The Catholic Church, which has been engaged in formation activities for many centuries, particularly the education of youth, will continue to serve mankind in this regard.

Turning to the subject of culture, the speaker expressed the appreciation of the Holy See for UNESCO's efforts to preserve the beautiful works of nature and the highest creations of human genius as part of the world's patrimony. But as important as those efforts are, UNESCO should work on behalf of culture in an even more profound sense. UNESCO ought to consider what constitutes the soul of different cultures—that is to say, how each people asserts its identity and expresses an aspect of culture that, by its nature, assumes varied forms likely to encounter each other. This encounter can be a source of grave difficulty and danger to cultures of less numerous populations. Here UNESCO can help considerably to preserve what is of value in the different cultures.

The speaker concluded his remarks by noting that the huge strides made by science and technology in the last decades can serve mankind in a wonderful way as long as they are placed at the service of mankind and its integral development. But history teaches that science and technology can be used to man's detriment. The Holy See invites scientists and politicians to use all their influence to see that science and research always respect human life from the moment of conception to its natural end.[12]

10

Disarmament and Peace

Disarmament

The Charter of the United Nations confers specific responsibilities in the matter of disarmament on the General Assembly and the Security Council. The assembly is empowered to consider "principles governing disarmament and the regulation of armaments" and to make "recommendations with regard to such principles to the members or to the Security Council or to both" (art. 11.1). The Security Council, "in order to promote the establishment of peace and maintenance of international peace and security with the least diversion for armaments of the world's human and economic resources," is responsible for formulating, with the assistance of the Military Staff Committee, "plans to be submitted to the members of the United Nations for the establishment of a system of regulating armaments" (art. 26).

Originally, the United Nations set up the Atomic Energy Commission in 1946 and the Commission for Conventional Armaments in 1947 to deal with the problem of disarmament. The two commissions strove for two goals: the use of atomic energy for peaceful purposes only and the reduction of armaments and armed forces under an international system of control and inspection.

The work of the two commissions was frustrated by the tensions of the Cold War, and in 1952 the General Assembly consolidated the two of them into a single Disarmament Commission with the same general goals. The ultimate goal of the United Nations has remained general and complete disarmament under effective international control, but measures that will bring about partial disarmament are viewed as integral to that goal.

The United Nations and various governments have taken limited but important steps in the control of armaments. For example, the Antarctic Treaty of 1959 prohibits in the Antarctic region any military maneuvers, weapons tests, building of installations, or disposal of radioactive wastes produced by military activities. The 1967 Treaty for the Prohibition of Nuclear Weapons in Latin America (Treaty of Tlatelolco) created the first nuclear-weapon-free zone in a densely populated area and was the first arms control agreement whose implementation is overseen by an international organization. The 1968 Treaty on the Non-Proliferation of Nuclear Weapons aims at limiting the spread of nuclear weapons from nuclear to nonnuclear countries, at promoting the process of disarmament by the nuclear nations, and at guaranteeing all countries access to nuclear technology for peaceful purposes. The 1972 Convention on the Prohibition of the Development, Production and Stockpiling of Bacteriological (Biological) and Toxin Weapons and on Their Destruction was the first international agreement providing for genuine disarmament—that is, the destruction of existing weapons. The 1985 South Pacific Nuclear-Free-Zone Treaty (Treaty of Rarotonga) establishes a large nuclear-free zone in the South Pacific.

In 1978, the General Assembly, deploring the meager results of past efforts at disarmament, held its first session devoted entirely to that subject. The conclusions of the session were embodied in what is called the Final Document. According to the Final Document, the United Nations should play a central role in disarmament efforts, disarmament was of fundamental importance to international peace and security, and "disarmament and arms limitation agreements should provide for adequate measures of verification satisfactory to all parties." The Final Document offered a Program of Action that identified matters that required immediate and urgent attention: nuclear weapons; other weapons of mass destruction, including chemical weapons; conventional weapons; and the reduction of armed forces. The program went on to outline the steps toward disarmament to be taken in each area.

The Final Document also noted the urgent need to revitalize existing machinery working for disarmament and to establish appropriate forums for disarmament negotiations and deliberations. In this connection, the General Assembly established a new Disarmament Commission as a deliberative body composed of all members of the United Nations. The commission considers and makes recommendations on various disarmament problems, and it reports annually to the assembly. There is also a Conference on Disarmament, which consists of forty members, including all the major nuclear powers. It serves as a multilateral negotiating forum to carry on efforts of earlier negotiating bodies.

In 1982, the General Assembly held a second special session on disarmament. More than 140 states took part in the general debate. The assembly was unable to agree on several important agenda items, but it unanimously affirmed the validity of the Final Document of the first special session. A third special session on disarmament was held in 1988 and was attended by 159 member-states. Nuclear disarmament was the principal subject of discussion. The atmosphere of the session was improved by arms reduction agreements reached earlier by the United States and the Soviet Union, but no substantive final document was approved.

At its regular sessions, the General Assembly has continued to call for a comprehensive nuclear test-ban treaty, the cessation of the nuclear arms race, the establishment of nuclear-free zones in the Middle East and South Asia and the denuclearization of Africa, increased security for non-nuclear-weapons states, the banning of chemical weapons, the reduction of armed forces and conventional weapons, the prevention of the arms race in outer space, the prohibition of new types of weapons of mass destruction, the reduction of military budgets, and consideration of the impact of science and technology upon international security.

Since the end of the Cold War, substantial progress toward disarmament has been made on various long-standing issues. The two major nuclear powers have concluded two treaties on the reduction of nuclear weapons, START I in 1991 and START II in 1993. The 1995 Conference of Parties to the Treaty on the Non-Proliferation of Nuclear Weapons decided to extend the treaty indefinitely. The 1993 Chemical Weapons Convention prohibits the production, use, and spread of chemical weapons and provides for the destruction of existing stockpiles.

The efforts of the United Nations to achieve disarmament by the nations of the world have been encouraged by the Holy See. In 1978, Pope Paul VI sent a message to the first special session of the General Assembly devoted to disarmament. To disarm, the Pope said, is to deprive war of its means. However, statesmen ask themselves: Isn't the balance of forces the best way to maintain peace? Don't nations without protection and the means of defense invite attack? Ever new and dreadful means of mass destruction fuel the arms race, but it cannot continue indefinitely without causing a catastrophe. What can be done to lessen the danger?

The problem of disarmament, the Pope said, is substantially a problem of mutual trust. One can promote disarmament by replacing "the balance of terror" with "the balance of trust." A first step in the process is improvement of relations among the great powers and blocs of nations. Then balanced and supervised disarmament measures together with international structures that secure and guarantee everyone's rights will support the improvement. The present generation has a moral responsibility before God and man to act even if action demands immense efforts and new ways of thinking. A step-by-step strategy toward the goal of disarmament seems best in the circumstances. Nuclear weapons must be dealt with first, then other existing or possible weapons of mass destruction such as chemical and radiological weapons, and then conventional weapons. The latter, too, cause much suffering and destruction.

The Holy Father noted the scandal of the arms race, which devotes so much money and brainpower to death rather than to life. He hoped that the reduction of arms expenditures would release more resources for development. Disarmament, a new world order, and development are obligations that rest upon the whole world and are inseparably linked. The Holy See, for its part, will not reject any appeal for help in overcoming the obstacles to peace, it will continue to proclaim untiringly the obligation of peace and the means by which it is achieved, and it will continue to pray for peace, which is, above all, a gift of God.[1]

In 1982, Pope John Paul II sent a message to the second special session of the General Assembly devoted to disarmament. Pope John Paul had seen very little progress toward disarmament. In the four years that had elapsed since the first special session on disarmament, there had been even greater expenditures for weapons—nuclear, chemical, and specialized.

By sending a personal message to the second special session of the General Assembly on disarmament, the Pope wished to express some ethical principles bearing upon peace and disarmament. The world wants peace; it needs peace; but modern warfare could involve the devastation and destruction of entire regions. The major powers of the world have invoked the ancient Roman principle: *"Si vis pacem, para bellum."*[2] This principle expresses the idea of deterrence, or "balance of terror," as some call it. In accordance with this principle, the parties involved seek military superiority and thus spark the arms race. Now, the Pope said, the General Assembly seeks to reverse this race, for the world wants and needs peace and disarmament. May God grant the members of the assembly the light and strength to pursue this goal despite the failures of the past and the uncertainties of the present! The Catholic Church, the Pope promised, will continue to struggle for peace, and it will not rest until there is a general, verifiable disarmament and the human race is committed to those ethical choices that guarantee a lasting peace.

Pope John Paul went on to say that even small steps are helpful in achieving peace. Moreover, there is no place for exaggerated speech or threatening stances. Governments need to respect the wishes of their people, who are more and more fearful of nuclear war. Witness the peace movements that are springing up everywhere! Still, in the present conditions, deterrence based on a balance of arsenals is morally acceptable if it is accompanied by progressive disarmament. In the absence of the supranational authority of which Pope John XXIII wrote in *Pacem in Terris,* negotiation remains the only realistic response to the threat of war. Negotiation should include the whole range of weapons, nuclear and conventional. When he was writing, the Pope said, 80 percent of arms expenditures went for conventional weapons.

Pope John Paul agreed with Pope Paul VI when the latter said in his address to the General Assembly in 1965 that peace is the product not only of politics and the balance of power, but also of ideas and the works of peace. So Pope John Paul urged that bonds linking people be forged and strengthened. The products of the mind and culture and the creative powers of peoples are meant to be shared. What is more, the resources devoted to the development of arms ought to be diverted to the development of peoples.

In conclusion, Pope John Paul noted that the arms race is a consequence of an ethical crisis—namely, a disrespect for ethical principles. True disarmament, which will guarantee the peace, will come about only with the resolution of the ethical crisis. We shall have to overcome the narrow-minded pursuit of personal interest and privilege, the great disparity between the rich and the poor, and the denial of human rights. Only then can we eliminate the true causes of the insecurity of which the arms race is an effect. Halting the arms race requires a struggle on two fronts: on the one hand, a gradual and verifiable reduction of armaments by all parties; and on the other, the removal of conditions that cause the race.

Peace is not a utopian dream, nor is war an inevitable calamity.[3]

The Holy See continued to take part in the debate on disarmament at the 1984 session of the Disarmament Conference at Geneva. At that time, Archbishop Achille Silvestrini spoke for the papal delegation. The conference was meeting to promote general and complete disarmament under the safeguard of international inspection. Pope John Paul II was deeply interested in the work of the conference, and he did not believe that war was inevitable; rather, the differences between nations could and must be settled by means other than war and violence. Young people and young married couples were asking about the meaning of life when total warfare threatens to destroy it. Simultaneous and progressive disarmament, accompanied by genuine international inspection, would do much to lessen the tension. Less money spent on nuclear and conventional weapons would release more resources for the relief of poor nations.

Monsignor Silvestrini went on to list a number of priorities that, in the judgment of the Holy See, were likely to lead to real disarmament and a genuine peace. These included a willingness to negotiate, the restoration of trust among nations, and working to place science and technology at the service of life instead of war. Banning weapons in outer space and banning radiation and chemical weapons is a matter of particular urgency because of their possible devastating results. In this context, the speaker recalled the words of Vatican II in *Gaudium et Spes:* "Any act of war aimed indiscriminately at the destruction of entire cities or of extensive areas, along with their populations, is a crime against God and against man himself."

What contribution to disarmament and peace can the Catholic Church make? It can invite all men and women of goodwill to make the ethical choices so necessary in this regard. This invitation has been extended in recent documents not only by the Holy See, but also by episcopal conferences in several countries, including the United States. Pope John Paul expressed the hope that the international community could come up with a system of law that regulates relations and maintains peace among nations, just as civil law regulates relations and maintains peace among the citizens of an individual country. Is this a utopian dream? By no means, for there are countless men and women who aspire to form one universal family.[4]

In 1991, Archbishop Jean Louis Tauran, the papal Secretary for Relations with States, addressed the First Committee of the United Nations General Assembly on the subject of disarmament. He referred to two recent conflicts with sadness—the Gulf War, between UN forces and Iraq, and the civil war that was devastating Yugoslavia. After the tragedy of World War II, the colonial wars, and the crises in the Middle and Far East, one would have thought, he said, that national leaders finally understood what Pope John Paul II had said at the beginning of that year: "A peace obtained by arms could only prepare new acts of violence." In any case, it remains true: it is absolutely necessary to exhaust all peaceful means provided by international law before unleashing a war of any kind. One must always ask: Is the evil entailed in waging war proportional to its objectives?

However, the speaker noted certain hopeful signs. The new international climate tended to promote dialogue and mutual trust. The signing of the START Treaty between the United States and the Soviet Union could only be a cause for rejoicing. The major nuclear powers had decided to eliminate short-range nuclear missiles. Finally, we would soon achieve an agreement on a verifiable, total, and universal ban on chemical warfare. Yet there was a dark side: nations continued to modernize nuclear weapons, and the arms trade was flourishing.

For forty-six years, the speaker said in conclusion, the United Nations has persevered in its quest for peace. The organization deserves our homage and support for its noble mission. The Catholic Church is convinced that war is not inevitable. However, peace will never be achieved and disarmament will be impossible if human rights and basic freedoms are ignored, if justice, solidarity, respect for one's neighbor, and the aspiration of peoples to self-determination are denied.[5]

Peace

According to the preamble of the UN charter, the peoples of the United Nations are determined

> to practice tolerance and live together in peace with one another as good neighbors, and to unite their strength to maintain international peace and security, and to ensure, by the acceptance of principles and the institution of methods, that armed force shall not be used, save in the common interest. . . .

Under the charter, the Security Council is given the primary responsibility for the maintenance of international peace and the peaceful solution of disputes. First of all, it can call upon the parties to a dispute to settle their differences "by negotiation, inquiry, mediation, conciliation, arbitration, judicial settlement, resort to regional agencies or arrangements, or other peaceful means of their own choice" (art. 33). If stronger measures are necessary to deal with the threat to international peace and security, the Security Council may call upon the members of the United Nations to break economic and diplomatic relations with the offending parties or even resort to force (arts. 39–51).

The elaboration of principles or norms for the promotion of peace is carried out primarily by the General Assembly under article 11 of the charter, which states in part: "The General Assembly may consider the general principles of cooperation in the maintenance of peace and security . . . and may make recommendations with regard to such principles to the members or to the Security Council or both."

Some of the main resolutions and declarations on peace and related matters adopted by the General Assembly over the years include the following:

- The 1957 resolution on peaceful and neighborly relations among states, which stresses the need to develop friendly cooperation and peaceful relations among states irrespective of their divergencies.
- The 1965 Declaration on the Inadmissibility of Intervention in the Domestic Affairs of States and the Protection of Their Independence and Sovereignty, which condemns all forms of such intervention as contrary to the principles of the charter and threats to universal peace.
- The 1974 Declaration on Aggression, which calls upon states to refrain from all acts of aggression and recommends that the Security Council should be guided by the definition in determining the existence of an act of aggression.

- The 1987 Declaration on the Enhancement of the Effectiveness of the Principle of Refraining from the Threat or Use of Force in International Relations, which declares that principle to be universal in character and binding, regardless of states' political, economic, social, or cultural systems or alliances, and which calls upon states to build their international relations on the basis of mutual understanding, trust, respect, and cooperation.

The assembly designated the opening day of its regular annual session, the third Tuesday in September, as International Day of Peace. The year 1986 was proclaimed the International Year of Peace.

The United Nations has frequently been called upon to deal with situations that threaten to erupt, or have erupted, into armed conflict. In such circumstances, the world organization tries to bring the opposing parties to the conference table and halt fighting if it has occurred. Despite frustrations and setbacks, the UN has made progress in its peacemaking and peacekeeping activities. For these purposes, the United Nations has employed, in addition to negotiation and quiet diplomacy, various means such as peacekeeping forces, observer or fact-finding missions, the supervision of plebiscites, conciliators, mediators, and special representatives.

The Secretary-General of the United Nations has acted as a peacemaker in several instances—for example, in the cases of Afghanistan, the Iran-Iraq war, Namibia, and the dispute between France and New Zealand following the *Rainbow Warrior* affair. The Secretary-General may act at the request of the Security Council or the General Assembly or, in exceptional circumstances, on his own initiative.

To preserve or restore peace, the United Nations also provides military observer missions and peacekeeping forces whose mandates are defined by the Security Council. Military observer missions are composed of unarmed officers made available to the United Nations by member-states. Peacekeeping forces are composed of contingents of armed forces made available to the United Nations by member-states and financed by the international community. These forces are sent in, normally with the consent of the parties involved, to prevent recurrence of hostilities and provide humanitarian assistance. Peacekeeping forces must act in an impartial manner and do nothing that might affect the claims or positions of the parties. While they are armed, peacekeeping forces may use their weapons only in self-defense. UN peacekeeping forces have played a significant role in the Congo (now Zaire), Cyprus, the Middle East, and elsewhere. UN peace-keeping forces were awarded the Nobel Peace Prize in 1988.

The United Nations broke new ground in 1989 when, as part of its peacekeeping operation, it monitored the entire electoral process in Namibia. Since then, the United Nations has monitored, at government request, elections in Nicaragua and Haiti (1990), Angola (1992), Cambodia (1993), El Salvador, South Africa, and Mozambique (1994) as well as the 1993 referendum in Eritrea. UN action has involved all aspects of the electoral process, including voter registration, poll organization, voting, ballot counting, and the announcement of results. In each case the goal was to be able to determine that the electoral process was "free and fair at every stage."

Of course, the Holy See, along with the United Nations, is vitally interested in peace. In 1983, Cardinal Agostino Casaroli, the papal Secretary of State, delivered a lecture on the Holy See and peace at the University of

San Francisco in California. In this lecture the Cardinal did not make an official statement on behalf of the Holy See; rather, he simply recalled and synthesized certain ideas already known.

How, he asked, does the Catholic Church contribute to the establishment of peace? For one thing, the Church exercises a teaching ministry explaining the nature and conditions of peace. The speaker recalled the doctrinal statements of recent Popes with regard to peace: the Christmas messages of Pius XII, the encyclical *Pacem in Terris* of John XXIII, the messages and homilies of Paul VI for each World Day of Peace at the beginning of the new year, and the statements and addresses of John Paul II on many occasions. From this material we can extract the essential and basic elements of the Holy See's position on peace—namely, that peace is a supreme good for humanity, is necessary, possible, and obligatory, is gravely threatened by social injustice and the arms race, and requires mutual trust and cooperation.

As a practical means of ensuring peace, the speaker noted, the Second Vatican Council and recent Popes have called for some universal public authority that is acknowledged by all and is capable of effective action on behalf of justice and human rights. For the moment at least, even the United Nations does not have this capability. In principle, then, we cannot deny to states the right to military action in self-defense.

However, the existence of nuclear weapons requires a reevaluation of the conditions of a just war. Indeed, the effects and consequences of nuclear war are always such as to exclude even the hypothesis of recourse to them. The use of such weapons would be a kind of collective murder-suicide. To be sure, the possession of nuclear weapons by one state is a deterrent to aggression by another, but there is always the real danger that possession will lead to use. Science is not to be blamed for the present situation; it is man's abuse of science that is at fault. In any event, we all remember the statement of Pope John Paul II in his message to the second special session of the General Assembly on disarmament: "In current conditions, deterrence based on balance, certainly not as an end in itself but as a step toward progressive disarmament, may still be judged morally acceptable."

The policy of deterrence, according to papal teaching, is necessarily a provisional one. Up to this point, deterrence has enabled the parties involved to avoid the worst, and it affords them the opportunity to reach agreements about disarmament and to cooperate for the good of the human race by diverting resources from the arms race. Winning the peace demands no less valor and commitment than winning a war.

We all know the difficulties of dialogue about the knotty problems of the international community, problems that have to do with vital rights and interests, with deep feelings and strongly rooted convictions. True dialogue requires sincerity, frankness, understanding, patience, and confidence in the goodwill of the other side. Public opinion can encourage the process, especially public opinion that is understanding and open to the needs of others. Hence the importance of educating the sons and daughters of the Church and, indeed, all people to be peacemakers. Surely Catholic colleges and universities have a part to play in this regard. Dialogue often needs mediation, and the Holy See offers its assistance in accordance with its nature and capabilities.

The papal Secretary of State concluded his remarks by noting the profoundly religious and almost prophetic tone of papal statements about the problems of peace. He recalled the words of Pius XII at the beginning of World War II: "Nothing is lost with peace; everything can be lost by war," and also the words of Paul VI before the General Assembly of the United Nations: "No more war; war never again!" The Holy See seeks to remind everyone again and again of the conditions that make peace possible, and it calls everyone, especially believers, to conversion, since hatred, injustice, and war are the "social" fruit of sin. Of course, there is One who has conquered sin—namely, Christ the Redeemer, the Prince of Peace. It is Christ whom the Church and the Holy See strive to hold up for all to see.[6]

In 1987, Pope John Paul II addressed the United Nations Committee on Coordination at the Vatican. The Pope said that the UN organization that the committee serves

has a vital role in today's world. We are all aware that increasing global interdependence and intercommunication create an ever greater potential for peace and understanding, but also multiply the risks of wider conflict. Your Organization is uniquely suited to foster the possibilities for peace and to reducing the dangers created by injustice and aggression.

The UN serves as a useful forum for discussion, and as an effective instrument for action, in promoting the common good of the human family. It owes its very existence to the desire of people of good will for peace, security, and the freedom to seek legitimate human development for themselves, their families and their communities. Each of the agencies you represent was initiated in order to insure true human progress, that is, progress based on respect for fundamental God-given rights, on mutual cooperation, and on the promotion of justice and peace.

196

The Pope went on to say that the United Nations deserves praise for its service to humanity on many levels. For example, the United Nations, as part of its regular activities, has called international attention to the needs of the poor, the homeless, those deprived of their human rights, refugees, children, the handicapped, and women. It has likewise called attention to cultural, economic, scientific, and public health issues. These and other problems of mankind can be solved only by international cooperation, which is facilitated by the United Nations. The organization must exercise patience and perseverance as it carries on its work, given the many social, political, and economic differences of the human family.

The United Nations, the Pope maintained, must continue to find inspiration in the ideals and values upon which it was founded. Only in this way can it preserve its credibility. An ethical approach to the problems that confront us is crucial if we are not to lose sight of the dignity and rights of human beings. For too long the world has been driven by conflicting ideologies and economic interests. Therefore, a twofold challenge confronts the United Nations at this time: to overcome ideological competition and to foster an ethical approach to human development and the resolution of social problems. In other words, human beings and the quality of their life should be at the center of the world body's thought and action.

In the name of the Catholic Church, the Pope expressed his appreciation for the efforts of the United Nations on behalf of peace, and he restated his understanding of the enormous problems facing the organization. With the United Nations, the Church, too, believes in peace. Truly, human development and progress are rooted in the divine creation and redemption of the world. For these reasons the Church is always ready to cooperate with the United Nations in any initiative that promotes human dignity, social justice, and peace.[7]

11

Development

Development is an important concept for both the United Nations and the Holy See, both of which have acted vigorously for its implementation.

The United Nations

The United Nations understands development to mean economic and social progress, especially in developing countries, where two-thirds of the world's population live, often in the grip of poverty, hunger, ignorance, and disease. Most of the work of the United Nations, measured in terms of money and personnel, goes into programs aimed at development. With a view to the creation of conditions of stability and well-being so necessary to peace, the Charter of the United Nations pledges the organization to promote "higher standards of living, full employment, and conditions of economic and social progress and development" (art. 55.a).

Since 1960, the General Assembly has proclaimed four successive United Nations Development Decades to focus international attention on the problems of development. There is general agreement that urgent problems of development require a world plan of action and international cooperation.

In 1974, at a special session on development, the General Assembly adopted the Declaration and Program of Action on the Establishment of a New International Economic Order. Member-states solemnly proclaimed their determination to work urgently for

the establishment of a new international economic order based on equity, sovereignty, interdependence, common interest and cooperation among states, irrespective of their economic and social systems [that would] correct inequalities and redress existing injustices, make it possible to eliminate the widening gap between the developed and developing countries and insure steadily accelerating economic and social development in peace and justice for present and future generations.

In the same year, 1974, the General Assembly adopted the Charter of Economic Rights and Duties of States. The charter stipulates that every state has the right freely to exercise full permanent sovereignty over its wealth and natural resources, to regulate foreign investments within its national jurisdiction, and to nationalize, expropriate, or transfer the ownership of foreign property. It also provides that appropriate compensation should be paid in cases of nationalization and that any controversies should be settled under the domestic laws of the nationalizing states unless all states concerned agree to other peaceful means.

Unfortunately, efforts to implement the New International Economic Order and the Charter of Economic Rights and Duties have not been generally agreed upon.

The UN family—the United Nations and the various agencies connected with it—has undertaken many practical measures to assist developing countries. Such practical measures included technical cooperation, surveys, studies, convening international conferences, development planning and special projects in individual fields such as trade, industry and agriculture.

Among the global conferences convened in recent years were conferences on desertification, water, technical cooperation among developing countries, science and technology, agrarian reform and rural development, women, renewable resources of energy, least developed countries, aging, population, nuclear energy, drug abuse and illicit trafficking, and trade and development:

> The United Nations Development Program (UNDP) [which was established as an agency of the United Nations in 1965] is the world's largest channel for multilateral technical and pre-investment cooperation. It is active in more that 150 developing countries and territories. Its five-year country and inter-country programs coordinate development activities in virtually every economic and social sector, including farming, fishing, mining, manufacturing, power, transport, communications, housing and building, trade and tourism, nutrition, health, sanitation, environmental protection, education and training, community development, social welfare, economic planning and public administration.[1]

The UNDP administers the United Nations Volunteers (UNV) program. The volunteers are recruited in many countries, and they are sent to a country only at the request and with the approval of the host country. The volunteers represent many professions, and they are, for the most part, practitioners who share skills at the working level, rather than theoreticians or advisers. They are paid a monthly allowance for their needs rather than a salary commensurate with their qualifications and experience.

Another agency of the United Nations concerned with development is the United Nations Conference on Trade and Development (UNCTAD). It was founded in 1964, and its Secretariat is located at Geneva. It includes all the member-states of the United Nations plus a few others:

UNCTAD is a principal instrument of the General Assembly for the deliberation and negotiation of international economic cooperation. Its mandate is to promote international trade, and particularly that of developing countries, with a view to accelerating their economic development. In addition to its role as an inter-governmental forum, UNCTAD is involved with research, conceptual innovation and policy analysis; the implementation of, or follow-up to, decisions of inter-governmental bodies; technical cooperation, *inter alia* as an executing agency of UNDP; and information exchanges and consultations.[2]

In effect, UNCTAD seeks to expand the export of goods and services from developing countries, stabilize and strengthen international commodity markets, promote investment in Third World countries, enhance their technological capabilities, reduce Third World debt, afford special support for the least developed countries, and increase trade and economic cooperation among developing countries.

A third agency of the United Nations concerned with development is UNIDO (the United Nations Industrial Development Organization). It was established by the General Assembly in 1966 with headquarters in Vienna:

The organization is the United Nations system's central coordinating body in industrial development. It encourages and assists developing countries to promote and accelerate their industrialization; and it coordinates, initiates, and follows up United Nations activities to this end. It contributes to cooperation between industrialized and developing countries in accelerating world industrial development by: providing a forum for contracts, consultations and negotiations; encouraging investment promotion activities; and promoting and facilitating the transfer of technology to and between developing countries.[3]

More specifically, UNIDO provides technical assistance for industrial development, organizes industrial training programs, offers advisory services, and assists in obtaining fair external financing for industrial development. UNIDO also serves as a clearinghouse for industrial information by collecting, analyzing, publishing, standardizing, and improving industrial statistics.

The efforts of the United Nations on behalf of development go beyond the work of UNDP, UNCTAD, and UNIDO. A large program of technical cooperation for developing countries in the fields of energy, water and mineral resources, and infrastructure is executed by the Department of Technical Cooperation for Development (DTCD), an operational arm of the United Nations Secretariat:

In the field of energy, the DTCD implements projects in developing countries for the exploration, development and utilization of petroleum and gas, coal, electric power (thermal and hydropower), new and renewable sources of energy (geothermal, solar, wind energy, biomass and small-hydropower) . . .

In the field of water resources, the DTCD implements a broad range of technical assistance projects which focus on such areas as the planning and management of water resources development, rural water supply, the establishment and strengthening of national water resources institutions, ground water exploration and exploitation, and river basin development. . . .

The DTCD is the United Nations' principal agency for mineral resources development and provides technical assistance on such matters as policy and legislation, exploration and evaluation, mining, processing and marketing. . . .[4]

The Holy See

Development was and is a major concern of the Holy See too. A noteworthy expression of that concern was Paul VI's encyclical letter *Populorum Progressio* (The development of peoples) (1967). In the first part, Pope Paul wrote about the nature of authentic and complete human development. Developing nations that had recently gained their independence found that political freedom was not enough. Indeed, they also needed to acquire the social and economic structures that allowed their citizens to live in human dignity. Unfortunately, this process was going forward only at a slow pace in most developing nations. An acute restlessness was engulfing the poorer classes, a situation that was aggravated by the conflict between the traditional culture and the demands of the industrial age. The older moral, spiritual, and religious values were giving way without a worthy replacement.

The Church makes a distinctive contribution to development when it offers a global perspective on human beings and their situation. The development that the Church espouses is not only economic, but also holistic. Each person is primarily responsible for his self-fulfillment, of which a transcendent humanism—one that surpasses nature—is the highest goal. This transcendent humanism is really the fullness of life bestowed by Christ. The humanism espoused by the Church permits men and women to escape from the inhuman conditions of economic and political oppression and enables them to have the material, intellectual, cultural, and spiritual goods required for a truly human life.

In *Populorum Progressio,* Pope Paul quoted the words of the Second Vatican Council: "God intended the earth and everything in it for the use of all human beings and peoples. Thus, under the leadership of justice and in the company of charity, created goods should flow fairly to all."[5] All other rights, whatever they may be, including the rights of property and free trade, must be subordinated to this principle. Industrialization is necessary for economic growth and human progress, and it is both a sign of and an incentive to development. However, industrialization itself cannot be blamed for the unrestrained pursuit of profit, cutthroat competition, and irresponsible ownership of the means of production that have sometimes accompanied it. Generally, revolution is not a solution to unjust conditions, but a new state of affairs must be created without delay.

Development cannot be left to private initiative alone, important as this is, but public authorities need to coordinate goals and plans. Everything should be directed to the good of human beings; economics and technology are meaningless if they do not serve men and women. Basic education, the capacity to read and write, is absolutely necessary for any nation seeking to develop itself. The family continues to be the basis of society, and it is up to the parents to make a responsible decision about the number of children they will bring into the world.

In the second part of *Populorum Progressio*, Pope Paul wrote about development as the goal and common task of the human race as a whole. In this matter, wealthier nations have a duty to assist poorer nations so that they can live a truly human life. Again, there must be a coordinated effort on the part of all to define goals and identify ways and means. A world fund, created by reduced expenditures for arms, could provide funds for development. Moreover, a dialogue between those who contribute aid and those who receive it would permit a balanced assessment of support available and needed.

Free trade, the Pope wrote, is not always fair to developing nations because, in a free market, they do not always receive a just price for their raw materials and agricultural crops. In this case, international agreements on a broad scale can help a great deal. A selfish nationalism and racism can also be the cause of injustice, division, and hatred. The Pope looked forward to the day when an ever more effective international solidarity would allow all peoples to become the artisans of their own destiny.

What can be done to strengthen brotherly ties between nations? Many things can be done. Students and workers from developing countries can be welcomed in other countries. Business people who travel to newly industrialized countries can be sensitive to the needs of the host country. Visiting experts can act as helpers and fellow workers and not as overlords. Young people can help developing nations by social service. Development is the new name of peace, which is fashioned by a more perfect form of justice among individuals and nations. Then the Pope returned to an idea that he had expressed before the General Assembly in New York: "Who can fail to see the need of a world authority capable of taking effective action on the juridical and political planes?"

The Pope concluded his encyclical with an appeal to various groups:

- to Catholics that they might act without waiting passively for directions from others;
- to other believers that they might promote living conditions truly worthy of the children of God;
- to all men and women of goodwill that they might look upon civil progress and economic development as the only roads to peace;
- to governments that they might abandon the senseless arms race;
- to thoughtful men and women that they might blaze a new trail of mutual cooperation among human beings;
- and to all promoters of development to continue their work on behalf of needy nations.

Then, in his apostolic letter, *Octogesima Adveniens* (1971), written on the eightieth anniversary of Leo XIII's *Rerum Novarum,* Pope Paul proposed to deal with a number of new problems that were (and are) particularly urgent, extensive, and complex. The subjects that drew the Pope's attention were these: urbanization, Christians living in the city, youth, the role of women, workers, victims of change, discrimination, the right to emigrate, unemployment, the social communications media, and the environment. The Holy Father did not attempt to offer any final conclusions about these subjects, but he urged Christians to attend to them and seek improvement.

In the following section of the apostolic letter, the Pope noted the profound changes in modern civilization caused by scientific and technological progress. In the midst of the changes, two human aspirations have surfaced as men and women become better informed and better educated—namely, the aspiration to equality with others and the aspiration to participate in the decisions that affect one's life. The Pope reaffirmed the necessity of subordinating economic activity, as beneficial as it is, to legitimate political authority in the interest of the common good. Moreover, there is a need for new approaches and new structures to achieve greater justice in international economic life. The idea is "to allow each country to promote its own development within the framework of a cooperation free from any spirit of domination whether economic or political."

Pope Paul concluded his letter *Octogesima Adveniens* with a ringing call to action. Let each one examine himself to see what he has done up to now and what he ought to do in the future. In the face of what seems a limitless task, the Christian will find hope in the fact that the Lord and other men and women of goodwill are also working in the world for justice and peace. In specific situations, Christians will differ about options and commitments, but the bonds that unite them are mightier than anything that divides them.

In 1987, Pope John Paul II wished to commemorate the twentieth anniversary of Pope Paul's *Populorum Progressio* and did so by publishing his own encyclical, *Sollicitudo Rei Socialis* (Social concern). Pope John Paul noted that the hopes for development expressed in 1967 had not been realized in 1987; indeed, realization was still far off. An innumerable multitude of people in developing countries still suffered under the burden of severe poverty. Various parts of the world were separated by a widening economic gap. The situation was aggravated by other signs of underdevelopment: illiteracy, exclusion from the political process, suppression of human rights, and discrimination of every kind.

However, there were signs of underdevelopment even in developed countries—two in particular. One is the housing crisis, which is due in large measure to the growing phenomenon of urbanization, and the other is the widespread unemployment and underemployment even in developed countries. The Pope also mentioned the huge debt that many nations incurred in order to promote development. That debt must now be serviced and acts as a brake upon development.

There was also a political factor that hindered development. That was the "Cold War" between two powerful political blocs in the West and East. These two blocs were driven by conflicting ideologies: the West by liberal capitalism and the East by Marxist collectivism. The conflict between West and East affected developing countries adversely by compelling them to choose between parties when they needed the help of both. Moreover, the arms race between West and East consumed resources that might otherwise have gone to development. In his negative assessment of the situation prevailing at that time, the Pope also referred to the problems created by burgeoning populations.

Yet there were also positive aspects to the actual situation. One was the growing awareness of human dignity and the creation of many private groups to monitor what was happening in this sensitive field. The United Nations' Declaration of Human Rights has played an important role in this regard. Other positive aspects included a growing conviction about the interdependence of human beings and nations, a greater respect for life in all its phases, a resolute desire for peace on the part of many, a greater concern for the environment, the generous commitment of many individuals and organizations to the solution of human problems, and the progress made by some Third World countries in food production and industrialization.

Having surveyed the progress of development up to that point (1987), Pope John Paul then asked in effect: What is the nature of authentic human development? Experience teaches us, he replied, that the accumulation of material goods and the very real benefits of science and technology do not of themselves produce genuine happiness. Material possessions are not helpful unless they contribute to the realization of one's humanity in all its fullness. The problem is that the relatively few who possess so much are hindered by the cult of "having," while the many who possess so little are deprived of essential goods. Therefore, authentic human development is not only economic development, although it includes that, but also means improving the lot of the whole human being and that of all men and women who are made in the image and likeness of God.

Our personal and collective effort to elevate the human condition is part of God's plan for the world revealed in Christ. The Church is concerned with development because she wishes to place herself at the service of the divine plan that is meant to order all things to the fullness that dwells in Christ. What is more, the Church desires to respond to her fundamental vocation of being a "sacrament"—that is to say, a sign and instrument of intimate union with God and the unity of the whole human race. The obligation to commit oneself to the development of peoples obliges each and every man and woman as well as societies and nations. However, not even the need for development may be used as an excuse for imposing one's way of life or religious belief on others.

Nor would a type of development that does not respect and promote human rights be really worthy of human beings. Within each nation, if there is to be true development, there must be respect for life in all its stages, respect for the family, justice in employment, and political and religious freedom. On the international level, there must be complete respect for the historical and cultural identity of each people and recognition of its fundamental equality with other peoples. Finally, a true concept of development cannot ignore the use and renewability of natural resources and the consequences of haphazard industrialization.

At this point, Pope John Paul recalled an idea that he had articulated two years earlier, in 1985, in a document called *Reconciliation and Penance.* In that document the Pope had spoken of sinful social structures that are ways of buying, selling, trading, and promoting development that oppress the poor and restrict human rights. Sinful social structures are the result and concentration of many personal sins. Often enough, these personal sins are an all-consuming desire for profit and a thirst for power. Obviously, not only individuals but also nations and blocs of nations are guilty of these sins.

To dismantle these sinful social structures there has to be a change of heart—what Christians call conversion—on the part of believers and nonbelievers alike. Even now, however, there are certain hopeful signs of conversion. One is the growing awareness of interdependence among individuals and nations. When interdependence is recognized as a *moral* category, it gives rise to solidarity. Solidarity, as the Pope describes it, is "a firm and persevering determination to commit oneself to the common good; that is to say, to the good of each and every individual, because we are really responsible for all."

Solidarity is practiced within a society when its members recognize each other as persons. The poor practice solidarity among themselves when they support one another, and their public demonstrations express their needs and rights in the face of the inefficiency or corruption of public officials. Solidarity is practiced on the international level by the implementation of the principle that created goods are meant for all. Solidarity helps us to see the "other" as a neighbor, a helper, and an equal and transforms mutual distrust into collaboration. Finally, in the light of faith, solidarity takes on the added Christian dimension of forgiveness and reconciliation.

The Church makes a contribution to the urgent problems of development when she proclaims the truth about Christ, about herself, and about human beings, applying this truth to concrete situations. The Church's social doctrine is not a "third way" between liberal capitalism and Marxist collectivism; rather, it is a statement about the complex realities of human existence in the light of faith.

Today, more so than in the past, the Church's social teaching must express an option for the growing number of poor people throughout the world. To correct the imbalances between richer and poorer nations the Pope advocated the reform of the international trade system, changes in the world monetary and financial system, a careful look at the transfer of technology, and a review of the methods, costs, and effectiveness of international organizations. Above all, development demands a spirit of initiative on the part of poorer countries. Some of them will have to increase food production, others will have to reform their political institutions to achieve greater participatory democracy, and still others should promote cooperation with nations in their own geographical area.

In the concluding section of the encyclical, Pope John Paul noted that the human desire to be free from all forms of slavery is something noble and legitimate. However, human beings are totally free only when they are completely themselves in the fullness of their rights and duties. The principal obstacles to be overcome on the way to authentic freedom are sin and the degrading structures created by sin. The process of true development goes forward in the love and service of neighbor, especially of the poorest. We are all called, indeed obliged, to face the tremendous challenges of the present moment. At stake is the dignity of the human person, the indestructible image of God the Creator, which is identical in each one of us.

In this enterprise, the sons and daughters of the Church should serve as examples, but the Pope also invited the collaboration of other believers and men and women of goodwill. All that we do to make the lives of people more human is connected with the kingdom of God already present in mystery. All of us who take part in the Eucharist are called to discover, through this sacrament, the profound meaning of our actions in the world in favor of development and peace. And we continue to look to Mary, the mother of Jesus, whose maternal care extends to the personal and social aspects of people's lives on this earth.

Subsequently, in March of 1995, the United Nations organized a World Summit for Social Development at Copenhagen, Denmark. It was the first time in history that the international community, under the aegis of the United Nations, met in the framework of a conference to deal with the topic of social development. The Copenhagen Summit, in which the heads of state or government from all over the world took part, drafted strategic policies and concrete measures to promote social development on a world scale.

Cardinal Angelo Sodano, the papal Secretary of State, addressed the World Summit in the capacity of head of government. From the moment that the World Summit was announced, the speaker said, Pope John Paul II gave it his firm support. More than 270,000 Church educational and welfare institutions, spread across all the continents, work for the objectives of the Summit. The Holy See was pleased that the Summit had committed itself to promote a vision of social development that is political, economic, ethical, and spiritual, with full respect for religious and ethical values and the cultural patrimony of persons. What is needed to promote social development is a sense of community, interdependence, and solidarity on the part of all—governments and individuals alike.

Cardinal Sodano reaffirmed a principle stated several times in the documents of the summit, that "the person is at the center of sustainable development." As Pope John Paul II wrote in *Centesimus Annus,* even prior to the system of the exchange of goods and the free market something is due a person by reason of his nature and dignity. Moreover, in order to guarantee worldwide economic development, international participation and cooperation, including that of the poorer nations, are needed. Nor may the fundamental rights of migrant workers and their families be overlooked.

Development can be achieved only when women, in equal partnership with men, are enabled to participate fully in the social and economic order, especially through their access to education. If development is to be achieved, the scourge of war must be removed. In various parts of the world, war continues to debase the dignity of many people. Without peace, the development of peoples will never come about, just as without development there will never be peace. Now more than ever, the Holy See wishes to join with all states and all men and women of goodwill in the task of promoting the integral development of humanity.[6]

12

Food and Agriculture

The FAO

The FAO (Food and Agricultural Organization) is a specialized agency of the United Nations. It developed out of a conference on food and agriculture held at Hot Springs, Arkansas, in May 1943, and it was founded at a conference in Quebec on October 16, 1945. Since 1979, that date has been observed annually as World Food Day. More than 150 countries are members of the FAO.

The organization is governed by a Conference composed of the entire membership, which meets every two years to determine the budget and plot the program of work. The Conference elects a Council (consisting of forty-nine members), which serves as an interim governing body. The Conference also elects the Director-General, who is head of the Secretariat. Committees and commissions report to the Council on specific issues. For example, the Committee on Commodity Problems works to bring greater stability to world trade with agricultural commodities. The FAO has no mandatory powers. Its motto is: *"Fiat panis"* (Let there be bread).

The headquarters of the FAO are in Rome. Speaking to representatives of the organization at the Vatican in 1959, Pope John XXIII said that he often used to pass near the large FAO building in Rome. Seeing the many windows lighted at night, he never failed to send a grateful thought to those who were working there for the good of humanity. And from his apartment in the Vatican he could see the imposing headquarters of the agency rising on the horizon, so the FAO was very present to him in mind and heart.

The member-states of the FAO have pledged themselves to four goals: to raise the level of nutrition and standards of living of their people; to improve the production and distribution of all food and agricultural products; to improve the condition of rural people; and, by these means, to eliminate hunger. In effect, the FAO seeks world food security so that all people, at all times, may have physical and economic access to the food they need.

A publication of the United Nations notes that in pursuing these goals the

> FAO promotes investment in agriculture, better soil and water management, improved yields of crops and livestock, and the transfer of technology to, and the development of agricultural research in, developing countries. It promotes the conservation of natural resources, particularly plant genetic resources, and rational use of fertilizers and pesticides; combats animal diseases, promotes the development of marine and inland fisheries and of new and renewable sources of energy, particularly rural energy; and encourages the rational use of forest reserves. Technical assistance is provided in all these fields and in others such as nutrition, agricultural engineering, agrarian reform, development communications, remote sensing for natural resources, and the prevention of food losses.[1]

The Global Information and Early Warning System on Food and Agriculture of the FAO provides current information on the world food situation. Special alerts identify countries threatened by food shortages for the information of governments and relief organizations. The Food Security Assistance Scheme of the FAO is designed to assist developing countries in setting up national food reserves.

The FAO gives direct, practical help to countries in the developing world through technical assistance projects in all areas of food and agriculture. Two-thirds of some three thousand professionals employed by the FAO are based in the field on project sites or at country and regional offices in the Third World. The field projects in which they cooperate—there can be several thousand at any moment—may last ten years and involve a team of international experts and local technicians, or they can last two months and involve a single FAO officer. Billions of dollars of foreign and domestic capital plus food have been channeled through the FAO to developing countries.

In 1948, by a unanimous vote of its Conference, the FAO accorded the Holy See the status of Permanent Observer.

The Holy See

On at least five different occasions—in 1948, 1951, 1953, 1955, and 1957—Pope Pius XII addressed the representatives of the FAO whom he had received at the Vatican. In 1948, he praised the vision that inspired the foundation of an institution to deal with food and agricultural problems. Collaboration between nations on common problems means closer attention to the well-being and needs of all. The work of the FAO helps to free nations from poverty and the humiliation of begging from others. Rural peoples deserved special consideration because they are the first victims of natural and man-made calamities.

In 1951, Pope Pius noted that these calamities, so numerous in the 1940s, were a source of discouragement to many; yet it seemed to the Pope that the FAO was undaunted in the face of a very complex situation. The FAO's concern has to do with the production, conservation, allocation, transport, and distribution of food and with the best possible use of the immense riches of the earth, including agriculture, fisheries, and cattle. The Pope was distressed by so much land that was unproductive for lack of tools and skills and by the lack of transport that in some cases prevented useful products from reaching the market.

In 1953, the FAO reported that in developing countries the production of food was growing, the levels of consumption were rising, and exports were increasing, while in less developed countries, particularly in the Far East, production remained weak and food deficient. According to the Pope, the FAO provides an important service in solving the problems of hunger by gathering precise data. Seventy percent of the world's population was undernourished. Surely help would be forthcoming from developed nations, but the best way to help was to enable hungry people to help themselves by growing their own food. Teaching self-help may necessitate an effort to create new social conditions in which workers are more self-reliant and gain new skills, but such an effort would have ramifications beyond the production of food. The civilized world looks with profound sadness at the pitiful victims of famine when the earth is capable of feeding all human beings. The objectives of the FAO reflect the prayer of Christ, who taught us to pray for our daily bread.

In 1955, Pope Pius congratulated the FAO on its tenth anniversary. Its objectives remained the same: to raise the level of nutrition, to facilitate the distribution of food and agricultural products, and to contribute to the expansion of the world economy. After World War II, the FAO went to work to deal energetically with the hunger that was the aftermath of the war. Agricultural production increased significantly in the decade after the war, but formidable needs and obstacles remain. Efforts at soil conservation are surely necessary, and they must be augmented by agrarian and credit reform and by improvement of the living conditions of rural populations. There must also be vigilance over the manner in which forests are exploited. In any event, where once the problems of hunger seemed insoluble, the collaboration of governments offers much hope. In the effort to solve the problem of hunger one sees the charity of Christ.

Finally, in 1957, Pope Pius, speaking to the representatives of the FAO at the Vatican, noted that market changes had generally affected farmers adversely. The prices of manufactured goods continued to rise, while those of agricultural products had gone down. Farmers were migrating to the city, provoking a new series of social and religious problems. This state of things worried the Pope because it threatened a farming population that is numerous, brave, and deserving, a population whose qualities of stability and fidelity to the best traditions were more than ever necessary to maintain balance in a rapidly evolving society. The Pope blessed the efforts of the FAO to reverse this process of deterioration.[2]

The successor of Pope Pius XII, Pope John XXIII, was no less warm in his support of the FAO. In 1959, the Pope addressed the representatives of the organization at the Vatican. The technicians of the organization, he said, were working all over the world to organize the struggle against hunger. It was a great and wonderful thing; indeed, the entire activity of the FAO is an immense work of mercy on a worldwide scale. The Church highly esteems the FAO's spirit of positive achievement and disinterested service. The FAO wishes to raise the standard of living in rural areas. Coming from a rural family himself, the Pope had seen with his own eyes the fatigue and suffering of those who worked the land. Easing the burden of rural workers was a beautiful work of mercy. Finally, the Pope remarked that the good deeds of the FAO surely promote unity and peace among peoples.

Six months later, in 1960, Pope John XXIII spoke again to those who had come to Rome under the auspices of the FAO. They were organizing a worldwide "Campaign against Hunger." The Church could only support such a campaign, for she warmly recommends the corporal works of mercy, and the first on the list is feeding the hungry. The gospels tell us how Christ multiplied the loaves and fishes because he had compassion on the multitudes. The Campaign against Hunger was motivated by similar feelings of compassion. Then the Pope recalled all that he had said in praise of the FAO a few months earlier. Moreover, what had been done in the past should be an incentive to do what remains to be done.

The first thing that remains to be done is to draw the attention of the entire world to the immense problem of hunger. Millions of people go hungry, while others do not have sufficient nourishment even if they are not actually starving. Consciences must be awakened to the responsibility that rests on all, especially on those who have many advantages, to feed the hungry. The second thing that remains to be done is to raise the levels of production and consumption where the hungry are. New lands must be devoted to agriculture, and the production of lands already under cultivation must be increased. The

Pope rejoiced over the possibilities of the Campaign against Hunger.

Then, in 1963, three years after the FAO had launched the Campaign against Hunger, it sponsored the "World Freedom from Hunger Week" and the "World Food Congress" within the framework of the campaign. Pope John heartily recommended an effort on the part of all to teach human beings to utilize fully the superabundant gifts of God. Every day new, modern methods of exploration uncover treasures hidden in the depths of the earth and seas. It is our duty to develop these immense riches, but it is the immediate duty of society to bring relief to those deprived of essential goods. Two obstacles stood in the way of this relief: the failure to distribute properly the bountiful supply of food already available throughout the world and the failure of developing countries to utilize their own resources properly. In conclusion, the Pope invoked God's blessing on all those involved in the work of the FAO.[3]

Pope Paul V, the successor of Pope John XXIII, maintained the cordial relations of the Holy See with the FAO. In 1963, he urged the representatives of the FAO, whom he received at the Vatican, to increase the supply of bread and refrain from suppressing human life. Hadn't the Creator said to his creatures, "Be fruitful and multiply and fill the earth"? The Pope congratulated the FAO for its remarkable development over the years. It was a development characterized by generous, disinterested initiatives aimed at combating malnutrition, which keeps a large part of humanity in physical and mental weakness. The hungry appeal for help to their more fortunate brothers and sisters. May the worthy agenda of the FAO be translated increasingly into action![4]

Again, in 1965, Pope Paul received the representatives of the FAO at the Vatican. The organization was observing the twentieth anniversary of its foundation. The Pope referred to the traditional friendship and respect between the Holy See and the FAO over the years. The aims of the FAO seem to be purely temporal, without reference to the spiritual mission of the Church, but nothing that affects the welfare of human beings is alien to the Church. The FAO has made an important contribution by calling attention to the serious problem of hunger: half the world does not have enough to eat. The only permanent solution is enabling developing countries to feed themselves. The preceding twenty years had demonstrated the will of the FAO to overcome the problem of hunger, a will that was manifested by many happy initiatives. The hierarchy and faithful of the Church consider the FAO to be a necessary and effective organization. May God bless the FAO as it tries to ensure that "sufficient bread is available for the table of mankind."[5]

Six years later, in 1971, the Pope addressed at the Vatican those who had come to participate in the fifteenth session of the Conference of the FAO convened at Rome. In the preparatory documents of the conference, Pope Paul had noted an increasing awareness of human solidarity and a greater determination to encourage peoples and governments to help others live a fully human life. The Church cannot fail to rejoice! The Pope went on to speak about young people in rural areas. They were becoming more impatient with the disparities between rich and poor. These young people wanted "to do more, to know more and have more in order to be more." Economic and social action is not enough, for it must be sustained and promoted by a plan that is at once psychological, pedagogical, and spiritual.

Many young rural persons, the Pope said, wanted those things that assured them a truly human life, which means exercising a well-defined profession and having a clearly marked social status, a house equipped with at least a minimum of comfortable surroundings, free time that is a source of legitimate satisfaction, living conditions that they are not ashamed to share with their mate, schools that educate their children, and holidays that make it possible for them to renew their daily horizon. Only then will rural families find their natural balance, and only then will villages become places of cultural and religious life. Can't human beings use their immense talents to make the earth more productive, as they are now using them to devise instruments of destruction? Finally, when some are tempted to retire to a selfish and absolute nationalism can't the FAO find and open up new ways to international cooperation?[6]

Three years later, in 1974, the United Nations convened a World Food Conference in Rome, where the Pope addressed the members at the Vatican. The Pope shared the concerns of the conference. The problem of hunger had grown more severe. Countless millions of people remained undernourished, with all the consequences of malnutrition. Recent catastrophes of every kind—droughts, floods, and wars—had aggravated the shortage of food, and more fortunate nations had reduced the amount of food they had once furnished. And all this happened despite the marvelous technological progress in the production of food, a progress that was manifested in the form of new fertilizers, mechanization, distribution and transport. The Pope offered the members two guiding principles for confronting the situation: face the problem squarely without being discouraged, and act immediately, without settling for delays and half-measures. In

1965, before the General Assembly in New York, the Pope had said, "Never again war"; now on this occasion, he said, "Never again famine!"

Famine and malnutrition are not inevitable. Fifty percent of the land capable of producing food has never been cultivated, the seas offer huge, largely untapped, stores of fish, and some nations destroy vast quantities of food for economic reasons. The present crisis is really one of civilization and human solidarity. It has come about partially because industry has been favored to the neglect of agriculture. Moreover, those who have the tools of food production seem unwilling to share with others the abundance they enjoy. We need to acknowledge that every human being has the right to eat his fill, for the resources of the world are intended, first and foremost, for the good of all and only secondarily for private appropriation. One of the most evident causes of the present disorder is the increased price of foodstuffs and materials needed to produce them. However, scarcity and high prices spring from the profit motive and not from the desire to meet the needs of mankind.

Pope Paul repeated his appeal to the rich and powerful nations to devote a part of their military budgets to feeding the poor. Forbidding the birth of the poor or allowing their children to starve is not a just solution to the problem of hunger. Is it not a new form of war when some nations seek to impose restrictive demographic policies on others? The Pope applauded those who are prepared to sacrifice some of their resources for needy individuals and peoples. Moreover, the food crisis cannot be resolved without the help of farmers. This help will not be forthcoming unless the modern world attaches greater importance to agriculture. Farm youth must see agriculture as an attractive alternative to the city and industry.

Of course, farmers need to be trained in using the newer methods, machinery, and approaches to their work if they are to succeed, and they must be able to get the financial credit they need.

The present moment, the Pope said, calls for a long-range effort to enable each people to secure for itself what it needs for a truly human existence. The present moment also calls for an immediate sharing of goods to meet the pressing need of a large part of humanity. Also, we must be firmly determined not to waste precious resources. The Holy Father recalled how the Lord bade his disciples gather up what was left over after he had fed the multitude (Jn 6:12). What a splendid lesson in thrift! It rejects the idea that consumption is an end in itself. Finally, the Pope noted, what is lacking is a noble unrest caused by the sight of so many hungry brothers and sisters and the deeply rooted conviction that the whole human family suffers when one of its members is in distress.[7]

Pope Paul addressed the delegates to the Conference of the FAO for the last time at the Vatican in 1977. It was a joy for him to greet the delegates from so many countries who had come to study the needs of the hungry. The food problem was still one of the principal concerns of the time. To be sure, droughts, famine, and floods had helped to create the problem. However, the Director-General of the FAO had himself noted that while some attempts to improve food production had produced some spectacular results, they were often ephemeral and did not measure up to what was promised.

The Pope recalled that one of the primary objectives of the FAO was the advancement of rural areas and peoples, especially in developing countries. Better to improve the lot of people in the agricultural sector than to transplant them into industry. Furthermore, it is of the highest importance that developing countries themselves should produce the food they need. The disparity between the cost of imports and the price of exports was hurting developing countries. In conclusion, the Pope urged the delegates never to lose sight of the ethical aspects of the problems before them. May the Lord one day reward the delegates for their response to the cry of the hungry![8]

The food problem is also a major concern of Pope John Paul II. On the occasion of the first World Food Day, in 1981, the Pope sent a message to Mr. Edward Saouma, the Director-General of the FAO. The Pope wished to join all those who recognized and proclaimed the fundamental right of every person to nourishment. Corresponding to this right is the duty to create an international order capable of ensuring sufficient food in the various countries of the world. Yes, natural calamities have contributed to the problem of hunger, but human beings are also responsible for it by their failure to take certain steps—namely, exploit the immense riches of the earth, appreciate the importance of agriculture, curb expenditures on nonessential goods, and halt the arms race. New ways should be found that will permit each country to provide for its own needs. May the FAO carry out its noble mission with new energy and receive increased support from the nations of the world![9]

A month later, in keeping with a happy tradition, Pope John Paul II addressed the delegates to the current session of the Conference of the FAO at the Vatican in 1981. The Pope called for the elimination of the "absolute poverty" that afflicts so many nations of the world. "Absolute poverty," he said, "is a condition in which life is so limited by the lack of food, malnutrition, illiteracy, a high infant mortality rate and a low life expectancy as to be beneath any rational definition of human decency." The conditions of poverty and underdevelopment in many places are maintained and fostered by rigid and backward economic and social structures, both national and international, which need to be changed through a long and gradual process. True development takes as its criterion the human person with all his or her needs, just expectations, and fundamental rights.

The Pope cited the words of his recently published encyclical, *Laborem Exercens* (1981), to the effect that "in many situations radical and urgent changes are needed to restore to agriculture and rural people their just value as the basis for a healthy economy." Developing countries must define and put into effect their own national strategy for development with a plan adapted to the actual conditions, capacities, and unique culture for each country, but more prosperous countries may not leave the burden of development to the poorer countries alone.

There can be no doubt that developing countries require technical and financial assistance in order to become self-sufficient in food production. Fortunately, a few are beginning to reach a level of self-sufficiency. To help developing countries, however, more is needed than the distribution of what is surplus, for the resources of the whole earth are intended for all. Justice demands that each nation should assume its share of responsibility for the development of poor nations, in the awareness that all peoples have equal dignity and that together all nations constitute a worldwide community.[10]

In 1983, Pope John Paul addressed again the current session of the Conference of the FAO. He received the delegates at the Vatican and reaffirmed his esteem for the work being done by the organization. The right to have enough food, he said, was certainly an inalienable human right. Food security for all includes three objectives: sufficient production, the availability of emergency resources, and provision for development. Food production was increasing, but the problem remained serious in poorer countries where the growth of the population was outstripping the production of food. However, according to a FAO report, the lands of developing countries are capable of producing sufficient food to sustain at least one and one-half times their population in the year 2000.

Over and above the increased production of food on a worldwide scale, what was urgently needed, the Pope said, was to ensure increased production in the developing countries themselves. The latter needed to avoid still further dependence upon developed countries. Besides production, there are other major concerns: the concentration of food reserves in a small number of countries, reductions in the acreage of cultivated land, roadblocks to the distribution of available food, excessive consumption in some countries, and the maintenance of artificially high food prices. What is needed are loans for developing countries on favorable terms and more training to develop the skills of local farmers. In all this the Church can help by collaborating in the formation of public opinion.[11]

In 1989, the twenty-fifth session of the Conference of the FAO met in Rome, where Pope John Paul addressed the members at the Vatican. According to the Pope, the FAO and other organizations continued to play an indispensable role in safeguarding the basic human right to food. Experience has demonstrated the complexity of mounting an adequate and effective campaign against hunger and malnutrition. An effective campaign against hunger and malnutrition will depend upon a united course of action undertaken, first of all, by those organizations and agencies directly involved with food and agriculture.

The struggle against hunger has ramifications in the area of investment as well. International monetary and financial organizations, in coordinating loans and payments, are called to demonstrate a cooperation born of solidarity. The struggle against hunger requires that the international community devise norms that allow less developed countries to have access to markets, especially for their agricultural products. The Pope noted that even with a significant increase in world population, there has been a reduction of food supplies that provide a guarantee against crises of hunger and malnutrition.

The protection of the environment has become a new and integral aspect of development. Concern for ecology demands that in every economic enterprise there be a rational and calculated use of resources. Economic activity carries with it the obligation to use the goods of nature reasonably. The relationship between the problems of development and ecology also demands that economic activity accept the expenses entailed by environmental protection measures required by the community. Such expenses must not be accounted as an incidental surcharge, but rather as an essential element of the actual cost of economic activity.

The Pope went on to say:

Today, there is a rising awareness that the adoption of measures to protect the environment implies a real and necessary solidarity among nations. It is becoming more apparent that an effective solution to the problems raised by the risk of atomic and atmospheric pollution and the deterioration of the general conditions of nature and human life can be provided only on the world level. This in turn entails a recognition of the increasing interdependence which characterizes our age. Indeed, it is increasingly evident that development policies demand a genuine international cooperation, carried out in accord with the decisions made jointly and within the context of a universal vision, one which considers the good of the human family in both the present generation and in those to come.

In conclusion, the Pope expressed his satisfaction with the attention that the FAO was giving to the role of women in agricultural and rural development. Apart from women's strictly economic contribution to agricultural production, the organization was mindful of their human dignity as the basis for their integration into the life of society as a whole.[12]

In 1990, Pope John Paul II sent a message to Mr. Edward Saouma, the Director-General of the FAO, on the occasion of the annual World Food Day. The theme chosen for the day was "Food for Tomorrow." The theme, according to the Pope, emphasized the right of every person to adequate nourishment; and it placed in relief all the problems tied to feeding the population of the world today and tomorrow. Malnutrition is chronic for millions upon millions of human beings, yet the supply of available food is sufficient to meet the needs of the world's population. It is a matter of great urgency to confront the problem of hunger in a practical way. The problem must be dealt with in the larger framework of economic and social development on the national and international levels.

It was necessary, the Pope wrote, that each country utilize and augment its own resources so that it could feed its own people. Meanwhile, it would be good to stockpile in advance supplies of food in those regions where shortages and famines are likely to occur. Doing so supposes the elimination of those trade barriers that impede less developed countries from marketing their products. Richer countries ought to show their solidarity with poorer ones by avoiding production and trade policies that harm them. At the same time, it is the duty of less developed countries to implement those internal measures that will lead to economic progress. The Pope expressed the wish that the observance of World Food Day would renew the efforts of governments and international organizations to work together for the resolution of the problem of hunger and malnutrition. One should not be discouraged by the magnitude of the difficulties. Much has been accomplished; much remains to be done.[13]

In 1991, the Holy Father, Pope John Paul II, once again addressed the delegates to the Conference of the FAO at the Vatican. The organization was observing the fortieth anniversary of the establishment of its headquarters in Rome. The Pope noted that even after four decades of unremitting efforts by men and women of goodwill, the objectives of the FAO continued to have pressing urgency, for hunger remained a very serious problem. Concern for the environment is closely related to the FAO's concerns. We must find the path that lies between the extremes of asking too much of the environment and asking too little, either of which would have disastrous consequences for the human family. Developing the skills of farmers vastly increases the otherwise limited potential of the earth.

According to the Pope, development that is worthy of the human person must aim at advancing people in every aspect of life, the spiritual as well as the material. One implication of this principle is that we must respect the dignity of those who work to produce our food. The latter need to be involved in formulating the policies that affect them directly. Moreover, projects that are aimed at eliminating hunger must be in harmony with the fundamental right of couples to establish and foster a family. Rather than forbidding the poor to be born, we ought to ensure that the poor share even now in the material goods they need and receive the necessary training to produce these goods by their own labor. We hope the lessening of world tensions will enable governments to spend less on armaments and more on the fight against hunger. In any event, the nobility of the FAO's goal justifies the effort and sacrifice in pursuing it.[14]

The meeting between the Pope and the participants in the twenty-seventh Conference of the FAO again took place at the Vatican in 1993. The meeting recalled the decision of the FAO, forty-five years earlier, to admit the Holy See to participation in the activity of the organization with the status of "Permanent Observer." In his address to the conference, the Pope said that the Holy See wished to propose the ethical guidelines that ought to inspire the international community. Just as at Hot Springs, fifty years ago, so this session of the conference was taking place at a time when the international community was undergoing profound changes. At the Hot Springs conference the participants acknowledged that "the first cause of hunger and malnutrition is poverty." Today that same awareness must motivate the work of the FAO. Even though the FAO had admitted a conspicuous number of new states, the membership was still characterized by a great disparity between very wealthy nations and very poor ones. Often it was the selfishness of a few that was responsible for the hunger and malnutrition of a large part of humanity.

Data collected by the conference show yet again that the world production of food is sufficient to respond, now and in the longer run, to the demand of the world's population considered as a whole. It is the agricultural policies of individual countries or groups of countries that generally determine the availability of food. Protectionism in its various forms constitutes the principal obstacle to trade and to markets for developing countries. A new world order of trade that does not penalize agricultural progress in developing countries should be created as soon as possible. Article 55 of the UN charter states that conditions of stability and well-being are necessary for peaceful and friendly relations among nations. Sometimes intervention or even interference is necessary as a response to a moral obligation to come to the aid of individuals, peoples, or ethnic groups whose fundamental right to nutrition has been denied to the point of threatening their existence. The Pope concluded his address by invoking God's blessing on the work of the FAO.[15]

According to their custom, the participants in the twenty-eighth Conference of the FAO met with Pope John Paul II at the Vatican in 1995. The FAO was observing its fiftieth anniversary. This anniversary, the Pope said in his address to the participants, was a suitable occasion to reflect on the international community's responsibility for a fundamental good and duty—namely, freeing human beings from malnutrition and the threat of starvation. People were dying of starvation even then because of evil mechanisms within economic structures, because of unjust criteria in the distribution of resources and production, and because of selfish forms of protectionism. Moreover, the provision of emergency help for refugees is not enough; this kind of help does not permit a satisfactory solution as long as extreme poverty persists. At the worldwide level sufficient food can be produced to satisfy everyone's needs. Why, then, are there so many people threatened by starvation? Among other causes are national policies that reduce the production of food, widespread corruption in public life, unreasonable expenditures for armaments, and a consumerist culture in certain countries.

According to the Pope, an effective campaign against hunger supposes the dignity of the human person and a culture of giving that should make every country prepared to meet the needs of the less fortunate. In addition, there must be concern for environmental issues such as limiting the damage to the ecosystem and safeguarding food production from desertification and erosion. The goods of creation are meant for all peoples. Daily bread for every person on earth is an essential condition for world peace and security, for only when people consider the struggle against hunger as a priority and commit themselves to providing everyone with the means of gaining their daily bread, instead of amassing weapons, will conflicts and war come to an end. This is the sublime task to which the FAO is called. May God bless its work abundantly![16]

13

Justice and Law

The International Court of Justice

The preamble of the Charter of the United Nations expresses the determination of the members "to establish conditions under which justice and respect for the obligations arising from treaties and other sources of international law can be maintained." Article 1 of the charter states that one purpose of the United Nations, among others, is "to bring about by peaceful means, and in conformity with the principles of justice and international law, adjustment or settlement of international disputes or situations which might lead to a breach of the peace." Among the means of peaceful settlement, the charter cites, in article 33, arbitration and judicial settlement. Under article 13, one of the General Assembly's functions is "encouraging the progressive development of international law and its codification."

The International Court of Justice (ICJ), whose seat is at The Hague, Netherlands, is the principal judicial organ of the United Nations. It was established by chapter 14 of the UN charter. The Court's functions are defined in its statute, which is an integral part of the UN charter and is based on the Statute of the Permanent Court of International Justice, which functioned at the time of the League of Nations. All members of the United Nations are ipso facto parties to the Statute of the Court, and other states may be permitted to adhere to the statute.

According to the Statute of the ICJ, the Court is composed of a body of independent judges, elected regardless of their nationality from among persons of high moral character, who possess the qualifications required in their respective countries for appointment to the highest judicial offices. The Court is composed of fifteen members, no two of whom may be nationals of the same state. The members of the Court are elected by the General Assembly and the Security Council, voting independently, from a list of persons nominated by government-appointed national groups of highly reputed international-law experts. At every election, the electors should see to it that the main forms of civilization and the principal legal systems of the world are represented on the Court as a whole.

Judges are elected for terms of nine years and are eligible for reelection. The terms of five of the fifteen judges expire at the end of every three years. The Court itself elects its President, who directs its administration, and a Vice President. All questions are decided by a majority of the judges present, with nine constituting a quorum. The President does not vote except in the event of a tie.

The Court has jurisdiction over all cases that the parties refer to it and over all matters specifically provided for in the Charter of the United Nations. To decide disputes that are submitted to it, the Court applies several criteria—namely, international conventions, whether general or particular, establishing rules expressly recognized by the contending states; international custom, as evidence of a general practice accepted as law; the general principles recognized by civilized states; and judicial decisions and teachings of the most highly qualified publicists of the various nations. The charter also provides that members of the United Nations may entrust the solution of differences to other tribunals. Much concern has been expressed, however, about the small number of cases that nations have been willing to submit to the Court.

A decision of the Court has no binding force except between the parties and in respect of that particular case. The decision is final and without appeal. An application for the revision of a judgment may be made only when it is based upon the discovery of some fact of such a nature as to be decisive. The fact must have been unknown to the Court and also to the party claiming revision, always provided such ignorance was not due to negligence. If a member of the United Nations fails to comply with a judgment of the Court, the other party may call upon the Security Council for assistance.

Apart from its competence to deal with contentious cases, the Court also has the authority to give advisory opinions—that is, its views on any legal question, at the request of the General Assembly, the Security Council, and other bodies authorized by the charter. An opinion given by the Court is in principle advisory, but the requesting body may be bound by it in certain circumstances.

The Court is not open to private individuals. It has always refused to entertain the petitions and requests that have been addressed to it by individuals. However, it is always possible for a state to take up the complaint of one of its citizens against another state, but what is then involved is a dispute between states.

Since its beginning, the Court has handed down dozens of judgments and advisory opinions. In contentious cases, the disputes decided by the Court have dealt with a wide variety of subjects, including territorial rights; the delimitation of territorial waters and continental shelves; fishing rights; questions of nationality and the right of individuals to asylum; territorial sovereignty; and the right of passage over foreign territory.

The Court's advisory opinions have addressed such issues as the competence of the General Assembly to admit a state to the United Nations, the competence of the organization to claim reparation of damages, the reservations that could be attached by a state to its signature on an international convention, appeals against judgments of the administrative tribunals that consider staff issues in the United Nations and the ILO, the presence of South Africa in Namibia, and the status of Western Sahara.

Two important cases dealt with by the International Court of Justice involved the United States. In the case brought by the United States against Iran concerning the seizure of the U.S. embassy in Teheran and the detention of its diplomatic and consular staff, the Court first indicated provisionally (December 1979) that the embassy should be immediately given back and the detained staff released. Subsequently (May 1980) the Court decided on the merits that Iran had violated its obligations to the United States and must release the hostages, hand back the embassy, and make reparations. However, before the Court had occasion to fix the amount of reparation, the case was withdrawn following the settlement reached by the two states.

In a second case, in April 1984, Nicaragua filed an application instituting proceedings against the United

States on the grounds that the United States was using military force against Nicaragua and intervening in its affairs, in violation of its sovereignty. The United States denied the Court's jurisdiction.

In May 1984, the Court called on the United States to refrain from action against Nicaraguan ports and, in particular, from the laying of mines. The United States disputed the jurisdiction of the Court as well as the admissibility of the case. In November 1984, the Court found that it had jurisdiction to adjudicate the case and that Nicaragua's application was admissible.

In June 1986, the Court handed down its ruling, having determined that the actions of the United States toward Nicaragua were in breach of its obligations under international law and that it was under obligation to desist from those actions and to make reparation to Nicaragua. In a further development, the new Nicaraguan government informed the Court that it was studying the different matters it had pending before the Court, and in 1991 the request by Nicaragua that the Court determine the form and amount of reparation was withdrawn.

The United Nations and the Development and Codification of International Law

Under article 13 of the UN charter, one of the General Assembly's functions is "encouraging the progressive development of international law and its codification." The International Law Commission was established in 1947 to work toward this goal. The commission, which meets annually, is composed of thirty-four members who are elected by the assembly for five-year terms. The members serve in their individual capacity and not as representatives of their governments.

Most of the commission's work consists in the preparation of drafts on topics of international law. Some topics are chosen by the commission, while others are referred to it by the General Assembly or the Economic and Social Council. When the commission completes a draft on a particular topic, the General Assembly usually convenes an international conference of plenipotentiaries to incorporate the draft articles into a convention that is then opened to states to become parties.

The result has been conventions dealing with the law of the sea, the reduction of statelessness, diplomatic and consular relations, treaties, the prevention and punishment of crimes against internationally protected persons, the relationship between states and international organizations, the succession of states in respect of treaties and state property, archives and debts, and other topics.

The current work of the commission includes the codification and progressive development of the law of state responsibility, the law of the nonnavigational use of international watercourses, the status of the diplomatic courier and the diplomatic bag not accompanied by a diplomatic courier, jurisdictional immunities of states and their properties, international liability for injurious consequences arising out of acts not prohibited by international law, relations between states and international organizations (second part of topic), and the draft code of crimes against the peace and security of mankind.[1]

International Trade Law

In response to the need for the United Nations to play a more active role in removing or reducing legal obstacles to the flow of international trade, the General Assembly established the United Nations Commission on

International Trade Law (UNCITRAL) in 1966 to promote the progressive harmonization and unification of international trade. The thirty-six-nation commission, whose members represent the various geographical regions and principal economic and legal systems of the world, reports annually to the General Assembly and also submits reports to the UNCTAD for comments.

The functions of the commission include coordination of the work of international trade organizations active in the field of international trade law, promotion of wider participation in existing international conventions, and the preparation of new conventions and other instruments relating to international trade law. The commission also offers training and assistance in international trade law, taking into account the special needs of developing countries.

The commission's attention has been principally directed to the study and preparation of uniform rules in the following fields: international sale of goods; international payments, including a legal guide on electronic fund transfers; international commercial arbitration; and international legislation on shipping.[2]

The Catholic Tradition of Law and Justice

For centuries the Catholic Church has held a position on law and justice as they pertain to the international community. In this matter, there is an analogy between individuals and nations. Individuals need to live together for their mutual advantage. Each individual performs a service that fulfills the need of another. For example, one must be farmer, a second a teacher, and a third a fireman. When, however, individuals live and work together, they must be guided by laws that direct their activities to the common good. For example, there must be traffic laws for the safety of drivers and pedestrians, residence laws for the good of owners and renters, and pure-food laws for the health of all. These laws are made by those in charge of the community, no matter how the latter are chosen. All this is simply a matter of common sense based on the rational desires and needs of human beings flowing from their nature.

Law is, or should be, an expression of justice. Justice is a virtue that inclines a person to render to others what is due a person in light of the fact that he is a human being and needs certain things for personal fulfillment. For example, there are laws forbidding murder and theft. Indeed, every human being is entitled to whatever he needs in order to live a decent human life, and it is the function of law to guarantee what is just or due in this regard.

What has been said about law and justice with respect to individuals is applicable to states after making the necessary allowances. The ease of communication and travel, the dependence of one state upon another for certain resources, the development of trade, and the growth of populations have brought states more closely together. As citizens live together in the same city or state, so peoples and states live together on this earth. If they are to live together for their mutual advantage, they must be guided by laws that direct their activities to the common good. These laws form the body of international law. They are the result of agreements between nations or simply reflect the manner in which states have commonly dealt with each other over the years. Conceivably, such laws might stem from an international organization, such as the United Nations, to which individual states have delegated legislative authority. All this, too, is a matter of common sense based on the nature of states and their mutual relationship.

Of course, justice must prevail between states, too. Each state is entitled to its due—what it needs to provide a decent human life for all its citizens. For example, each state has a right to sufficient food for all its citizens, to adopt the form of government chosen by its people, to possess equality with other states before international bodies, and to live in peace and security. These rights are demanded by the nature of the state itself, and it is a matter of justice that other states observe these rights. International law will formulate what is just in this regard.

Surely disputes will arise between states just as they arise between individuals. To settle these disputes there must be a judicial body that will adjudicate the matter in accordance with the principles of international law.

Pope John Paul II

In 1985, Pope John Paul addressed the ICJ at The Hague, Netherlands. The Pope recalled the close personal involvement of his predecessor, Leo XIII, with the peace conference held at The Hague in 1899, which paved the way for the Permanent Court of Arbitration, the Permanent Court of International Justice,and, eventually, the ICJ. As soon as Pope Leo learned of the initiative of Czar Nicholas II to convene a peace conference, he supported it. Through his Secretary of State, Cardinal Rampolla, the Pope made it clear why he considered the establishment of an international system of mediation and arbitration so important:

The international community lacks a system of moral and legal means to establish and maintain the rights of everyone. There is therefore no alternative but an immediate recourse to force. This explains the rivalry between states to develop military strength. . . . The establishment of mediation and arbitration would seem to be the most appropriate way of dealing with this disastrous situation; in every respect it satisfies the wishes of the Holy See.

According to Pope John Paul, the Church has consistently supported the development of an international administration of justice and arbitration as a way of peacefully resolving conflicts and as a part of the evolution of the world legal system.

The Pope went on to say that the current situation of the world makes it even more imperative to resolve conflicts peacefully. Modern warfare could mean the total annihilation of an enemy. Moreover, there is a new quality of interdependence among nations. What is needed now is the will to achieve true peace. Unfortunately, however, in today's world, even the peaceful settlement of disputes is often the province of a diplomacy determined more by self-interest than by the requirements of the common good of the international community. Nonetheless, the judicial organs of the United Nations have an extremely important role to play by settling disputes and contributing to the development of law. The task of these organs is to bring an element of objectivity and impartiality to bear on dealings between states.

According to the Pope, there are a number of ways in which the judicial element can play a wider role in international relations:

- by states and international organizations making more extensive use of the ICJ;

- by a wider acceptance of the so-called compulsory jurisdiction of the Court;
- by more frequent use of arbitration;
- by development of legal and political/humanitarian organizations at the regional level to supplement and support those at the world level;
- and by development of the law of humanitarian and
  criminal responsibility toward the international community.

The Pope believed that these elements were clearly
discernible in many recent developments.

One of the services provided by the Church is to identify the criteria that the development of an international
system of law must satisfy. In *legal* terms, these criteria
can be expressed as the recognition of human rights: the
right to life of every individual, his right to a decent existence worthy of a human being, the right to protection
by the law, recognition of the rights of peoples to self-
determination and independence, and their right to a fair
share in the world's economic wealth. *Pacem in Terris*
expresses the basic criteria in *moral* terms such as truth,
love, freedom, justice, and solidarity. These criteria must
find expression in international relations in the form of
treaties and the work of international organizations. All
this must be supported by a growing awareness among
ordinary people of the duty to respect in all circumstances
the fundamental rights of human persons. The support
of governments in these matters is also very important.

However, a proper legal system cannot exist without
an understanding of the source of law and the reasons
for law and the object of law. The law of God written in
the hearts of people and proclaimed by the Church provides the norms and incentives for improving laws and
legal institutions. Peace comes only when human beings

strive for truth and love in their dealings with one another, when they discover who they truly are, and when they recognize one another's purpose. The Church speaks in the name of he who will come one day to judge all people on the basis of truth. Sent by him, the Church wants to help form the consciences and behavior of human beings.

The absence of solidarity within a country encourages a lack of solidarity in the world. Modern societies are characterized by increasing fragmentation and alienation. This leads to a situation in which people expect more of a system than they do of their own efforts and collaboration.

The Pope concluded his remarks with praise for the Netherlands, which plays host to the ICJ, and for the judges of the Court. The words of the Psalmist are appropriate: "The just man will flourish like the palm tree and grow like a cedar of Lebanon" (Ps 92:13).[3]

Then, in May 1992, the Holy Father, Pope John Paul II, received the members of the World Jurist Association of the World Peace through Law Center at the Vatican. They were observing World Law Day. The Pope commended the members of the association for their efforts. The Pope went on to say that peace is the work of justice and efforts to attain lasting peace must be linked to the patient and persistent defense of human rights. The human person is by nature the subject of certain rights that no individual, group, or state may violate.

Moreover, the efforts of the association to obtain peace through law must be based upon the demands of truth, especially the truth about man himself. In the past, disregard for the truth led some regimes to sacrifice the rights of individuals to the rights of the state and its programs. Today, however, disregard for truth leads to a dangerous moral relativism that looks to public opinion or electoral advantage.

According to the Pope, in any consideration of fundamental human rights a primary place must always be accorded freedom of religion, which is in a sense their source and synthesis, as the Pope noted in his encyclical *Centesimus Annus*. This is true about freedom of religion because it involves the right of each individual to seek truth in accordance with his conscience and to live in conformity with that truth, in a spirit of respect and tolerance for others.

While the Pope was speaking, whole peoples were being liberated from oppression, but old hostilities between certain ethnic and religious groups were reappearing. There was an urgent need to strengthen, within an internationally recognized legal order, the juridical means to protect the rights of individuals and groups, including the right to freedom of religion. The Pope concluded his remarks by invoking abundant blessings upon all who were present.[4]

14

Population, Human Settlements, and the Environment

Population

Population questions have been a major concern of the United Nations since its earliest years. The Population Commission was established and attached to the Economic and Social Council in 1947 to study such matters as the size and structure of populations, the policies that influence them, the interplay of demography on economic and social factors, and other demographic questions on which the United Nations and related agencies might ask advice.

The commission also reviews and appraises progress toward achieving the goals of the World Population Plan of Action. The plan of action was adopted in 1974 at the World Population Conference held in Bucharest. The plan stressed the fundamental relationship between population factors and overall economic and social development. The commission also follows up on the recommendations of the 1984 International Conference on Population held at Mexico City. The 1984 conference affirmed the validity of the 1974 plan, appraised the progress made in achieving it, and made further recommendations. A third international meeting on population was convened in Cairo in 1994 to assess the progress made in attaining the goals of the previous conferences.

In the beginning the United Nations concentrated on gathering reliable demographic statistics, which were lacking for large parts of the world. In the 1960s, the rapid growth of populations was a matter of particular concern. The rate of population growth peaked in the late 1960s but declined moderately during the 1970s and remained steady during the 1980s. The world population grew from 2.5 billion in 1950 to over 5 billion by 1988.

In 1967, the General Assembly established a Trust Fund for Population Activities, which was renamed in 1969 as the United Nations Fund for Population Activities (UNFPA). In 1987, the name was again changed to United Nations Population Fund, although the acronym UNFPA was retained. Almost all of UNFPA's funds come from voluntary governmental contributions:

> UNFPA's role is to build up nations' capacity to respond to needs in population and family planning, to promote understanding on population factors (population growth, fertility, mortality, spatial distribution and migration), to assist governments to develop population goals and programs, and to provide financial assistance to implement them. Its areas of work include family planning, communication and education, data collection and analysis, formulation and implementation of policies and programs, special programs (for women, youth, the aged, the handicapped, etc.), support for conferences, documentation centers and clearing-houses, and training.[1]

In 1974, the year designated by the General Assembly as World Population Year, Pope Paul VI received at the Vatican Mr. Antonio Carillo-Flores, Secretary-General of the World Conference on Population, and Mr. Rafael Salas, Executive Director of the UNFPA. The World

Population Conference was to be held later in the year at Bucharest. Population problems, the Pope said, have to do with people, and the Church is vitally interested in people because of its commission from the Author of Life. Of course, the growing number of people and their needs present a challenge to the human community and governments. However, solutions to population problems must respect the dignity of human beings and the divine laws governing life. Any population program must shun everything that is opposed to life itself or that harms man's full and responsible freedom. Any population policy should also guarantee the dignity and stability of the family. Married couples themselves and not the state should determine the size of their families in the light of their duties toward God, themselves, the family, and society.

The Pope went on to speak about the need for social justice if all men and women are to enjoy a fully human life. The Population Year should see the rededication of all to justice through out the world. Some say that population growth must be slowed radically if less developed countries and future generations are to have a life worthy of human beings. Government authorities may surely intervene in this matter by furnishing appropriate information and promoting economic development and social progress, provided, though, that they safeguard true human values and respect the moral law. The history of the world proves that human beings can find correct answers to the questions that face them, and the sphere of possibility always increases when one goes forward with God.[2]

In 1984, Pope John Paul II received at the Vatican Mr. Rafael M. Salas, Secretary-General of the 1984 International Conference on Population and Executive Director of the UNFPA. The Pope spoke to Mr. Salas about the population conference to be held in Mexico City a few months later. According to the Pope, the Holy See had studied the implications of population growth for the entire human family. It is a complex problem having ramifications in many areas, such as the quality of human life, education, health care, and economic development. The Church recognizes the role of government and the international community in these areas, but people are more than statistics; they have fundamental rights and human dignity. The Church is called to promote and defend human life against all attacks and rejects contraception, sterilization, and abortion as solutions to the population problem.

According to the Pope, the Church stresses the importance of the family, which is the natural and fundamental group unit of society. The family is a community of love and solidarity uniquely suited to transmit values essential to the well-being of its members and society. The Pope spoke of the contribution that today's children can make to the entire human family and of the joy we all find in children. Married couples themselves should determine the size of their families, but they ought to use acceptable means of spacing or limiting births. Governments will create a socioeconomic order conducive to family life. Continued efforts should be made to ensure the full integration of women into society while giving due recognition to their important role as mothers. Finally, the Pope called for a development policy that satisfies both the material *and* spiritual needs of all.[3]

In 1984, Bishop Jan Schotte, Vice President of the Pontifical Commission for Justice and Peace, led a delegation of the Holy See to the International Conference on Population held at Mexico City. In his statement, Bishop Schotte wished to offer the Holy See's ethical and moral perspective on the human problems under consideration at the conference. Briefly, the Holy See wished to make life more human for all. All population policies and strategies, in the judgment of the Holy See, must be evaluated in the light of the sacredness of human life, the dignity of every human being, the inviolability of all human rights, the value of marriage, and the need for economic and social justice.

Experience reminds us of the complexity and uncertainties of long-range population projections. The spiritual as well as the material well-being of the person should be taken into account in the developmental process. Surely each person and couple has a responsibility to the local and world community; but to see all progress as dependent on a decline in population growth betokens a shortness of vision and a failure of nerve. Economic aid for the advancement of peoples should never be conditioned on a decline in birthrates or on participation in family planning programs.

According to Bishop Schotte, the Holy See agrees that continued efforts should be made to control infectious and contagious diseases, improve nutrition and health care systems, and ensure greater access to health care for both adults and children. The family, based on marriage, is the basic unity of society that the state must juridically protect, support, and foster. Population problems cannot be solved without reference to the family, and marriage is the only place in which both sexual intimacy and parenthood are appropriately and responsibly pursued. It is a positive duty of governments to create economic and social conditions in which couples can responsibly bear and rear their children and follow objective moral principles with respect to the spacing of births and the size of their families. In making these decisions, couples should be able to rely on morally licit methods of family planning.

Bishop Schotte stated that the Holy See continues to be opposed on moral grounds to abortion, sterilization, and contraception. Recent scientific studies underscore the validity and reliability of the newer natural methods of spacing births, and pedagogical techniques that can be properly implemented in various cultures have been developed. In matters pertaining to family life and sex education, parents have the right to impart values and establish standards of conduct for their children in the context of ethical principles. Educational programs, either in schools or under the auspices of voluntary agencies, should respect parental rights and be carried out under the supervision and with the participation of parents. Such programs need to be accompanied by instruction in ethical standards and values.

The Bishop continued:

> The Holy See has repeatedly advocated appropriate social and personal advancement for women in order to ensure the dignity of women and provide for genuine human development for future generations. While we ought to support programs which aim at the advancement of women in all areas of their life, it is important to remember that the advancement of women is not to be identified exclusively with work outside the home. Adequate recognition must be given to motherhood and the work of mothers in the home because of their value for the woman herself, for the family and society, not only on the material level but also in other aspects, particularly in the field of education.
>
> Mothers must be afforded all the necessary social protection and assistance during pregnancy and for a reasonable time afterwards, so that they can be with their

children during this vital period of their development. Education of women and particularly of mothers is one of the critical determinants of the health, welfare and development of children. Mothers should receive the necessary training so that they can carry out their roles in the areas of education, nutrition and primary health care with both competence and satisfaction. Policies should aim at reducing the heavy work load which many women have to bear in various societies, both developed and developing; and programs of education for fathers should lead them to assume fully their role of effective collaboration in family and parental duties and responsibilities.

Bishop Schotte concluded his remarks by speaking of two other groups of the population—namely, migrants and the aging. Migrants have a right to respect for their culture, to be integrated into the community to which they contribute, and to see their families united as soon as possible. The aging are entitled to respect and recognition of their place and proper role in society. They should be considered an integral part of society, to which they make many valuable contributions. These and other groups of the population should always be regarded as a precious good to be cherished and not as mere objects of governmental policies.[4]

The Cairo Conference on Population and Development was convened in September of 1994. Archbishop Renato Martino, Permanent Observer of the Holy See at the United Nations, spoke to the assembled delegates on behalf of the Holy See. Population policy, the Archbishop said, must always be seen as a part of a more comprehensive development policy. Both are, in fact, about the same reality—namely, the centrality of the human person and the responsibility of all to guarantee that every individual person can live in a manner that respects his dignity.

Development strategies require equity in the distribution of resources and technology within the international community and access to international markets.

According to the speaker, the Cairo conference addressed in a special way the position of women. Population policies must address as a priority the advancement of women's education and health care, especially primary health care. Further, population policies need to address the responsible use of human sexuality and the mutual responsibility of men and women concerning human reproduction. Parents alone ought to determine the size of their families as their circumstances warrant, and parents should be free of all coercion in reaching a decision in this matter. Lack of responsibility in the area of human sexuality can only be a cause of concern to everybody. It is women and children who are most often the principal victims of such irresponsible behavior. In fact, much remains to be done to educate and inform men concerning the procreation and education of children.

New human life, from its very beginning, has the right to be welcomed into the loving and stable community of the family, the natural and fundamental group unit of society. The family is the place where the stable relationship of a man and a woman is transformed into a caring institution for the responsible transmission and nurturing of life. Society ought to recognize the importance of the family by supporting it on the level of cultural, fiscal, and social policy.

The Holy See rejects family planning methods that separate the unitive and procreative aspects of human sexuality. The Holy See rejects sterilization and abortion as legitimate means of family planning. The concept of a "right to abortion" would be entirely innovative in the international community. Unfortunately, the documents of the conference make only passing reference to the natural methods of family planning, which have so much to recommend them.

According to the speaker, the Holy See supports efforts to provide for the reduction of maternal and infant mortality and to ensure improvement in the conditions of women's health and child survival. The Holy See supports the concept of "reproductive health," which is understood as a holistic vision of health concerns in the area of reproduction—that is, a vision that embraces men and women in the entirety of their personality, mind, and body, a vision that is oriented towards a mature and responsible exercise of their sexuality.

The speaker concluded his address by saying that the Holy See and the institutions of the Catholic Church throughout the world would continue to collaborate with the international community in the matter of concrete service to basic education and care, in complete respect for human life and for the development of peoples in solidarity.[5]

Archbishop Martino also addressed the final session of the Cairo Conference on Population and Development. He expressed the Holy See's "partial consensus" to the Final Document of the conference but also indicated certain reservations about its contents.[6] Subsequently, Pope John Paul II noted that the initial proposals of the Cairo conference included abortion among other means of birth control. Fortunately, according to the Pope, the worrisome proposals were later reworded, and a call for respect for religious and ethical values was included among the principles that inspired the Final Document. The Pope said that the Church did everything possible to make her voice heard in order to reawaken consciences.[7]

Human Settlements

A Conference on Human Settlements was convened in Vancouver, Canada, in 1976, and it adopted the Vancouver Declaration on Human Settlements. The declaration expressed the determination of the international community to improve the quality of life for all people by, among other things, working for decent human dwellings for all. A recommendation of the conference led the General Assembly in 1977 to transform the Committee on Housing, Building and Planning into a Commission on Human Settlements, and in 1978 it established the United Nations Center for Human Settlements (Habitat), with headquarters in Nairobi.

Habitat's major concerns are the planning, financing, and management of human settlements; energy requirements and conservation; rural settlement development; the upgrading of slums and squatter settlements; low-cost building technology; technologies for urban and rural water supply and sanitation systems; and the establishment or strengthening of government institutions concerned with human settlements.

When governments cannot increase their investment in low-cost housing, Habitat believes that they should encourage self-help efforts for building, maintenance, and upgrading of human settlements. Habitat warns against excessive reliance on legislation and institutions, recommending that they be replaced with more imaginative participatory arrangements. Habitat also suggests that the building industry is probably the best single source of productive jobs for rural migrants to urban areas, because the building trades employ a high proportion of unskilled and semiskilled workers and are labor-intensive.

The General Assembly adopted the Global Strategy for Shelter to the Year 2000 in 1988 and launched it in 1989. The strategy seeks to enable people—by a facilitating legal, institutional, and regulatory environment—to provide and improve their own shelter.

The first Monday in October of each year is World Habitat Day, a global observance coordinated by the center. On that day, governments, nongovernmental organizations, community groups, academic institutions, and other bodies are urged to undertake activities focused on themes that address national shelter needs and the means to satisfy them.

Pope Paul VI took up the subject of human settlements in 1975. In that year he received at the Vatican Dr. Enrique Peñalosa, Secretary-General of the United Nations Conference on Human Settlements. The conference was to be held in Vancouver in the following year. Speaking to the Secretary-General, the Pope noted that men and women need not only shelter from the elements, but also a home in which they can develop their material, cultural, and spiritual resources. A home should afford privacy and also facilities for social contact to the family and its members. Over and above these things, a family will need certain public facilities, such as nurseries for the children of working mothers, sports grounds, cultural centers, meeting places, especially for the young, and houses of worship. However, absolute priority must be given to ensuring everyone the minimum conditions for a decent life. The Pope was thinking particularly of the large number of families and migrant workers who live in conditions unworthy of human beings.[8]

The following year, in May of 1976, the year of the United Nations Conference on Human Settlements, Pope Paul VI sent a message to the President of the conference.

The Pope spoke once more of the family's need for a worthy and attractive dwelling along with the normal services of health, hygiene, and communication. The Pope expressed his confidence in the capability of human beings to enlarge the areas of what is possible once they have committed themselves to providing truly human living conditions for all. "Human beings," as the General Principles of the conference stated, "constitute the most important element in the universe." Surely all persons have the same fundamental dignity and the home must remain the first concern of every program having to do with the human environment. In the home, children need to be educated about the meaning and value of life and about the means of reaching true happiness. All people, even the most humble and not only technicians, should be mobilized in the implementation of programs. International cooperation, of which the conference was a fine example, is needed to achieve justice and carry out resolutions.[9]

The following month, June 1976, the head of the delegation of the Holy See to the United Nations Conference on Human Settlements, Msgr. Eduard Gagnon, read a statement to the delegates assembled at Vancouver. According to the speaker, the problems and challenges connected with the human "habitat" are immense and complex. In the days to come, civilization will become even more urbanized, industrialized, migratory, and technological, with profound economic and political changes. Clearly there is need for a deliberate strategy at the national and international levels to provide adequate housing for all. We cannot continue to tolerate the vast settlements of people in slums and barrios where life is now so contaminated. Nor can we countenance the massive and depersonalized buildings that, in theory or in practice, offend the dignity of human beings.

Monsignor Gagnon continued: The development of habitats ought not to be a marginal corollary to economic decisions, but rather a strategic priority geared to the welfare of human beings. Such a priority requires that every individual enjoy the minimum conditions for a decent human life. Minimum conditions for a decent human life include whatever is needed for good nutrition, hygiene, and health, and whatever is needed to fulfill one's basic social needs for employment, family stability, literacy, just social relations, peace, respect for human rights, and the possibility of a spiritual life. The large numbers of people who have no homes or live in hovels require particular attention. Their situation is particularly ironic because they often coexist in proximity to the luxury and waste of large residences located in the districts of privileged minorities. Furthermore, individuals need housing that not only shelters them from the elements, but also meets their material, cultural, and spiritual needs.

It is desirable that in some way privacy, tranquillity, and intimacy be possible amid the din and congestion of cities; that cities become truly livable, with convenient transportation, attractive housing, and harmony between human dwellings and the environment; and that there be nurseries for the children of working mothers, sports facilities, cultural centers, meeting places for young and old, and places of worship. The Catholic Church wishes to be involved in the immense effort needed to achieve these goals, for her Founder will identify himself at the Final Judgment with those in need of housing: "I was a stranger and you made me welcome" (Mt 25:35). May the earthly habitat reflect, if only in an obscure way, the heavenly habitat that has been prepared for all those who love God![10]

The Environment

For decades there has been increasing concern about the deterioration of the environment. This deterioration is the result of air and water pollution, erosion, waste, noise, biocides, and other agents. In 1972, the United Nations convened a Conference on the Human Environment in Stockholm. The conference sought to encourage international action to protect and improve the environment, and it adopted a Plan of Action to be undertaken by governments and international organizations. The opening day of the conference, June 5, is observed annually as World Environment Day.

Later in 1972, as a result of the Stockholm conference, the General Assembly created the United Nations Environmental Program (UNEP), with headquarters in Nairobi, the first UN agency to be based in a developing country. The aims of the program are to facilitate international cooperation in the environmental field, to further international knowledge in this area, to keep the state of global environment under review, and to bring emerging environmental problems of international significance to the attention of governments. The program comprises a Governing Council (drawn from fifty-eight countries), a Secretariat headed by an Executive Director, and a Fund, which provides financing for environmental programs.

Among UNEP's comprehensive programs are the Global Environmental Monitoring System (GEMS), the International Register of Potentially Toxic Chemicals (IRPTC), and a worldwide data network: Infoterra. UNEP programs also include a wide range of environmental management activities and supporting systems in environmental law, education, and information. UNEP's regional seas programs help bring countries together to protect the common seas.

UNEP has had substantial influence on environmental treaties and conventions. The Montreal Protocol, negotiated under UNEP's auspices in 1987, is designed to help reduce chemical damage to the atmospheric ozone layer, which shields life on earth from harmful ultraviolet radiation. The Basle Convention, negotiated by UNEP in 1989, provides controls on the international movement and disposal of hazardous wastes.

UNEP is working with governments and other agencies to limit global climate change and to preserve and restore tropical forests, whose protection is essential in limiting climate change and maintaining species diversity. UNEP is active in the areas of desertification control, genetic resources, water conservation, and environmental education. It promotes environmentally sound plans and actions by developing countries to sustain the productivity of their natural resources, including forests, species, soils, and water.[11]

In 1992, the United Nations sponsored an "Earth Summit" in Rio de Janeiro to deal with problems of the environment. At the close of the summit, which was attended by leaders of 152 nations, five significant documents were published: a Climate Treaty, to slow global warming by cutting "greenhouse" gas emissions; a Biodiversity Treaty, to conserve threatened plants, animals, and habitats; Forest Principles, a pledge to protect and conserve forests; Agenda 21, an eight-hundred-page plan covering more than one hundred issues for environmentally sound development into the twenty-first century; and the Rio Declaration, a worldwide declaration of the rights and responsibilities of countries toward the environment.[12]

In 1972, on the occasion of the opening of the United Nations Conference on the Environment at Stockholm, Pope Paul VI sent a message to Mr. Maurice F. Strong, Secretary-General of the conference. According to the Pope, there was a growing awareness that human beings and their environment essentially condition man's life and development while man, in his turn, perfects and ennobles the environment through his presence, work, and contemplation. However, the uncontrolled advance of material progress must be replaced with a newly found respect for the earth's biosphere. There is a growing interdependence among all peoples and all parts of the earth, and an abuse of the environment in one part of the world can spoil the quality of life in another. We cannot ignore the imbalances created by the disorderly exploitation of the physical resources of the planet. We must prepare a hospitable earth for future generations.

Pope Paul went on to say that interdependence must now be accompanied by joint responsibility and common destiny by solidarity. Technical measures, such as pollution control, are indispensable to deal with environmental problems, but a radical change of attitude is also necessary to restore man's respect for his environment. No one may use the environment in a selfish way, for it is a *res omnium,* the patrimony of mankind, and should be used in a way that redounds to the good of all. Human beings are surely the best and truest treasures of this earth. The Pope concluded his message by saying that the Stockholm conference should pursue not only ecological equilibrium, but also a just balance of prosperity between the developed and developing nations, for want, it has been rightly said, is the worst of pollutions.[13]

Pope Paul took up the same subject again in 1977 on the occasion of the fifth World Environment Day. The

Pope began his message by citing the words of Genesis 1:31: "And God saw everything he had made, and behold it was very good." The world we live in is good, and it is the environment in which we live our lives in solidarity with one another. The environment, as the Pope had said on another occasion, essentially conditions man's life and development while man, in his turn, perfects and ennobles the environment through his presence, work, and contemplation.

The Pope continued:

> Consciousness of the environment around us is more pressing today than ever before. For men who have the means and ability to construct and ennoble the world about them can also destroy it and squander its goods. Human science and technology have made marvelous gains; but care must be taken that they are used to enhance human life and not diminish it. Human effort has brought forth much wealth from the earth; but this wealth should not be squandered superfluously by a small minority, nor selfishly hoarded for a few at the expense of the rest of mankind in need of it.

According to the Pope, World Environment Day should be a day for rededicating ourselves to the task of preserving, improving, and handing over to future generations a healthy environment in which every person is truly at home. Such a task requires a change of mentality that places greater emphasis on simplicity of lifestyle, on conservation rather than consumption, and on our interdependence in protecting the environment.[14]

In 1985, Pope John Paul II visited the United Nations Center for the Environment at Nairobi. There he greeted and addressed the assembled staff and friends. According to the Pope, the Church's commitment to the

265

environment is linked to divine providence, which created all things and entrusted them to the care of human beings (Gn 1:28). God is glorified when creation, under the stewardship of human beings, serves the integral development of the whole human family. With the rapid acceleration of science and technology, the possibilities for enhancing or destroying the environment have increased enormously each year. Human beings will ultimately determine the future of the planet.

Today threats to the environment are numerous—deforestation, water and air pollution, soil erosion, desertification, acid rain, and many others. These threats affect all nations, but especially the developing ones. The Catholic Church approaches the care and protection of the environment from the point of view of the human person. It was the Pope's conviction, therefore, that all ecological problems must respect the dignity and freedom of those who might be affected by such programs. The ultimate purpose of environmental programs is to enhance the quality of human life.

According to the Pope, we can hardly overstate the character of ecological problems or the benefit of their solution. Surely these problems require the expertise and assistance of scientists and technicians from industrialized countries, but only when trained personnel from the local population are present on the scene can the problems be dealt with adequately. Environmental problems also include the problems of housing and shelter. Christians cannot remain indifferent to the homeless or poorly sheltered, with whom the Savior shared a common lot (Mt 8:20).

The Pope took the occasion to speak about the drought on the African continent. Two kinds of assistance were needed: that which met the immediate need for food and shelter and that which would make it possible for the people who were suffering to reclaim their land and make it productive once more.

In conclusion, the Pope recalled the words of Paul VI in *Populorum Progressio:* "Development is the new name of peace." Integral development of the whole person is a condition of peace, and environmental programs for food and housing are concrete ways of promoting peace. Peace is built up slowly through goodwill, trust, and persevering effort; it is built up when national budgets are diverted from the creation of more powerful and deadlier weapons to provide food and raw materials to meet basic human needs. It is built up when men and women of the mass media make known the plight of those who suffer. And those who make peace and foster conditions for peace shall be called the children of God (Mt 5:9).[15]

In 1992, Archbishop Renato R. Martino, the Holy See's Permanent Observer at the United Nations in New York, led a delegation of the Holy See to the United Nations Conference on Environment and Development, the "Earth Summit," in Rio de Janeiro. Speaking to the distinguished gathering, Archbishop Martino said that the Catholic Church approached both the care and protection of the environment and all questions of development from the point of view of the human person. The purpose of every environmental and developmental program should be the integral advancement of the human person with all his needs, just expectations, and fundamental rights. Indeed, the problems of environment and development are, at their root, issues of a moral, ethical order,and proposed solutions must meet the criteria of truth and justice.

The earth is ultimately the common heritage of the human race; hence, the necessity of developing in everyone a true sense of stewardship and solidarity. Stewardship requires that all of us care for the goods entrusted to us and do not squander them; solidarity requires that all human beings, as a kind of "cosmic family," share the goods and beauty of the one world. Stewardship and solidarity together require that we achieve a just balance between protection of the environment and the right to development. Moreover, the scandalous pattern of wasteful consumption by a few must be corrected to ensure justice and sustainable development for all.

Archbishop Martino noted that when considering the problems of environment and development one must also pay due attention to the complex issue of population. The Catholic Church does not propose procreation at any cost; rather, it insists that the transmission of and caring for human life must be exercised with the utmost sense of responsibility, but it is the right of the spouses themselves to decide on the size of their family and the spacing of births, without pressure from governments and organizations. "People are born not only with mouths to be fed, but also with hands that can produce, and minds that can create and innovate."[16]

Finally, the Holy See invited the international community to discover and affirm that there is a spiritual dimension to the issues at hand. Human beings need more than clean air and fresh water; we may not permit them to be robbed of their souls. An alarm must be sounded against the poison of hatred, falsehood and vice, narcotic drugs, and the ruthless self-centeredness that disregards the rights of others. The problems facing today's world are serious indeed and even threatening. All forces must be joined in a positive adventure of unprecedented magnitude and cooperation that will restore hope to the human family and renew the face of the earth.[17]

15

Atomic Energy, Crime and Drugs, Financial Matters, Disaster Relief, and Outer Space

Atomic Energy

In 1953, Pres. Dwight D. Eisenhower of the United States proposed the establishment of an organization devoted exclusively to the peaceful uses of atomic energy. In 1954, his proposal was unanimously endorsed by the General Assembly. The Statute of the IAEA (International Atomic Energy Association) was approved in 1956 at an international conference held at UN headquarters in New York, and the agency came into existence in Vienna in 1957. Later in the same year, 1957, the General Assembly approved an agreement concerning the IAEA's relationship with the United Nations.

In accordance with its Statute, the two main objectives of the IAEA are to "seek to accelerate and enlarge the contribution of atomic energy to peace, health and prosperity throughout the world" and to "ensure, so far as it is able, that assistance provided by it or at its request or under its supervision or control, is not used in such a way as to further any military purposes."

The IAEA fosters and guides the development of peaceful uses of atomic energy, establishes standards for nuclear safety and environmental protection, aids member-countries through technical cooperation, and fosters the exchange of scientific and technical information on nuclear energy.

The IAEA's policies and programs are directed by the General Conference, which is composed of the IAEA's member-states and meets annually, by a thirty-five-member Board of Governors, and by a Secretariat. The headquarters are located in Vienna.

The Holy See has also been concerned about the use of atomic energy. In 1980, Msgr. Mario Peressin, head of the delegation of the Holy See, made a statement to the Twenty-fourth Regular Session of the General Conference of the IAEA at Vienna. The statement was based, Monsignor Peressin said, on anthropological and social principles inspired by the Catholic faith. He went on to say that the specter of past abuses of science haunts the modern world. We must guarantee that nuclear energy is employed solely and exclusively for the benefit of mankind. We cannot be sure that even a limited use of nuclear weapons in self-defense will not lead to all-out nuclear destruction.

The speaker held out a vision of hope for the future based upon the cooperation and collaboration of peoples and nations, but this hope can be realized only if it is linked to the political will of national leaders. The world cannot renounce the atom, but it must ensure that it is used for the common good. The IAEA can play a significant role in three areas: disarmament, a new world order in which all nations and peoples share equitably in the benefits of nuclear energy, and development.[1]

In 1982, Monsignor Peressin addressed the Twenty-sixth Regular Session of the General Conference of the IAEA, convened in Vienna. He noted that the advantages of the peaceful uses of atomic energy are generally recognized, the most important being the supply of energy. The economic growth of Third World countries demands an increasing use of nuclear power, but overdependence upon one source of energy should be avoided. The use of nuclear energy constitutes a risk for mankind because of the danger of accidents in nuclear power plants and the problems of nuclear waste disposal. Perhaps "zero risk" situations are unattainable and unrealistic, since all human efforts necessarily involve some risk. The speaker noted the remarkable fact that up to that point in time no fatal accident caused by radiation had occurred in nuclear power plants for civilian use. The public should be kept fully informed of developments to avoid a climate of unnecessary fear and mistrust.

Finally, Monsignor Peressin took up the military aspect of the atomic problem. Nuclear weapons were becoming more deadly and increasing in number. They could easily lead to horror and holocaust. In the future, war should find no place on the agenda of humanity. The Treaty on the Non-Proliferation of Nuclear Weapons concluded in 1968 commits nuclear-weapons states to a general and complete disarmament. A comprehensive test ban treaty is a sine qua non for reducing the threat of nuclear war. The effort to achieve peace must be carried out on two fronts—the reversal of the arms race and the struggle against the material and spiritual inequalities of our world. Peace is possible; and because it is possible, it is our duty.[2]

In 1984, the representative of the Holy See, Msgr. Giovanni Ceirano, addressed the Twenty-eighth Regular Session of the General Conference of the IAEA, which was meeting in Vienna. The speaker wished to call attention to some basic and general aspects of the agency's work. He expressed satisfaction that in the course of the previous year the agency had taken an important step in achieving that universality of membership that is called for by the very matter with which it is concerned. The speaker appealed to all members to unite in common effort to control, restrict, and finally ban nuclear weapons.

With respect to the peaceful use of nuclear energy, Monsignor Ceirano noted, there is opposition in some quarters because of the fear of the unknown. Public authorities should make a greater effort to inform public opinion about nuclear power with realism and honesty. They should draw attention to the benefits provided by nuclear energy such as greatly increased electrical capacity, greater food production, and medical advances.

Finally, all of us, including scientists, must be committed to wedding knowledge to the overriding values of the human person in society. According to Saint Bernard of Clairvaux, there are some persons who wish to acquire knowledge for vain reasons, but there are others who wish to know in order to edify, and this is charity, and there are still others who wish to know in order to be edified, and this is wisdom. May the scientific investigations of those assembled at the conference serve the whole of humanity![3]

In 1985, Monsignor Ceirano addressed the Twenty-ninth Regular Session of the General Conference of the IAEA, convened at Vienna. The head of the papal delegation wished to address certain current basic issues connected with the use of nuclear energy. He stated that the buildup of nuclear weapons, horizontally and vertically, impedes the development of nuclear energy for peaceful uses. Nuclear energy should serve the spiritual and material development of human beings. As a general rule, each country should decide for itself whether and to what extent it will utilize nuclear energy. In addition to producing nuclear energy for peaceful purposes, nuclear technology can and should be utilized for the benefit of all mankind in other fields, too, such as agriculture, medicine, geology, and scientific research. The Holy See would prefer to see a large number of smaller projects in many countries, for justice would be better served in that way.

Finally, the speaker touched upon the delicate question of choosing personnel for the IAEA. The agency needs to maintain technical expertise while at the same time securing as wide a representation as possible. In any event, the real fruit of the agency, apart from the concrete good of this or that project, will be the growth of a spirit of cooperation and harmony among peoples and nations.[4]

In September 1994, Msgr. Mario Zenari, the new Permanent Representative of the Holy See, addressed the Thirty-eighth Session of the General Conference of the IAEA. He recalled that the agency was created with the aim solely to develop the peaceful use of nuclear energy. He mentioned the enormous progress that has been achieved by means of nuclear research in practically all fields, including energy supply, agriculture, hydrological research, and medicine. He praised the efforts of the agency to draw up safety standards for nuclear activities and ensure the peaceful use of nuclear energy. All this has been done to enhance the quality of human life and, in the words of Pope John Paul II, "to make the earth more habitable, more fertile, and more fraternal."[5]

The following September, 1995, Monsignor Zenari addressed the Thirty-ninth Session of the General Conference of the IAEA in Vienna. The delegation of the Holy See welcomed the extension of the Non-Proliferation

Treaty with respect to nuclear weapons. In order to attain the objective of a nuclear-weapon-free world, state parties to the Non-Proliferation Treaty have to accept IAEA safeguards and cooperate in all manners required. But an important question remains: Can the IAEA promote the peaceful use of nuclear energy without endangering the environment? Every country needs to provide its citizens with sound technical and ethical knowledge to answer this question satisfactorily.

However, there are further problems. There is the danger that adventurers and swindlers may try to smuggle fissionable material. Aged reactors need to be upgraded, and additional safety precautions need to be introduced. Compensation to victims for harm done by nuclear activities cannot be overlooked; and radioactive waste management has to be taken into account.

The speaker went on to say that the policy of energy production has to allow all human beings to participate while preserving the environment and other energy sources for the future. There is general agreement about the necessity of reducing drastically the production and consumption of fossil energy not only because of the limited supply, but mainly because of the consequences for the atmosphere. Future patterns of energy production need to weigh both the benefits and undesirable side effects. As a matter of fact, the almost universal membership in the IAEA manifests that the majority of countries consider atomic energy to be a suitable means of development or at least an unavoidable bridge between traditional sources of energy—coal and oil—and renewable sources. In any event, an efficient international authority is needed not just to guarantee nonproliferation, but also to help avoid the dangers of crime, negligence, human failure, and ignorance.[6]

Crime and Drugs

The United Nations is involved in the field of crime prevention and criminal justice, in line with the charter's provision that it should seek to achieve international cooperation in solving global problems of an economic, social, cultural, or humanitarian nature. To provide a world forum in the field of crime and criminal justice, the General Assembly in 1950 authorized the convening every five years of a United Nations Congress on the Prevention of Crime and the Treatment of Offenders. Participants include criminologists, penologists, and senior police officers, as well as experts in criminal law, human rights, and rehabilitation. The Economic and Social Council's Committee on Crime Prevention and Control acts as the preparatory body for the congresses. The committee meets every year in Vienna to report on the progress made in implementing the resolutions of the congress.

UN research and training activities are furthered by the United Nations Interregional Crime and Justice Research Institute, headquartered in Rome, and by regional training and research institutes in Africa, Asia, including the Far East, Latin America, Arab states, and Europe.

The control of narcotic drugs has been of global concern since the first international conference on the subject was held in Shanghai in 1909. Despite increasingly strict national and international controls, the illicit international traffic in drugs has increased greatly. Massive production of cocaine in some Latin American countries and of opium, morphine, and heroin in Southeast and Central Asia has led to a rapid increase in exports to the United States and Western Europe, the main markets for such drugs, while the local populations in the source countries have become increasingly susceptible to drug abuse. What is more, greater numbers of developing countries have begun to point to drug abuse and trafficking as a threat to their social and political stability, citing the involvement of organized crime and the corruption of government officials.

A series of treaties adopted under the auspices of the United Nations require that governments exercise control over the production and distribution of narcotic drugs and psychotropic substances, combat drug abuse and illicit traffic, maintain the necessary administrative machinery, and report to international organs on their actions. The central objective of these treaties is to limit the supply of and demand for narcotic drugs and psychotropic drugs to medical and scientific purposes.

The Commission on Narcotic Drugs, one of the functional commissions of the Economic and Social Council, considers all matters pertaining to the aims of the treaties and the implementation of their provisions and makes recommendations to the council on the control of narcotic drugs and psychotropic substances. The commission is thus the main policymaking body for international drug control within the UN system.

The International Narcotics Control Board, which began operation in 1968, is responsible for the continuous evaluation and overall supervision of governmental implementation of drug control treaties. In 1971, the Secretary-General created the United Nations Fund for Drug Abuse Control (UNFDAC). It has the mandate to develop drug control programs and provide funds for their execution. In 1984, the assembly adopted a Declaration on the Control of Drug Trafficking and Drug Abuse, calling for intensified efforts and coordinated strategies aimed at the control and eradication of complex drug problems.

Based on the premise that both the demand and the supply of drugs have to be addressed if the problem is to be attenuated, the first International Conference on Drug Abuse and Illicit Trafficking was held at Vienna in 1987. The principal document adopted by the conference was a Comprehensive Multidisciplinary Outline of Future Activities in Drug Abuse Control. It contained recommendations for practical action to be taken by governments and organizations to prevent and reduce demand for narcotic drugs and psychotropic substances, control supply, suppress illicit drug trafficking, and promote policies for effective treatment and rehabilitation. A declaration adopted by the conference committed the participants to taking vigorous international action against drug abuse and illicit trafficking.

Crime and criminals were also the concern of the Holy See. In 1982, the Holy See submitted a document having to do with arbitrary and summary executions to the United Nations Committee on Crime Prevention and Control. Subsequently, the document was published in a report of the Secretary-General of the United Nations. According to the Holy See, the problem of arbitrary and summary executions is a typical example of the excesses of some political regimes. Already in 1953, Pope Pius XII acknowledged the state's right to punish wrongdoers, but such punishment must be commensurate with the crime and subject to legal safeguards that protect the rights of the accused. Legal provisions for dealing with the accused and guilty should not be arbitrary or depend on purely personal judgment, but should be in accord with sound reason and the universal sentiment of justice. Then, in 1979, Pope John Paul II urged that there should be a strict commitment to respecting the physical and moral integrity of the person, even in the case of those guilty or accused of having broken the law.[7]

The Holy See has also spoken about the problem of drugs. In 1985, Monsignor Giovanni Ceirano, the representative of the Holy See, delivered a statement at the Thirty-first Session of the United Nations Commission on Narcotic Drugs, held at Vienna. He spoke of the tragic dimensions of the drug problem. It is linked to a crisis of civilization and a great malaise. Why are so many young people affected? Because they reject a society incapable of offering valid reasons for living or making strong commitments. Everyone knows that the drug traffic is one of the biggest illegal businesses in the world today. Is it possible that some people use drugs as a means of destabilizing and destroying society for military and political purposes? According to Pope John Paul II, what is needed is prevention, suppression, and rehabilitation. Exemplary measures in this regard have been undertaken by some governments, but there is still too much complacency, superficiality, and fear of facing the problem squarely.[8]

In 1987, Pope John Paul himself sent a message to the International Conference on Drug Abuse and Illicit Trafficking held at Vienna. The Pope described the phenomenon of drug abuse as one of the greatest tragedies plaguing the modern world, especially its young people. The human cost is steadily increasing, and no country, rich or poor, has been spared. Many factors contribute to the dramatic increase in drug abuse: the breakdown of the family, the weakening of traditional ways of life, unemployment, subhuman standards of living, the fear of nuclear warfare, and numerous other social factors. Drug abuse impoverishes every community where it exists.

The Pope praised the great, even heroic, efforts being made in many quarters to counter the plague of drug addiction. The criminal activity of drug production and trafficking should be directly opposed and stopped. Those who work to impart preventive education in the home, at school, or in places of work are to be applauded. Other initiatives, such as making crop substitution a feasible alternative to illicit plant cultivation, should be considered. Special consideration must also be given to the treatment and rehabilitation of drug addicts. A key factor in successful rehabilitation, particularly in the case of young people, is the restoration of self-confidence and healthy self-esteem. Drug abusers must be helped to re-establish trusting relationships with their families and friends. They must also be helped to resume their work or education or job training. In any event, the Church wishes to offer every possible support to the many and varied efforts being made by so many in this regard.[9]

Financial Matters

The World Bank is a group of four separate institutions: the International Bank for Reconstruction and Development (IBRD), established in 1945; the International Finance Corporation (IFC), established in 1956; the International Development Association (IDA), established in 1960; and the Multilateral Investment Guarantee Agency (MIGA), established in 1988. The common objective of all four agencies is to reduce poverty and raise the standards of living in developing countries by promoting sustainable economic growth and development.

The IBRD

The bank's charter spells out the basic rules that govern its operations: it must lend only for productive purposes (such as agriculture, energy, education, health, family planning and nutrition, roads and railways, tele-communications, urban ports, and power facilities) and must pay due regard to the prospects for repayment; each loan must be guaranteed by the government concerned and, except in special circumstances, must be for specific projects; the bank must assure itself that the necessary funds are unavailable from other sources on reasonable terms; the use of loans cannot be restricted to purchases in any particular member-country or -countries; and the bank's decisions to lend must be based on economic considerations. The bank, whose capital is subscribed by its member-countries, finances its lending operations primarily from its own borrowings in world markets, as well as from retained earnings and the flow of repayments on its loans.

The IDA

The need for lending to very poor countries on much easier terms than the bank alone could give became apparent in the 1950s, and the IDA was therefore established in 1960, as an affiliate of the bank, to help meet this need. The bulk of the IDA's resources come from three sources: transfers from the bank's net earnings; capital subscribed in convertible currencies by members of the IDA; and contributions from the IDA's richer members.

Nearly all the IDA's "credits," as they are called to distinguish them from bank "loans," have been for a period of fifty years without interest, except for a small charge to cover administrative costs. Repayment of principal does not begin until after a ten-year grace period.

The IFC

The IFC, while closely associated with the bank, is a separate legal entity, and its funds are distinct from those of the bank. The IFC's aims are to assist in financing private enterprise, which could contribute to development by making investments, without guarantee of repayment by the member-government concerned; to bring together investment opportunities, domestic and foreign capital, and experienced management; and to stimulate the flow of private capital, domestic and foreign, into productive investment in member-countries.

The IFC's investments have been primarily in manufacturing but have included mining and energy, tourism, utilities, and projects related to agriculture. Its resources come mainly from subscriptions by its member-countries and from accumulated earnings.

The MIGA

The MIGA was established in 1988. The MIGA's basic purpose is to facilitate the flow of private investment for productive purposes to developing member-countries. It does so by offering long-term political risk insurance (that is, coverage against the risks of expropriation, currency transfer, and war and civil disturbance) to investors and by providing advisory and consultative services.

The IMF

Founded in 1945, the IMF (International Monetary Fund) is an intergovernmental organization that has three main functions: first, to administer a code of conduct regarding exchange policies and restrictions on payments for current account transactions; second, to provide members with financial resources to enable them to observe the code of conduct while they are correcting or avoiding payment imbalances; and, third, to provide a forum in which members can consult with one another and collaborate on international monetary matters.

The fund makes financial resources available to members with payment problems under a wide range of policies and facilities. In lending to its members, the fund is guided by two principles: first, the pool of currencies at the fund's disposal exists for the entire membership; and, second, before the fund releases any money from the pool, the member must demonstrate how it intends to solve its payment problems.[10]

In 1987, a document of the Pontifical Commission for Justice and Peace, dealing with the international debt question, was published as an official document of the United Nations General Assembly. The document noted that debt levels of developing countries constitute a serious, urgent, and complex problem with grave social, economic, and political repercussions. Some developing nations were at the breaking point because of their inability to meet their financial obligations. The Church wished to enlighten the consciences of decision makers and enkindle the hope and confidence of debtor nations. What is needed is a global perspective with an ethical approach.

What ethical principles should be invoked to deal with the debt question? The document of the Pontifical Commission identified these: create new forms of solidarity that reflect the interdependence between developed and developing countries as well as the need for international collaboration; accept coresponsibility for the causes and solutions to international debt; establish relations of trust between the parties involved; undertake to share efforts and sacrifices; foster the participation of all segments of society; and identify emergency and long-term measures to deal with the debt crisis.

Next, the document of the pontifical commission discussed action in emergency situations. Because some developing nations are at the brink of financial disaster, international solidarity calls for emergency measures to ensure the survival of these nations. One should respect the insolvent debtor and not burden him with demands he cannot meet. Just as the international community tries to foresee, prevent, and attenuate catastrophes in other areas, so the international community should try to foresee, prevent, and attenuate financial crises. The IMF has an important role to play in emergency situations; dialogue with all the parties concerned and the good of all are values that should guide the actions of the IMF. Other creditors, such as states and banks, are also responsible for emergency measures. The causes of financial crises in a country's debt situation should be identified, and emergency measures should be linked to medium- and long-term measures.

Then the document of the pontifical commission encouraged developed and developing countries to assume joint responsibility for the future. Surely financial relations between countries are quite complex. However, by reviewing the roles of the parties involved in the debt situation, it will be possible to bring out more clearly their respective responsibilities.

What are the responsibilities of industrialized countries with respect to the debt situation? They bear a heavier responsibility, which they must acknowledge and accept even if they are challenged by grave problems of reconversion and unemployment. The time is over when they can act without concern for the effects of their economic policies on other countries. If government officials wish to promote sharing with other countries, they will have to appeal to the values of brotherhood and solidarity for peace and development. Adopting measures to stimulate growth, reducing protectionism, lowering interest rates, and assigning a just value to raw materials—all these actions seem to be required of industrialized countries.

What are the responsibilities of developing countries for dealing with their indebtedness? Developing countries should determine both the external and internal causes behind their indebtedness, and political leaders will have to assign responsibility for the situation to each individual and social category. Leaders in developing countries must accept scrutiny of their actions relative to the debt situation. It is advisable for developing countries to mobilize all their available national resources to promote sustained economic growth. Nationalism can be an obstacle to growth. A developing country should try to import capital, technology, and equipment without increasing indebtedness unduly. Regional cooperation among developing countries can promote just solutions to the debt problem.

What are the responsibilities of creditors with respect to debtor nations? Creditors need to act with a view to the survival of a debtor nation that is unable to service its debt or meet its interest payments. All the parties involved should discuss the matter in order to find an equitable solution. However, creditors may not demand contract fulfillment by any and all means, especially if the debtor nation is in extreme need. Each country has to be left adequate financial leeway for its own growth, and this will help repay its debt. Creditors and debtors can reach agreement on new conditions and terms of payment in several ways, perhaps by arbitration or by converting loans into grants or by government guarantees of loans from commercial banks; still, it is possible for them to devise conditions for loans that go beyond profitability and security of capital. One might hope that multinational corporations could discover ways that will allow peoples still underdeveloped to break through the barriers that seem to enclose them.

What are the responsibilities of multilateral financial organizations, such as the IMF, the World Bank, and regional banks? These organizations will fulfill their roles if their decisions and actions are taken in a spirit of justice and solidarity at the service of all. Priority must be granted to peoples and their needs beyond the constraints that purely financial considerations might dictate. People themselves have the primary responsibility for their development, but they will not bring this about in isolation without assistance from others. In order to handle these new tasks, some new organizations are most assuredly necessary, but they will be successful only if people have confidence in them and perceive them to be motivated by impartiality and service to others. It is up to the member-states that have the preponderant influence on the decision-making process to support these new organizations and give them specific direction.

Each of the multilateral financial organizations has a specific function and responsibility. Greater participation of developing countries in major economic decisions affecting them is desirable. There are certain other considerations that should be of concern to multilateral organizations and those who work in them: reexamination of the loan conditions set by the IMF, the infusion of new capital into developing countries, the rescheduling of debts, special provisions for dealing with financial emergencies, planning for the future, and the selection and training of personnel who work in multilateral organizations. The fact that human lives are at stake should never be forgotten.

In conclusion, the document of the pontifical commission proposed a question: Just as there was a comprehensive plan to reconstruct Europe after World War II, should there not be a similar plan to help developing countries and their suffering populations?[11]

Disaster Relief

In the late 1960s, the international community responded to natural disasters in many countries throughout the world with vast quantities of assistance, but relief efforts were hampered by a lack of coordination in the handling and distribution of supplies. To deal with this situation, the General Assembly decided, in 1971, to establish the Office of the United Nations Disaster Relief Coordinator (UNDRO), which later gave way, in 1992, to the UN Department of Humanitarian Affairs (DHA).

The role of the DHA is to provide leadership in order to ensure a rapid response by the UN system to natural disasters, technological disasters such as the 1986 explosion of the Chernobyl nuclear power plant, and major humanitarian crises, many of which result from conflicts between states. The coordinating role of the DHA is crucial. It mobilizes and directs aid from all kinds of donors, including governmental, nongovernmental, and intergovernmental organizations. The DHA acts as a focal point and clearinghouse for information on relief needs and on what donors are doing to meet those needs. The agency seeks to mobilize relief more rapidly, coordinate it more systematically, reduce risks of waste or duplicated efforts, increase the supply of essential items, improve contingency planning and preparedness, and promote disaster prevention.

The Holy See has shared the concern of the United Nations for disaster relief. On the occasion of his first pastoral visit to Africa, Pope John Paul II went to Ouagadougou, Burkina Faso, in the heart of the Sahel region, and made a solemn appeal on behalf of those suffering from a devastating drought. In the wake of the appeal, there was a most generous response, so generous, in fact, that it became possible to set up a special program to assist the suffering in a more formal way. Thus the John Paul II Foundation was officially established in February 1984. The foundation would make available to the peoples of the Sahel region millions of dollars for programs of education and agricultural and technological development that ultimately would benefit everyone affected by the scourge of drought in that region. The foundation is but one example—an outstanding one, to be sure—of the Holy See's numerous contributions to disaster relief.[12]

Outer Space

Ever since the Soviet Union launched *Sputnik* into earth orbit in 1957, the United Nations has devoted close attention to the exploration and use of outer space. The organization's concern is that space be used for peaceful purposes and the benefit of all. To meet this concern, the General Assembly set up, in 1959, the Committee for the Peaceful Uses of Outer Space as the focal point of UN action in their field. The committee has two subcommittees, one dealing with legal issues and the other with scientific and technical matters.

The work of the committee and its subcommittees has resulted in five legal instruments, all of which have entered into force: the 1966 Treaty of Principles Governing the Activities of States in the Exploration and Use of Outer Space, Including the Moon and Other Celestial Bodies; the 1967 Agreement on the Rescue of Astronauts, the Return of Astronauts and the Return of Objects Launched into Outer Space; the 1971 Convention on International Liability for Damage Caused by Space Objects; the 1974 Convention on the Registration of Objects Launched into Outer Space; and the 1979 Agreement Governing Activities of States on the Moon and Other Celestial Bodies.

In 1982, the General Assembly adopted principles governing the use by states of artificial satellites for international direct television broadcasting; and in 1986, it adopted principles related to remote sensing of the earth from outer space, which stated that such activities were to be conducted for the benefit of all countries. Remote sensing was to be used to protect the earth's natural environment and protect mankind from natural disasters. In the scientific and technical fields, the committee has given priority to the implementation of the United Nations Program on Space Applications, started in 1969, and to the coordination of outer space activities within the UN system.

Two major conferences on outer space have been organized by the United Nations. The First UN Conference on the Exploration and Peaceful Uses of Outer Space was held at Vienna in 1968. The Second UN Conference on the Exploration and Peaceful Uses of Outer Space (UNISPACE 82), also held at Vienna, in 1982, reflected the growing involvement of all nations, developed and developing, in outer space activities. In the final report, adopted by consensus, UNISPACE 82 stressed that the prevention of the arms race and hostilities in outer space is an essential condition for the promotion and continuation of international cooperation in the exploration and use of outer space for peaceful purposes. The General Assembly, at its 1982 session, endorsed the recommendations of UNISPACE 82 and called for their implementation. The Committee on Outer Space has directed this implementation.[13]

The Holy See has followed the exploration of space with lively interest. In 1968, Pope Paul VI addressed a message to the First Conference on the Peaceful Use of Outer Space, held at Vienna. With the exploration and use of outer space, the Pope said, human life was acquiring a new dimension. Thanks to artificial satellites, there are new possibilities for the transmission of knowledge and information and for the demolition of the barriers between nations. The Holy See is concerned that space technology be placed at the service of all men and women.

To be sure, the new technology can be abused if, for example, it is used to spread subversion and hatred. There must be no delay in drafting a whole body of "space law" so that the common good is protected and furthered. Finally, the Pope expressed the hope that the new technology of the space age would contribute to the educational and cultural development of those who lag behind.[14]

In 1982, the Holy See sent a delegation to the Second United Nations Conference on the Exploration and Peaceful Use of Outer Space. Msgr. Mario Peressin spoke for the delegation. "What a fantastic scientific and technological adventure the exploration and use of space is!" the speaker said. He recalled the enthusiasm of Pope Paul VI in 1971 when the Apollo 14 mission landed successfully on the moon. "Honors to man, ruler of the earth and skies," the Pope had said. Capable of such scientific and technological feats, surely humanity is capable, if it so desires, of solving the great problems of unemployment and poverty.

Alas, Monsignor Peressin continued, there was the prospect that military confrontations would be transferred to outer space. The 1967 Treaty on Principles Governing the Activities of States in the Exploration and Use of Outer Space forbids the use of space for military purposes. What is still needed is an adequate system of verification by competent personnel. The military use of space could lead to the worst catastrophes.

All of which brought the speaker to a decisive point in his message. The 1959 Treaty on Antarctica and the Treaty on Outer Space refer to the common interest of humanity. Referring to the common interest of humanity represents a real change in international law, which is becoming, in effect, a law of humanity or planetary law. The common ideal of humanity requires that national egoisms give way to this primary consideration. Such an evolution corresponds to the deepest conviction of the Christian faith about the one origin, nature, and vocation of the human family. The Creator wills that the goods of creation should flow equitably into the hands of all. The resources of space belong first of all to humanity in general and must be used in the common interest; nor may we forget the generations to come.

The central concept of "humanity" demands that poor countries also participate in the benefits of space exploration and usage. This precise demand is also made by article 1 of the treaty of 1967. It has been very well said that "to the sharing of the world we must substitute, gradually but surely, the world of sharing."

With respect to remote sensing, its benefits have already been many, but some states complain that it allows an unchecked examination of their activities. Further, foreign broadcasting can result in a serious cultural imposition on a given population. Of course, each state has a right to act freely, but sovereignty is not an absolute right, because it must recognize and accept human solidarity. In any event, there must be institutions to regulate the use of space and preserve its supranational character. Every effort to organize international cooperation for the peaceful use of outer space will receive the warm support of the Holy See.[15]

In 1984, the Pontifical Academy of Sciences sponsored a study week on the impact of space exploration on mankind. Subsequently, the conclusions of the study week were published as a document of the United Nations. In the course of the study week, Pope John Paul II received the participants at the Vatican. The Pope expressed his admiration for the exceptional development of space technology. In a sense, the work of Galileo,

Kepler, Newton, and two former members of the Pontifical Academy, Colombo and Marconi, had paved the way. Now we must ask ourselves the question: To whom does space belong? The Pope did not hesitate to answer: "Space belongs to the whole of humanity; it is something for the benefit of all." The proper use of space must be studied by jurists and given correct solution by governments.

According to the Pope, one of the biggest tasks that can be accomplished by satellites is the elimination of illiteracy. Moreover, satellites can contribute to the dissemination of a culture that will promote the development of the whole person; but there should be no cultural or ideological colonialism that imposes the culture of rich nations on poor nations—rather, satellites can promote a dialogue between cultures. Modern space technology also provides observations that are useful for the cultivation of the earth, since satellites provide data regarding the conditions of the land, the flow of water, and the state of the weather. This so-called remote sensing is of fundamental importance in the fight against hunger. The harmony between man and nature must be restored, and we must strive for a technology that will free poor peoples from their poverty and relieve an oppressed nature. To these noble goals space technology can make a highly effective contribution.[16]

Then, in 1986, the Pontifical Academy of Sciences assembled again to study the impact of remote sensing on developing countries. Once again the conclusions of the study week were published as a document of the United Nations. Pope John Paul received the participants at the Vatican, where he addressed them. According to the Pope, the new technique of remote sensing makes it possible to survey anything from a few square meters to huge expanses of the earth's surface. Satellites with a network of ground tracking stations can provide a detailed picture of crops and offer technical help to combat the terrible phenomenon of desertification, with consequent famine and disease. With the help of remote sensing it is possible to obtain useful data for many projects relating to crops, forests, sources of energy, and food resources in the seas, lakes, and rivers.

The Pope expressed the hope of aiding all peoples, with the help of advanced technological methods, to share equitably in the resources of the earth. However, there is still a lack of firm determination in political circles to use the technological means to feed the human family. It was also the Pope's hope that by means of joint agreements and commitments all governments would promote the peaceful uses of space to secure the unification of the human family in justice and peace.[17]

A Final Word

As I wrote in the introduction, my hope for this book is to render the collaboration of the Holy See and the United Nations more understandable and promote the noble objectives of both.

That collaboration exists because the objectives of the two international entities are, to a considerable degree, the same. Both wish to promote the welfare of human beings, which includes the establishment and preservation of true peace, the practical recognition of human rights, and the creation of material conditions that foster the development of the whole person.

To be sure, the Holy See pursues another objective that is necessarily beyond the ken of the United Nations because of the latter's widely diverse membership. That objective is the eternal salvation of men and women as revealed by Jesus Christ, the Founder of the Catholic Church.

The Holy See looks upon the United Nations as an international organization that reflects the unity and solidarity of the human race. Indeed, the United Nations represents "the obligatory path of modern civilization and world peace," a phrase repeated by the Popes since Paul VI first expressed it in 1965. In turn, the United Nations recognizes the Holy See as a powerful ally by reason of its moral authority and worldwide influence.

Reading the messages and addresses of the representatives of the Holy See to the United Nations and its agencies, one hears certain recurrent ideas:

- that the nations of the world should never again resort to war to settle their differences;
- that men and women of all nations should regard themselves as one family standing in solidarity with other human beings;
- that every plan and program put forward by the United Nations should aim at safeguarding and promoting human dignity;
- that human beings have both a material *and* spiritual dimension that includes a profound need for truth, love, justice, beauty, and brotherhood;
- that the resources of the earth belong to all men and women and should be used for the benefit of all; and
- that the nations of the earth are becoming increasingly interdependent and one may not act without consideration for the rights of others.

The end of the Cold War affords renewed hope for peace and economic development. Perhaps a portion of the huge expenditures for weapons may now be diverted to the needs of the Third World. Speaking at the 1992 Convention of the Catholic Theological Society of America, Gustavo Gutiérrez remarked with wry humor that since the dissolution of the socialist bloc of nations, the "Third World" has been "promoted" to the status of "Second World." May the cooperation of the Holy See and United Nations over the next fifty years contribute to the formation of only "One World"!

Notes

Introduction

1. *Code of Canon Law,* cc. 360, 361.
2. When the United Nations celebrated its fiftieth anniversary, in October 1995, there were 185 member-nations.
3. Permanent Observer Mission of the Holy See to the United Nations, *Paths to Peace* (New York: Liturgical Publications, 1987), available from Liturgical Publications, Inc., 1025 S. Moorland Road, Brookfield, WI 53005. The material cited and summarized in this book was done so with the kind permission of the Permanent Observer of the Holy See at the United Nations.

1. The Holy See

1. Ireneaus of Lyons, *Against Heresies,* 3, 3, 2.
2. *Code of Canon Law,* cc. 331–35; 360–61.
3. Second Vatican Council, *Gaudium et Spes,* 16.
4. Recounted by Robert A. Graham, S.J., in his *Vatican Diplomacy* (Princeton, N.J.: Princeton University Press, 1959), 24.
5. For the full text see Ernesto Gallina, *Le Organizzazioni Internazionali e la Chiesa Cattolica* (Rome, 1967), 73–74.
6. *Code of Canon Law,* cc. 362–65.
7. A complete list of postings can be found in the *Annuario Pontificio,* published by the Libreria Editrice Vaticana, Vatican City.

2. The United Nations

1. *Everyone's United Nations,* 10th ed. (New York: Department of Public Information, United Nations), 399.
2. Ibid., 400.
3. From a speech by Ezequiel Padilla in *The United Nations Conference on International Organization: Selected Documents,* Department of State Publication 2490 (Washington, D.C.: Government Printing Office. 1946), 932.

3. The Catholic Church and the International Organization (I)

1. Later the Fathers and theologians of the Church will also see the image of God in man in the latter's capacity to know and will.
2. Ambrose, Sermon against Auxentius, 37.
3. Letter to the Emperor Anastasius I, A.D. 494 (DS 347).

4. The Catholic Church and the International Organization (II)

1. Thomas Aquinas, *Kingship,* book 1, chapters 1–3.
2. Dante Alighieri, *Monarchy,* book 1.
3. An English translation of these and other lectures may be found in J. B. Scott, *The Spanish Origin of International Law* (Oxford: Clarendon, 1934).
4. Vitorio is honored with a bust on the grounds of the United Nations in New York for his contribution to the development of international law.
5. Francis Suarez, *De lege humana et civili,* lib. 3, c. 2, n. 5, t. 5.
6. Ibid., lib. 2, c. 19. This quotation is inscribed in Latin on the wall of the Salle du Conseil of the Palais des Nations at Geneva.

7. J. B. Scott, *The Catholic Conception of International Law* (Washington, D.C.: Georgetown University Press, 1934), 484.

8. *The New Cyneas of Eméric Crucé,* ed. and trans. by T. W. Balch (Philadelphia: Allen, Lane and Scott, 1909), 84.

9. Louis Taparelli D'Azeglio, *Essai Théorique de Droit Naturel,* 3d French ed. (Tournai: Tome Second, 1883), nos. 1262–1398. There is an English translation in John Eppstein's book, *The Catholic Tradition of the Law of Nations* (Washington, D.C.: Catholic Association for International Peace), 266–272. Needless to say, there have been many other proposals for constructing an international organization of nations for preserving peace emanating from Catholic and non-Catholic sources. Here I have offered only a sample of Catholic thought on this important matter.

10. Cf. *The Catholic Mind* (New York: America Press, 1931), 34.

11. Cf. *The Pope Speaks* (New York: Harcourt, Brace, 1940), 285–89.

12. Ibid., 293.

13. John Eppstein, *The Catholic Tradition of the Law of Nations* (London, 1935), 320.

14. Cf. *The Pope Speaks,* op. cit., 307.

15. Pius XI, *The Promotion of True Religious Unity* (Washington, D.C.: N.C.W.C., 1928).

16. Pius XI, *Quadragesimo Anno* (Washington, D.C.: N.C.W.C., 1936), 29.

5. Papal Support of the United Nations

1. *Acta Apostolicae Sedis* (henceforth referred to as *AAS*) 31 (1939): 675.

2. *AAS* 32 (1940): 10.

3. *AAS* 36 (1944): 257.

4. *AAS* 37 (1945): 19.

5. *AAS* 37 (1945): 166.

6. *AAS* 41 (1949): 10.

7. *AAS* 41 (1949): 12.
8. *AAS* 44 (1952): 10.
9. *AAS* 55 (1963): 296.
10. Second Vatican Council, *Gaudium et Spes,* pt. 1, cc. 1–4.
11. Ibid., pt. 2, c. 5, no. 78.
12. Ibid., no. 84.
13. *AAS* 55 (1963): 653.
14. *AAS* 57 (1965): 877–85. One should read the Pope's magnificent address in its entirety to appreciate it fully. An English translation can be found in Permanent Observer Mission of the Holy See to the United Nations, *Paths to Peace* (New York: Liturgical Publications, 1987), 2–6.
15. *AAS* 62 (1970): 683–87.
16. *AAS* 64 (1972): 214–15; 69 (1977): 544–46.
17. *AAS* 71 (1979): 1143–60. The entire address may be found in *Paths to Peace,* op. cit., 16–24.
18. *AAS* 74 (1982): 711–14.
19. Cf. *Paths to Peace,* op. cit., 67–70.
20. *AAS* 81 (1989): 1329–31.
21. *AAS* 84 (1992): 1138–41.
22. *L'Osservatore Romano,* no. 41 (October 11, 1995): 8–10.

6. Human Rights (I)

1. *Everyone's United Nations*, 10th ed. (New York: Department of Public Information, United Nations, 1986), 305.
2. Cf. *The Pope Speaks* (New York: Harcourt, Brace, 1940), 159–60.
3. John XXIII, *Pacem in Terris,* pt. 1.
4. Ibid., pt. 4, toward the end.
5. Second Vatican Council, *Gaudium et Spes,* no. 26.
6. Ibid., no. 29.
7. Ibid., no. 41.
8. Second Vatican Council, *Dignitatis Humanae,* no. 2.
9. *AAS* 60 (1968): 283–86.
10. *AAS* 65 (1973): 673–77.
11. *AAS* 71 (1979): 1143–60.
12. *AAS* 72 (1980): 1252–60.

13. Cf. *L'Osservatore Romano,* English ed., no. 48 (December 1, 1993): 7; no. 9 (March 1, 1995): 4.

7. Human Rights (II)

1. Second Vatican Council, *Gaudium et Spes,* no. 29; Second Vatican Council, *Ad Gentes,* no. 15; Second Vatican Council, *Nostra Actate,* no. 5.
2. Permanent Observer Mission of the Holy See to the United Nations, *Paths to Peace* (New York: Liturgical Publications, 1987), 104–6.
3. Ibid., 380–81.
4. *AAS* 67 (1975): 437–39.
5. *Paths to Peace,* op. cit., 383–87.
6. Ibid., 393–97.
7. *L'Osservatore Romano,* no. 37 (September 13, 1995): 4–5.
8. *Everyone's United Nations,* 10th ed. (New York: Department of Public Information, 1986) 275.
9. *Paths to Peace* op. cit., 358–59.
10. Ibid., 359–62.
11. *AAS* 83 (1991): 358–61.
12. *L'Osservatore Romano,* no. 45 (November 10, 1993): 9.
13. *L'Osservatore Romano,* no. 44 (November 2, 1994): 2.
14. *Basic Facts about the United Nations* (New York: United Nations, 1989), 123.
15. *AAS* 78 (1986): 95–104.
16. *Paths to Peace,* op. cit., 372–76.

8. Human Rights (III)

1. *AAS* 74 (1982): 1172–79.
2. Permanent Observer Mission of the Holy See to the United Nations, *Paths to Peace,* (New York: Liturgical Publications, 1987), 397–403.
3. *AAS* 46 (1954): 714–18.
4. *AAS* 61 (1969): 491–502.

5. *AAS* 74 (1982): 992–1006.
6. *L'Osservatore Romano,* no. 32/33 (August 9–16, 1995): 3.
7. *AAS* 51 (1959): 481–83.
8. *AAS* 56 (1964): 996–97.
9. *Paths to Peace,* op. cit., 440–42.
10. Ibid., 434–36.
11. Ibid., 436–37.
12. *L'Osservatore Romano,* no. 43 (October 27, 1993): 6.
13. *Paths to Peace,* op. cit., 451–52.
14. *AAS* 60 (1968): 349–51.
15. *Paths to Peace,* op. cit., 454–55.
16. Ibid., 455–57.
17. Ibid., 457–59.
18. Ibid., 459–62.

9. Culture and Education

1. Permanent Observer Mission of the Holy See to the United Nations, *Paths to Peace* (New York: Liturgical Publications, 1987) 114–19.
2. *Gaudium et Spes,* no. 53.
3. *AAS* 63 (1971): 837–840.
4. Pope John XXIII, *Pacem in Terris,* pt. 5; *AAS* 66 (1974): 704–709.
5. *Paths to Peace,* op. cit., 140–43.
6. Ibid., 143–47.
7. Ibid., 147–49.
8. *AAS* 72 (1980): 735–52.
9. *AAS* 73 (1981): 420–28.
10. *AAS* 74 (1982): 1179–81.
11. *Paths to Peace,* op. cit., 149–51.
12. *L'Osservatore Romano,* no. 48 (December 1, 1993): 6.

10. Disarmament and Peace

1. *AAS* 70 (1978): 399–407.
2. "If you wish for peace, prepare for war."

3. *AAS* 74 (1982): 872–83.
4. Permanent Observer Mission of the Holy See to the United Nations, *Paths to Peace* (New York: Liturgical Publications, 1987), 180–34.
5. *L'Osservatore Romano,* (November 18, 1991).
6. *Paths to Peace,* op. cit., 502–11.
7. Ibid., 514–16.

11. Development

1. *Basic Facts about the United Nations* (New York: United Nations, 1989), 101.
2. Ibid., 104.
3. Ibid., 207.
4. Ibid., 111.
5. Second Vatican Council, *Gaudium et Spes,* no. 69.
6. *L'Osservatore Romano,* no. 11 (March 15, 1995), 2.

12. Food and Agriculture

1. *Basic Facts about the United Nations* (New York: United Nations, 1989), 188.
2. Permanent Observer Mission of the Holy See to the United Nations, *Paths to Peace* (New York: Liturgical Publications, 294–300.
3. Ibid., 300–304.
4. *AAS* 56 (1964): 40–42.
5. *AAS* 57 (1965): 995–97.
6. *AAS* 63 (1971): 875–79.
7. *AAS* 66 (1974): 644–52.
8. *AAS* 70 (1978): 95–97.
9. *AAS* 73 (1981): 733–35.
10. *AAS* 74 (1982): 35–39.
11. *L'Osservatore Romano,* (November 11, 1983), 1.
12. *AAS* 82 (1990): 670–74.
13. *AAS* 83 (1991): 361–363.

14. *L'Osservatore Romano,* (November 18, 1991, 3).
15. *L'Osservatore Romano,* no. 46 (November 17, 1993): 8.
16. *L'Osservatore Romano,* no. 44 (November 1, 1995): 7.

13. Justice and Law

1. *Basic Facts about the United Nations* (New York: United Nations, 1989), 178–79.
2. Ibid., 179–81.
3. *AAS* 78 (1986): 517–24.
4. *L'Osservatore Romano,* (May 20, 1992), 3.

14. Population, Human Settlements, and the Environment

1. *Basic Facts about the United Nations*, (New York: United Nations, 1989), 120.
2. *AAS* 66 (1974): 253–56.
3. Permanent Observer of the Holy See to the United Nations, *Paths to Peace* (New York: Liturgical Publications, 1987), 411–414.
4. Ibid., 414–19.
5. *L'Osservatore Romano,* no. 37 (September 14, 1994): 6–7.
6. *L'Osservatore Romano,* no. 38 (September 21, 1994): 7.
7. *L'Osservatore Romano,* no. 1 (January 4, 1995): 6.
8. *Paths to Peace,* op. cit., 420–21.
9. *AAS* 68 (1976): 403–06.
10. *Paths to Peace,* op. cit., 429–32.
11. *Basic Facts,* op. cit., 112–14.
12. *New York Times,* June 15, 1992, A5.
13. *AAS* 64 (1972): 443–46.
14. *Paths to Peace,* op. cit., 468–69.
15. *AAS* 78 (1986): 89–95.
16. Prince Malthus, "Review and Outlook," *Wall Street Journal,* April 28, 1992.
17. *L'Osservatore Romano,* (June 17, 1992), 13.

15. Atomic Energy, Crime and Drugs, Financial Matters, Disaster Relief, and Outer Space

1. Permanent Observer of the Holy See to the United Nations, *Paths to Peace* (New York: Liturgical Publications, 1987), 198–200.
2. Ibid., 204–06.
3. Ibid., 208–10.
4. Ibid., 210–12.
5. *L'Osservatore Romano,* (October 26, 1994), 2.
6. *L'Osservatore Romano,* no. 39 (September 27, 1995): 12.
7. *Paths to Peace,* op. cit., 462–63.
8. Ibid., 449–51.
9. Ibid., 516–18.
10. *Basic Facts about the United Nations* (New York: United Nations, 1989), 192–97.
11. *Paths to Peace,* op. cit., 342–56.
12. *AAS* 78 (1986): 89–95.
13. *Basic Facts,* op. cit., 75–78.
14. *AAS* 60 (1968): 570–72.
15. *Paths to Peace,* op. cit., 481–85.
16. Ibid., 491–93.
17. Ibid., 499–500.